www.EffortlessMath.com

... So Much More Online!

✓ FREE Math lessons

✓ More Math learning books!

✓ Mathematics Worksheets

✓ Online MAP Math Courses

Need a PDF version of this book?

Please visit www.EffortlessMath.com

MAP Grade 6 Math Full Study Guide

2024

Comprehensive Review + Practice Tests + Online Resources

By

Reza Nazari

Copyright © 2023

Effortless Math Education Inc.

All rights reserved. No part of this publication may be reproduced, stored in a retrieval system, or transmitted in any form or by any means, electronic, mechanical, photocopying, recording, scanning, or otherwise, except as permitted under Section 107 or 108 of the 1976 United States Copyright Ac, without permission of the author.

Effortless Math provides unofficial test prep products for a variety of tests and exams. It is not affiliated with or endorsed by any official organizations.

All inquiries should be addressed to:
info@effortlessMath.com
www.EffortlessMath.com

ISBN: 978-1-63719-481-2

Published by: **Effortless Math Education Inc.**

For Online Math Practice Visit www.EffortlessMath.com

Welcome to

MAP Grade 6 Math Prep 2024

Thank you for choosing Effortless Math for your MAP Grade 6 Math test preparation and congratulations on making the decision to prepare for the MAP Grade 6 test!

It's a remarkable move you are taking, one that shouldn't be diminished in any capacity. That's why you need to use every tool possible to ensure you succeed on the test with the highest possible score, and this extensive study guide is one such tool.

This study guide will help you prepare for (and even ACE) the MAP Grade 6 math test. As test day draws nearer, effective preparation becomes increasingly more important. Thankfully, you have this comprehensive study guide to help you get ready for the test. With this guide, you can feel confident that you will be more than ready for the MAP Grade 6 Math test when the time comes.

First and foremost, it is important to note that this book is a study guide and not a textbook. It is best read from cover to cover. Every lesson of this "self-guided math book" was carefully developed to ensure that you are making the most effective use of your time while preparing for the test. This up-to-date guide reflects the 2024 test guidelines and will put you on the right track to hone your math skills, overcome exam anxiety, and boost your confidence, so that you do your best to succeed on the MAP Grade 6 Math test.

This study guide will:

- ☑ Explain the format of the MAP Grade 6 Math test.
- ☑ Describe specific test-taking strategies that you can use on the test.
- ☑ Provide MAP Grade 6 Math test-taking tips.
- ☑ Review all MAP Grade 6 Math concepts and topics you will be tested on.
- ☑ Help you identify the areas in which you need to concentrate your study time.
- ☑ Offer exercises that help you develop the basic math skills you will learn in each section.
- ☑ Give **2 realistic and full-length practice tests** (featuring new question types) with detailed answers to help you measure your exam readiness and build confidence.

This resource contains everything you will ever need to succeed on the MAP Grade 6 Math test. You'll get in-depth instructions on every math topic as well as tips and techniques on how to answer each question type. You'll also get plenty of practice questions to boost your test-taking confidence.

In addition, in the following pages you'll find:

➢ **How to Use This Book Effectively** – This section provides you with step-by-step instructions on how to get the most out of this comprehensive study guide.

➢ **How to study for the MAP Grade 6 Math Test** – A six-step study program has been developed to help you make the best use of this book and prepare for your MAP Grade 6 Math test. Here you'll find tips and strategies to guide your study program and help you understand MAP Grade 6 Math and how to ace the test.

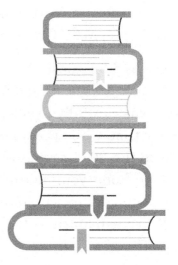

➢ **MAP Grade 6 Math Review** – Learn everything you need to know about the MAP Grade 6 Math test.

➢ **MAP Grade 6 Math Test-Taking Strategies** – Learn how to effectively put these recommended test-taking techniques into use for improving your MAP Grade 6 Math score.

➢ **Test Day Tips** – Review these tips to make sure you will do your best when the big day comes.

Effortless Math's MAP Grade 6 Online Center

Effortless Math Online MAP Grade 6 Center offers a complete study program, including the following:

- ✓ Step-by-step instructions on how to prepare for the MAP Grade 6 Math test
- ✓ Numerous MAP Grade 6 Math worksheets to help you measure your math skills
- ✓ Complete list of MAP Grade 6 Math formulas
- ✓ Video lessons for all MAP Grade 6 Math topics
- ✓ Full-length MAP Grade 6 Math practice tests
- ✓ And much more...

No Registration Required.

Visit effortlessmath.com/MAP6 to find your online MAP Grade 6 Math resources.

How to Use This Book Effectively

Look no further when you need a study guide to improve your math skills to succeed on the math portion of the MAP Grade 6 test. Each chapter of this comprehensive guide to the MAP Grade 6 Math will provide you with the knowledge, tools, and understanding needed for every topic covered on the test.

It's imperative that you understand each topic before moving onto another one, as that's the way to guarantee your success. Each topic provides you with examples and a step-by-step guide of every concept to better understand the content that will be on the test. To get the best possible results from this book:

- ➢ **Begin studying long before your test date.** This provides you ample time to learn the different math concepts. The earlier you begin studying for the test, the sharper your skills will be. Do not procrastinate! Provide yourself with plenty of time to learn the concepts and feel comfortable that you understand them when your test date arrives.
- ➢ **Practice consistently.** Study MAP Grade 6 Math concepts at least 20 to 30 minutes a day. Remember, slow and steady wins the race, which can be applied to preparing for the MAP Grade 6 Math test. Instead of cramming to tackle everything at once, be patient and learn the math topics in short bursts.
- ➢ Whenever you get a math problem wrong, **mark it off, and review it later** to make sure you understand the concept.
- ➢ Start each session by **looking over the previous material.**
- ➢ Once you've reviewed the book's lessons, **take the practice test at the back of the book** to gauge your level of readiness. Then, review your results. Read detailed answers and solutions for each question you missed.
- ➢ **Take another practice test** to get an idea of how ready you are to take the actual exam. Taking the practice tests will give you the confidence you need on test day. Simulate the MAP Grade 6 testing environment by sitting in a quiet room free from distraction. Make sure to clock yourself with a timer.

How to Study for the MAP Grade 6 Math Test

Studying for the MAP Grade 6 Math test can be a really daunting and boring task. What's the best way to go about it? Is there a certain study method that works better than others? Well, studying for the MAP Grade 6 Math can be done effectively. The following six-step program has been designed to make preparing for the MAP Grade 6 Math test more efficient and less overwhelming.

Step 1 - Create a study plan.
Step 2 - Choose your study resources.
Step 3 - Review, Learn, Practice.
Step 4 - Learn and practice test-taking strategies.
Step 5 - Learn the MAP Grade 6 Test format and take practice tests.
Step 6 - Analyze your performance.

STEP 1: Create a Study Plan

It's always easier to get things done when you have a plan. Creating a study plan for the MAP Grade 6 Math test can help you to stay on track with your studies. It's important to sit down and prepare a study plan with what works with your life, school, and any other obligations you may have. Devote enough time each day to studying. It's also a great idea to break down each section of the exam into blocks and study one concept at a time.

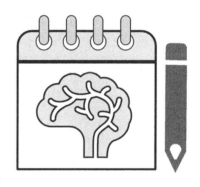

It's important to understand that there is no "right" way to create a study plan. Your study plan will be personalized based on your specific needs and learning style. Follow these guidelines to create an effective study plan for your MAP Grade 6 Math test:

* **Analyze your learning style and study habits** – Everyone has a different learning style. It is essential to embrace your individuality and the unique way you learn. Think about what works and what doesn't work for you. Do you prefer MAP Grade 6 Math prep books or a combination of textbooks and video lessons? Does it work better for you if you study every night for thirty minutes or is it more effective to study in the morning before going to school?

★ **Evaluate your schedule** – Review your current schedule and find out how much time you can consistently devote to MAP Grade 6 Math study.

★ **Develop a schedule** – Now it's time to add your study schedule to your calendar like any other obligation. Schedule time for study, practice, and review. Plan out which topic you will study on which day to ensure that you're devoting enough time to each concept. Develop a study plan that is mindful, realistic, and flexible.

★ **Stick to your schedule** – A study plan is only effective when it is followed consistently. You should try to develop a study plan that you can follow for the length of your study program.

★ **Evaluate your study plan and adjust as needed** – Sometimes you need to adjust your plan when you have new commitments. Check in with yourself regularly to make sure that you're not falling behind in your study plan. Remember, the most important thing is sticking to your plan. Your study plan is all about helping you be more productive. If you find that your study plan is not as effective as you want, don't get discouraged. It's okay to make changes as you figure out what works best for you.

STEP 2: Choose Your Study Resources

There are numerous textbooks and online resources available for the MAP Grade 6 Math test, and it may not be clear where to begin. Don't worry! This study guide provides everything you need to fully prepare for your MAP Grade 6 Math test. In addition to the book content, you can also use Effortless Math's online resources. (Video lessons, worksheets, formulas, etc.)

On each page, there is a link (and a QR code) to an online webpage which provides a comprehensive review of the topic, step-by-step instruction, video tutorial, and numerous examples and exercises to help you fully understand the concept.

You can also visit EffortlessMath.com/MAP6 to find your online MAP Grade 6 Math resources.

STEP 3: Review, Learn, Practice

This MAP Grade 6 Math study guide breaks down each subject into specific skills or content areas. For instance, the percent concept is separated into different topics–percent calculation, percent increase and decrease, percent problems, etc. Use this study guide and Effortless Math online MAP Grade 6 center to help you go over all key math concepts and topics on the MAP Grade 6 Math test.

As you read each topic, take notes or highlight the concepts you would like to go over again in the future. If you're unfamiliar with a topic or something is difficult for you, use the link (or the QR code) at the bottom of the page to find the webpage that provides more instruction about that topic. For each math topic, plenty of instructions, step-by-step guides, and examples are provided to ensure you get a good grasp of the material.

Quickly review the topics you do understand to get a brush-up of the material. Be sure to do the practice questions provided at the end of every chapter to measure your understanding of the concepts.

STEP 4: Learn and Practice Test-taking Strategies

In the following sections, you will find important test-taking strategies and tips that can help you earn extra points. You'll learn how to think strategically and when to guess if you don't know the answer to a question. Using MAP Grade 6 Math test-taking strategies and tips can help you raise your score and do well on the test. Apply test taking strategies on the practice tests to help you boost your confidence.

STEP 5: Learn the MAP Grade 6 Test Format and Take Practice Tests

The MAP *Test Review* section provides information about the structure of the MAP test. Read this section to learn more about the MAP test structure. When you have a prior understanding of the test format and different types of MAP Grade 6 Math questions, you'll feel more confident when you take the actual exam.

Once you have read through the instructions and lessons and feel like you are ready to go – take advantage of both of the full-length MAP Grade 6 Math practice tests available in this study guide. Use the practice tests to sharpen your skills and build confidence.

The MAP Grade 6 Math practice tests offered at the end of the book are formatted similarly to the actual MAP Grade 6 Math test. When you take each practice test, try to simulate actual testing conditions. To take the practice tests, sit in a quiet space, time yourself, and work through as many of the questions as time allows. The practice tests are followed by detailed answer explanations to help you find your weak areas, learn from your mistakes, and raise your MAP Grade 6 Math score.

STEP 6: Analyze Your Performance

After taking the practice tests, look over the answer keys and explanations to learn which questions you answered correctly and which you did not. Never be discouraged if you make a few mistakes. See them as a learning opportunity. This will highlight your strengths and weaknesses.

You can use the results to determine if you need additional practice or if you are ready to take the actual MAP Grade 6 Math test.

Looking for more?

Visit effortlessmath.com/MAP6 to find hundreds of MAP Grade 6 Math worksheets, video tutorials, practice tests, MAP Grade 6 Math formulas, and much more.

No Registration Required.

MAP Test Review

The Missouri Assessment Program (MAP) is a statewide assessment program designed to measure students' knowledge and skills in various subjects, including English Language Arts, Mathematics, Science, and Social Studies. The program is aligned with the Missouri Learning Standards (MLS), which outline what students are expected to know and be able to do at each grade level.

The MAP assessments are administered to students in grades 3-8 and high school. These assessments provide valuable information about a student's academic progress and growth over time, and they are used to evaluate schools and districts as well. The results of the MAP assessments are used to identify areas where students may need additional support or enrichment, to measure the effectiveness of instructional strategies and curriculum, and to identify areas where schools and districts may need additional resources or support.

At the student level, MAP assessments provide insights into a student's academic strengths and weaknesses, which can help teachers tailor their instruction to meet individual student needs. At the class level, MAP assessments provide information about how well students are mastering the MLS, which can help teachers adjust their instruction to better meet the needs of their classes. At the school, district, and state levels, MAP assessments provide valuable information about overall academic achievement and growth over time, which can be used to identify areas where schools and districts may need additional resources or support.

Unit #	Unit Name	Key Content	Standards
0	Beginning of Year	• Up to five days may be spent focusing on routines, expectations, and building classroom community.	
1	Area and Surface Area	• Reasoning to find area. • Parallelograms • Triangles • Polygons • Surface area • Squares and cubes	6. EE. A 6. EE. A. 1 6. EE. A. 2. a 6. EE. A. 2. c 6. G. A. 1 6. G. A. 4
2	Introducing Ratios	• What are ratios? • Equivalent ratios • Representing equivalent ratios • Solving ratio and rate problems • Part-part-whole ratios	6. RP. A. 1 6. RP. A. 2 6. RP. A. 3 6. RP. A. 3. a 6. RP. A. 3. b
3	Unit Rates and Percentages	• Using unit rate to solve problem • Unit conversions • Rates • Percentages	6. RP. A. 2 6. RP. A. 3 6. RP. A. 3. c 6. RP. A. 3. d 6. G. A. 6
4	Dividing Fractions	• Making sense of division • Meaning of fraction division • Algorithm for fraction division • Fractions in lengths, areas, and volumes	6. NS. A. 1 6. G. A. 1 6. G. A. 2
5	Arithmetic in Base Ten	• Warming up to decimals • Adding and subtracting decimals • Multiplying decimals • Dividing decimals	6. NS. B 6. NS. B. 2 6. NS. B. 3 6. EE. A 6. EE. A. 4

6	Expressions and Equations	• Equations in one variable • Equal and equivalent • Expressions with exponents • Relationships between quantities	6.EE.A.2.a 6.EE.A.2.c 6.EE.A.4 6.EE.B.5 6.EE.B.6 6.EE.B.7 6.EE.C.9 6.RP.A.3.b 6.RP.A.3.c
7	Rational Numbers	• Negative numbers and absolute value • Inequalities • The coordinate plane • Common factors and common multiples	6.NS.C.5 6.NS.C.6 6.NS.C.6.a 6.NS.C.6.c 6.NS.C.7.a 6.NS.C.7.b 6.NS.C.7.c 6.NS.C.7.d 6.EE.B.6 6.EE.B.8, 6.EE.B.5 6.EE.B.6 6.NS.B.4
8	Data Sets and Distribution	• Data, variability, and statistical questions • Dot plots and histograms • Mean and MAD • Median and IQR • Using box plots	6.SP.B 6.SP.A, 6.SP.A.1 6.SP.B.5.b 6.SP.B.4 6.SP.B.5.a 6.SP.A.2 6.SP.B.5.a 6.SP.A.3 6.SP.B.5.c 6.SP.B.5.d
9	Putting it All Together	• Synthesize and apply concepts of sixth grade math	6.SP.B 6.SP.A, 6.SP.A.1 6.SP.B.5.b 6.SP.B.4 6.SP.B.5.a 6.SP.A.2 6.SP.B.5.a 6.SP.A.3 6.SP.B.5.c 6.SP.B.5.d

MAP Grade 6 Math Test-Taking Strategies

Here are some test-taking strategies that you can use to maximize your performance and results on the MAP Grade 6 Math test.

#1: Use This Approach To Answer Every MAP Math Question

- Review the question to identify keywords and important information.

- Translate the keywords into math operations so you can solve the problem.

- Review the answer choices. What are the differences between answer choices?

- Draw or label a diagram if needed.

- Try to find patterns.

- Find the right method to answer the question. Use straightforward math, plug in numbers, or test the answer choices (backsolving).

- Double-check your work.

#2: Use Educated Guessing

This approach is applicable to the problems you understand to some degree but cannot solve using straightforward math. In such cases, try to filter out as many answer choices as possible before picking an answer. In cases where you don't have a clue about what a certain problem entails, don't waste any time trying to eliminate answer choices. Just choose one randomly before moving onto the next question.

As you can ascertain, direct solutions are the most optimal approach. Carefully read through the question, determine what the solution is using the math you have learned before, then coordinate the answer with one of the choices available to you. Are you stumped? Make your best guess, then move on.

Don't leave any fields empty! Even if you're unable to work out a problem, strive to answer it. Take a guess if you have to. You will not lose points by getting an answer wrong, though you may gain a point by getting it correct!

#3: Ballpark

A ballpark answer is a rough approximation. When we become overwhelmed by calculations and figures, we end up making silly mistakes. A decimal that is moved by one unit can change an answer from right to wrong, regardless of the number of steps that you went through to get it. That's where ballparking can play a big part.

If you think you know what the correct answer may be (even if it's just a ballpark answer), you'll usually have the ability to eliminate a couple of choices. While answer choices are usually based on the average student error and/or values that are closely tied, you will still be able to weed out choices that are way far afield. Try to find answers that aren't in the proverbial ballpark when you're looking for a wrong answer on a multiple-choice question. This is an optimal approach to eliminating answers to a problem.

#4: Backsolving

A majority of questions on the MAP Grade 6 Math test will be in multiple-choice format. Many test-takers prefer multiple-choice questions, as at least the answer is right there. You'll typically have four answers to pick from. You simply need to figure out which one is correct. Usually, the best way to go about doing so is "backsolving."

As mentioned earlier, direct solutions are the most optimal approach to answering a question. Carefully read through a problem, calculate a solution, then correspond the answer with one of the choices displayed in front of you. If you can't calculate a solution, your next best approach involves "backsolving."

When backsolving a problem, contrast one of your answer options against the problem you are asked, then see which of them is most relevant. More often than not, answer choices are listed in ascending or descending order. In such cases, try out the choices B or C. If it's not correct, you can go either down or up from there.

#5 : Plugging In Numbers

"Plugging in numbers" is a strategy that can be applied to a wide range of different math problems on the MAP Grade 6 Math test. This approach is typically used to simplify a challenging question so that it is more understandable. By using the strategy carefully, you can find the answer without too much trouble.

The concept is fairly straightforward–replace unknown variables in a problem with certain values. When selecting a number, consider the following:

- Choose a number that's basic (just not too basic). Generally, you should avoid choosing 1 (or even 0). A decent choice is 2.
- Try not to choose a number that is displayed in the problem.
- Make sure you keep your numbers different if you need to choose at least two of them.
- More often than not, choosing numbers merely lets you filter out some of your answer choices. As such, don't just go with the first choice that gives you the right answer.
- If several answers seem correct, then you'll need to choose another value and try again. This time, though, you'll just need to check choices that haven't been eliminated yet.
- If your question contains fractions, then a potential right answer may involve either an LCD (least common denominator) or an LCD multiple.
- 100 is the number you should choose when you are dealing with problems involving percentages.

MAP Grade 6 Math – Test Day Tips

After practicing and reviewing all the math concepts you've been taught, and taking some MAP Grade 6 mathematics practice tests, you'll be prepared for test day. Consider the following tips to be extra-ready come test time.

Before Your Test

What to do the night before:

- **Relax!** One day before your test, study lightly or skip studying altogether. You shouldn't attempt to learn something new, either. There are plenty of reasons why studying the evening before a big test can work against you. Put it this way–a marathoner wouldn't go out for a sprint before the day of a big race. Mental marathoners–such as yourself–should not study for any more than one hour 24 hours before a MAP Grade 6 test. That's because your brain requires some rest to be at its best. The night before your exam, spend some time with family or friends, or read a book.

- **Avoid bright screens** - You'll have to get some good shuteye the night before your test. Bright screens (such as the ones coming from your laptop, TV, or mobile device) should be avoided altogether. Staring at such a screen will keep your brain up, making it hard to drift asleep at a reasonable hour.

- **Make sure your dinner is healthy** - The meal that you have for dinner should be nutritious. Be sure to drink plenty of water as well. Load up on your complex carbohydrates, much like a marathon runner would do. Pasta, rice, and potatoes are ideal options here, as are vegetables and protein sources.

- **Get your bag ready for test day** - The night prior to your test, pack your bag with any gear that you need. Keep the bag right by your front door.

The Day of the Test

- Get up reasonably early, but not too early.

- **Have breakfast** - Breakfast improves your concentration, memory, and mood. As such, make sure the breakfast that you eat in the morning is healthy. The last thing you want to be is distracted by a grumbling tummy. If it's not your own stomach making those noises, another test taker close to you might be instead. Prevent discomfort or embarrassment by consuming a healthy breakfast. Bring a snack with you if you think you'll need it.

- **Follow your daily routine** - Do you watch TV each morning while getting ready for the day? Don't break your usual habits on the day of the test. Likewise, if coffee isn't something you drink in the morning, then don't take up the habit hours before your test. Routine consistency lets you concentrate on the main objective–doing the best you can on your test.

- **Wear layers** - Dress yourself up in comfortable layers. You should be ready for any kind of internal temperature. If it gets too warm during the test, take a layer off.

- **Get there on time** - The last thing you want to do is get to the test site late. Rather, you should be there 45 minutes prior to the start of the test. Upon your arrival, try not to hang out with anybody who is nervous. Any anxious energy they exhibit shouldn't influence you.

- **Leave the books at home** - No books should be brought to the test site. If you start developing anxiety before the test, books could encourage you to do some last-minute studying, which will only hinder you. Keep the books far away–better yet, leave them at home.

- **Make your voice heard** - If something is off, speak to a proctor. If medical attention is needed or if you'll require anything, consult the proctor prior to the start of the test. Any doubts you have should be clarified. You should be entering the test site with a state of mind that is completely clear.

- **Have faith in yourself** - When you feel confident, you will be able to perform at your best. When you are waiting for the test to begin, envision yourself receiving an outstanding result. Try to see yourself as someone who knows all the answers, no matter what the questions are. A lot of athletes tend to use this technique–particularly before a big competition. Your expectations will be reflected by your performance.

During your test

- **Be calm and breathe deeply** - You need to relax before the test, and some deep breathing will go a long way to help you do that. Be confident and calm. You got this. Everybody feels a little stressed out just before an evaluation of any kind is set to begin. Learn some effective breathing exercises. Spend a minute meditating before the test starts. Filter out any negative thoughts you have. Exhibit confidence when having such thoughts.

- **Concentrate on the test** - Refrain from comparing yourself to anyone else. You shouldn't be distracted by the people near you or random noise. Concentrate exclusively on the test. If you find yourself irritated by surrounding noises, earplugs can be used to block sounds off close to you. Don't forget—the test is going to last several hours. Some of that time will be dedicated to brief sections. Concentrate on the specific question you are working on during a particular moment.

- **Skip challenging questions** - Optimize your time when taking the test. Lingering on a single question for too long will work against you. If you don't know what the answer is to a certain question, use your best guess, and mark the question so you can review it later on. There is no need to spend time attempting to solve something you aren't sure about. That time would be better served handling the questions you can actually answer well. You will not be penalized for getting the wrong answer on a test like this.

- **Try to answer each question individually** - Focus only on the question you are working on. Use one of the test-taking strategies to solve the problem. If you aren't able to come up with an answer, don't get frustrated. Simply skip that question, then move onto the next one.

- **Don't forget to breathe!** Whenever you notice your mind wandering, your stress levels boosting, or frustration brewing, take a thirty-second break. Shut your eyes, drop your pencil, breathe deeply, and let your shoulders relax. You will end up being more productive when you allow yourself to relax for a moment.

- **Review your answer.** If you still have time at the end of the test, don't waste it. Go back and check over your answers. It is worth going through the test from start to finish to ensure that you didn't make a sloppy mistake somewhere.

After your test

- **Take it easy** - You will need to set some time aside to relax and decompress once the test has concluded. There is no need to stress yourself out about what you could've said, or what you may have done wrong. At this point, there's nothing you can do about it. Your energy and time would be better spent on something that will bring you happiness for the remainder of your day.

Contents

Chapter 1: Rational Numbers and Integers 1
- Using a Diagram to Classify Rational Numbers 2
- Opposite Integer 3
- Using Number Lines to Present Integers 4
- Using Vertical and Horizontal Number Lines to Represent Integers 5
- Chapter 1: Answers 6

Chapter 2: Fraction, Decimals and Mixed Numbers 9
- Using Number Lines to Represent Fractions 10
- Using Strip Diagrams to Represent Fractions 11
- Word Problems of a Number's Fraction 12
- Word Problems Involving Fractions of a Group 13
- Simplifying Fractions 14
- Using Number Lines to Present Decimal 15
- Repeating Decimals 16
- Convert Between Fractions and Decimals 17
- Unit Prices with Decimals and Fractions 18
- Convert Between Decimals and Mixed Numbers 19
- Convert Between Improper Fractions and Mixed Numbers 20
- Order of Decimals, Mixed Numbers and Fractions 21
- Chapter 2: Answers 22

Chapter 3: Rational Numbers 25
- Using Number Lines to Represent Rational Numbers 26
- Using Number Lines to Order Rational Numbers 27
- Word Problems of Ordering Rational Numbers 28
- Convert Rational Numbers to a Fraction 29
- Chapter 3: Answers 30

Chapter 4: Ratios and Proportions 33
- Write a Ratio 34
- Ratio Tables 35
- Using a Fraction to Write down a Ratio 36
- Matching a Model with a Ratio 37
- Word Problems Involving Writing a Ratio 38
- Finding Equivalent Ratio 39
- Word Problems Involving Comparing Ratio 40
- Word Problems Involving Equivalent Ratio 41
- Similarity and Ratios 42
- Equivalent rates 43
- Word Problems Involving Comparing Rates 44
- Word Problems Involving Rates and Ratios 45
- Make a Graph of Ratios and Rates 46
- Chapter 4: Answers 47

Chapter 5: Percentage 51

- Representing Percentage 52
- Using Number Line to Graph Percentages 53
- Using Grid Models to Represent Percent 54
- Using Strip Models to Explain Percent 55
- Using Grid Models to Solve Percentage Problems 56
- Using Strip Models to Solve Percentage Problems 57
- Word Problems of Determining Percentage of a Number 58
- Solving Percentage Word Problems 59
- Fractional and Decimal Percentages 60
- Using Grid Models to Convert Fractions to Percentages 61
- Word Problems: Comparing Percent and Fractions 62
- Word Problems: Conversion of Percent, Fractions, and Decimals 63
- Percent Problems 64
- Chapter 5: Answers 65

Chapter 6: Absolute Value 71

- Absolute Value Definition 72
- Integers and Absolute Value 73
- Using Number Lines to Present Absolute Value 74
- Integer Inequalities Involving Absolute Values 75
- Word Problems of Absolute Value and Integers 76
- Absolute Value of Rational Numbers 77
- Absolute Values and Opposites of Rational Numbers 78
- Chapter 6: Answers 79

Chapter 7: Expressions and Equations 81

- Identifying Expressions and Equations 82
- Identify Equivalent Expressions 83
- Using Properties to Write Equivalent Expressions 84
- Using Strip Models to Identify Equivalent Expressions 85
- Using Algebra Tiles to Identify Equivalent Expressions 86
- Using Exponents to Write down Multiplication Expressions 87
- Using Exponents to Write Powers of Ten 88
- Prime Factorization with Exponents 89
- Identifying Errors Involving the Order of Operations 90
- Writing down Variable Expressions Involving Two Operations 91
- Using Area Models to Factor Variable Expressions 92
- Using Distributive Property to Factor Variable Expressions 93
- Using Distributive Property to Factor Numerical Expressions 94
- Chapter 7: Answers 94

Chapter 8: Fundamentals of Computations 99

- Additive and Multiplicative Relationships 100
- Properties of Addition 101
- Using Area Models and the Distributive Property to Multiply 102
- Reciprocals 103
- Chapter 8: Answers 104

Chapter 9: Algebraic Operation of Integers 107

- Using Number Lines to Add Two Negative Integers 108
- Using Number Lines to Add two Different Signs Integers 109
- Using Input/Output Tables to Add and Subtract Integers 110
- Using Number Lines to Subtract Integers 111
- Using Number Lines for Multiplication by a Negative Integer 112
- Adding and Subtracting Integers 113
- Multiplying and Dividing Integers 114
- Multiply Three or More Numbers 115
- Order of Operations 116
- Chapter 9: Answers 117

Chapter 10: Operations of Fraction, Decimal, and Mixed numbers 121

- Scaling Whole Numbers by Fractions 122
- Using Models to Divide Whole Numbers by Unit Fractions 123
- Dividing Fractions by Whole Numbers in Recipes 124
- Using Models to Multiply Two Fractions 125
- Multiplying and Dividing Fractions 126
- Word Problem for Explaining Fractions as Division 127
- Word Problem of Dividing Fractions 128
- Multiplication and Division of Decimals by Powers of Ten 129
- Estimate Products of Mixed Numbers 130
- Scaling by Fractions and Mixed Numbers 131
- Multiplying Mixed Numbers 132
- Dividing Mixed Numbers 133
- Word Problem of Multiplying Mixed Numbers 134
- Multiplying and Dividing Decimals 135
- Multiplying Three Rational Numbers, and Whole Numbers 136
- Chapter 10: Answers 137

Chapter 11: Variables and Equations 143

- Independent and Dependent Variables in Tables and Graphs 144
- Independent and Dependent Variables in Word Problems 145
- Using Algebra Tiles to Model and Solve Equations 146
- Using Diagrams to Model and Solve Equations 147
- Evaluating One Variable 148
- Chapter 11: Answers 149

Chapter 12: One-Step Operations 151

- One–Step Adding and Subtracting of Decimals and Fractions 152
- One–Step Multiplying and Dividing of Decimals and Fractions 153
- Graphing One-Step Multiplication and Division Equations 154
- Graphing One-Step Inequalities with Rational Numbers 155
- One–Step Equations 156
- Matching Word Problems with the One-Step Equation 157
- Word Problems of the One-Step Equation 158
- Chapter 12: Answers 159

Chapter 13: Two-Variable Equation 163
- Using a Table to Write down a Two-Variable Equation 164
- Complete a Table and Graph a Two-Variable Equation 165
- Evaluating Two Variables 166
- Solving Word problems by Finding Two-Variable Equation 167
- Chapter 13: Answers 168

Chapter 14: Inequalities 171
- Write Inequalities from Number Lines 172
- Graphing Single–Variable Inequalities 173
- One–Step Inequalities 174
- Word Problems Involving One-step Inequalities 175
- Chapter 14: Answers 176

Chapter 15: Measurement System 179
- Mixed Customary Units Operations 180
- Mixed Numbers and Fractions Customary Unit Conversions 181
- Using Proportions to Convert Traditional and Metric Units 182
- Compare the Temperatures Above and Below Zero 183
- Chapter 15: Answers 184

Chapter 16: Geometry and Solid Figures 185
- Triangles 186
- Triangle Inequality 187
- Relationships Between Sides and Angles in a Triangle 188
- Definition of the Area of a Triangle 189
- Polygons 190
- Cubes 191
- Rectangular Prisms 192
- Definition of the Area of a Parallelogram 193
- Word Problems Involving Area of Quadrilaterals and Triangles 194
- Definition of the Area of a Trapezoid 195
- Finding Area of Compound Figures 196
- Finding Area Between Two Rectangles 197
- Finding Area Between Two Triangles 198
- Volume of Cubes and Rectangular Prisms: Word Problems 199
- Chapter 16: Answers 200

Chapter 17: Coordinate Plane 203
- Objects on a Coordinate Plane 204
- Understanding Quadrants 205
- Coordinate Planes as Maps 206
- Chapter 17: Answers 207

Chapter 18: Statistics and Data Analysis 209
- Pie Graph 210
- Graph The Line Plot 211
- Distributions in Line Plot 212
- Relative Frequency Tables 213
- Frequency Charts 214
- Mean, Median, Mode, and Range of the Given Data 215

www.EffortlessMath.com

Interpreting Charts to find mean, median, mode, and range 216
Finding an Outlier 217
Finding Range, Quartiles, and Interquartile Range 218
Interpreting Categorical Data 219
Identifying Statistical Questions 220
Completing a Table and Making a Graph: Word Problems 221
Chapter 18: Answers 222

Time to Test --- 227
MAP Grade 6 Math Practice Test 1 --- 229
MAP Grade 6 Math Practice Test 2 --- 241
MAP Grade 6 Math Practice Tests Answer Keys ------------------------------------- 253
MAP Grade 6 Math Practice Tests Answers and Explanations -------------------- 255

CHAPTER

1 Rational Numbers and Integers

Math topics that you'll learn in this chapter:

- ☑ Using a Diagram to Classify Rational Numbers
- ☑ Opposite Integers
- ☑ Using Number Lines to Present Integers
- ☑ Using Vertical and Horizontal Number Lines to Represent Integers

Rational Numbers and Integers

Topic	Using a Diagram to Classify Rational Numbers
Notes	✓ Whole numbers: a series of natural numbers are whole numbers, which includes zero. In other words, beginning at zero and then goes up. W is the symbol used to represent whole numbers. ✓ Integers: Integers are comprised of negative natural numbers (for instance, -3), positive natural numbers (for instance, 3), and zero. ✓ Rational numbers: These numbers can be seen as one fraction composed of integers. Diagram: Rational Numbers contains -2.3, $4.636363\ldots$, $\frac{5}{2}$, $\frac{1}{4}$, $\frac{3}{7}$; Integers contains $\sqrt{64}$, $+4$, -7; Whole numbers $\{0, 1, 2, 3 \ldots\}$, 0.
Example	*Which of the following numbers is a rational number but not an integer? Use the following diagram to find the answers.* All integers are rational numbers, but all rational numbers aren't integers. In the diagram, $\frac{3}{7}$ is outside the range of integers and is only in the range of rational numbers. So, $\frac{3}{7}$ is only a rational number, but not an integer. Diagram: Rational Numbers contains $\frac{3}{7}$; Integers contains $\sqrt{9}$, -1; Whole numbers contains 19.
Your Turn!	Use the following diagram to find the answers. 1) Which of the following numbers is a rational number, but not an integer? 2) Which of the following numbers is both an integer and a rational number, but isn't a whole number? 3) Which of the following numbers is an integer, a whole number, and a rational number? 4) Which of the following numbers is a rational number but not a whole number? Diagram: Rational Numbers contains -0.6, $\frac{1}{3}$; Integers contains -11, 0; Whole numbers contains 154.

bit.ly/3Jn6KUx

Find more at

www.EffortlessMath.com

Topic	**Opposite Integer**
Notes	✓ Opposite numbers are the same distance from zero, except they are from the opposite direction on a number line. ✓ An integer is a number that doesn't have fractional or decimal parts. The number may be negative, positive, or 0. Opposite integers are positive or negative forms of numbers.
Example	**What is the opposite of -8? Graph it on the number line.** Since the -8 is negative, the opposite of -8 will be on the right side of 0. Thus, the opposite of -8 is 8.
Your Turn!	1) $-4 =$ ___ 2) $+22 =$ ___ 3) $-13 =$ ___ 4) $+181 =$ ___ 5) $-99 =$ ___ 6) $-1 =$ ___ 7) $+4 =$ ___ 8) $-6 =$ ___ 9) $0 =$ ___ 10) $+34 =$ ___

bit.ly/40bH6ca

Rational Numbers and Integers

Topic	Using Number Lines to Present Integers
Notes	✓ Integers are whole numbers (not fractional numbers) and these may be shown as negative, positive, or as zero. ✓ To find integers on a number line: The 0 integer is placed in the middle of the number line. negative ← ... 0 ... → positive −9 −8 −7 −6 −5 −4 −3 −2 −1 0 1 2 3 4 5 6 7 8 9
Example	**What number does the y point on the graph show?** (Number line showing y at 3, with −3 −2 −1 0 1 2 y) The value g is larger than 0 (positive number), and each interval represents 1. Count the interval from 0. Since $0 + 3 = 3$, then $g = 3$.
Your Turn!	1) Number line: −9 −8 −7 −6 −5 −4 −3 −2 −1 0 1 2 3 4 y 6 7 8 9 2) Number line: −9 −8 −7 −6 −5 y −3 −2 −1 0 1 2 3 4 5 6 7 8 9 3) Number line: −9 −8 −7 −6 −5 −4 −3 −2 −1 0 y 2 3 4 5 6 7 8 9 4) Number line: −9 y −7 −6 −8 −4 −3 −2 −1 0 1 2 3 4 5 6 7 8 9 5) Number line: −27 −24 −21 −18 y −12 −9 −6 −3 0 3 6 9 12 15 18 21 24 27 6) Number line: −27 24 −21 −18 −15 −12 −9 −6 −3 0 3 6 9 12 15 18 y 24 27

bit.ly/3LvvFbb

www.EffortlessMath.com

Topic	**Using Vertical and Horizontal Number Lines to Represent Integers**
Notes	✓ Horizontal number lines: Draw a horizontal line, and then place a few points at identical distances on the line. Make one of the points 0. All the points on the right-hand side will be positive integers, while all of those on the left-hand side will be negative integers. ✓ Vertical number lines: Draw a vertical line, and then place a few points at identical distances along it. Make one of these points zero. The points above 0 will be positive integers, while those below 0 will be negative integers.
Example	*Graph 0 on the vertical number line.* Find 0 on the number line, then graph it with a point. *Graph 3 on the horizontal number line.* Find 0 on the number line, and then move to the right on the number line. Count 3 units of the distance and mark it with a dot.
Your Turn!	**Graph integers on the horizontal number line.**

1) -4	2) 7
3) -9	4) -6
5) 5	6) 13

Graph integers on the Vertical number line.

7) -1	8) 3

bit.ly/42dwT0x

Chapter 1: Answers

Using a Diagram to Classify Rational Numbers

1) $-0.6, \frac{1}{3}$
2) $-11, 0$
3) 154
4) $-11, 0, \frac{1}{3}, -0.6$

Opposite integer

1) $+4$
2) -22
3) $+13$
4) -181
5) $+99$
6) $+1$
7) -4
8) $+6$
9) 0
10) -34

Using Number Lines to Present Integers

1) 5
2) -4
3) 1
4) -8
5) -15
6) 21

Using Vertical and Horizontal Number Lines to Represent Integers

7)

8)

Chapter 2
Fraction, Decimals and Mixed Numbers

Math topics that you'll learn in this chapter:

- ☑ Using Number Lines to Represent Fractions
- ☑ Using Strip Diagrams to Represent Fractions
- ☑ Word Problems of a Number's Fraction
- ☑ Word Problems Involving Fractions of a Group
- ☑ Simplifying Fractions
- ☑ Using Number Lines to Present Decimal
- ☑ Repeating Decimals
- ☑ Convert Between Fractions and Decimals
- ☑ Unit Prices with Decimals and Fractions
- ☑ Convert Between Decimals and Mixed Numbers
- ☑ Convert Between Improper Fractions and Mixed Numbers
- ☑ Order of Decimals, Mixed Numbers and Fractions

Fraction, Decimals and Mixed Numbers

Topic	Using Number Lines to Represent Fractions
Notes	✓ Fractions are part of the whole. They have two parts: a numerator and a denominator. • A numerator is a number that is on the top. • A denominator is a number that is on the bottom. ✓ For instance, $\frac{1}{3}$ signifies one part out of three. Therefore, it's represented on a number line at $\frac{1}{3}$, and this number sits between 0 and 1.
Examples	**Graph $\frac{1}{4}$ on the number line.** Divide the distance between 0 and 1 by 4 (the denominator). Then jump to the 1st part (the numerator).
Your Turn!	1) 2) 3) 4) 5) 6) 7) 8)

www.EffortlessMath.com

Topic	Using Strip Diagrams to Represent Fractions
Notes	✓ It's a rectangular model used to represent numerical relationships. It can be used to display fractions or to solve problems that involve operations. Alternative names for it include bar model, length model, or fraction strip. One — 1 One half — $\frac{1}{2}$ One third — $\frac{1}{3}$ One — $\frac{1}{4}$ One fifth — $\frac{1}{5}$
Example	*Shade 1 part of the fraction bar and write what fraction it represents.* First, count the parts of the strip model; it is 6. And each part is $\frac{1}{6}$ of the whole. So, 1 parts of the fraction are $\frac{1}{6}$. Draw that. $\frac{1}{6}$ | $\frac{1}{6}$ | $\frac{1}{6}$ | $\frac{1}{6}$ | $\frac{1}{6}$ | $\frac{1}{6}$
Your Turn!	**Which models show fractions?** 1) $\frac{3}{10}$ a) 2) $\frac{1}{4}$ b) 3) $\frac{13}{20}$ c) 4) $\frac{3}{5}$ d) 5) $\frac{1}{2}$ e) 6) $\frac{5}{8}$ f) 7) $\frac{1}{6}$ g) 8) $\frac{7}{18}$ h)

bit.ly/42c26Bc
Find more at

Fraction, Decimals and Mixed Numbers

Topic	**Word Problems of a Number's Fraction**
Notes	✓ Some of the word problems on fractions that use fraction formulas are listed below: • Word problems on simplification of fractions. • Word problems on addition and subtraction of fractions. • Word problems on multiplication of fractions. • Word problems on dividing fractions. • Word problems on fractions, percentages, and decimals.
Examples	*Alice's sushi recipe calls for $\frac{2}{7}$ of a cup of rice. How much rice would Alice use to make 3 batches of sushi? Write your answer as a fraction or as a whole or mixed number.* Multiply 3 batches by $\frac{2}{7}$ cups of rice: $3 \times \frac{2}{7} = \frac{3}{1} \times \frac{2}{7} = \frac{3 \times 2}{1 \times 7} = \frac{6}{7}$ Alice would use $\frac{6}{7}$ cups of rice. *Kelly has 9 candy bars. She wants to share them with 3 brothers. How much will each get?* Divide 9 candy bars by 3 brothers + Kelly= 4: $$9 \div 4 = \frac{9}{1} \div \frac{4}{1} = \frac{9}{1} \times \frac{1}{4} = \frac{9 \times 1}{1 \times 4} = \frac{9}{4}$$ Then, simplify the product: $\frac{9}{4} = 2\frac{1}{4}$. They get $2\frac{1}{4}$ candy bars each.
Your Turn!	1) Mary needs to order fried chicken for 15 students. Each student should get $\frac{1}{3}$ of a fried chicken. How many fried chickens should Mary order?
	2) Five friends want to share 9 bananas so that they each get the same amount. How much banana would each friend get?
	3) Four children are sharing $\frac{1}{2}$ of a bottle of milk. How much will each child get?
	4) Samuel operates an orange juice stand. On Sunday he used 3 bags of oranges. On Friday he used $\frac{2}{5}$ as many oranges as on Sunday. How many bags of oranges did Samuel use on Friday?

Topic	Word Problems Involving Fractions of a Group
Notes	✓ The number on top (numerator) results from the number of items desired. The number on the bottom (denominator) results from the total amount of items in a group.
Examples	*Neil and his sister went for a walk. They saw 21 ducks along the way. 7 of the ducks they saw were white. What fraction of the ducks were white? Write the fraction in the lowest terms.* Since 7 out of 21 ducks were white, then $\frac{7}{21}$ of the ducks were white. To write the fraction in the lowest terms, divide both the numerator and denominator by 7. $$\frac{7 \div 7}{21 \div 7} = \frac{1}{3}$$
Your Turn!	1) Jules baked 48 cookies. He placed sprinkles on 6 cookies. What fraction of the cookies is covered in sprinkles?
	2) Nick painted his room walls. He divided the walls into 15 parts, and painted 3 parts of them purple. What fraction of the walls is purple?
	3) The fruit baskets contained 40 apples on the table. 5 of them were eaten by children in the afternoon. What fraction of the apples was eaten? Write the fraction in the lowest terms.
	4) 63 students went on a trip to New York City. 7 of them went to Broadway. What fraction of the students went to Broadway?
	5) There are 11 bottles on a shelf. 5 of the bottles are empty. What fraction of the bottles is empty?
	6) A refrigerator has 9 sections for organizing. 4 of the sections are for vegetables. What fraction of the sections is for vegetables?
	7) Karolina makes a necklace with 42 black and white beads. She uses 7 black beads. What fraction of the necklace has black beads?
	8) There were 25 butterflies in the garden. 15 flew away. What fraction of the butterflies flew away? Write the fraction in the lowest terms.

Fraction, Decimals and Mixed Numbers

Topic	Simplifying Fractions
Notes	✓ Simplifying a fraction means reducing it to its lowest terms. ✓ To simplify a fraction, evenly divide both the numerator and denominator of the fraction by 2, 3, 5, 7, etc. ✓ Continue until you can't go any further.
Example	**Simplify** $\frac{18}{30}$. To simplify $\frac{18}{30}$, find a number that both 18 and 30 are divisible by. Both are divisible by 6. Then: $\frac{18}{30} = \frac{18 \div 6}{30 \div 6} = \frac{3}{5}$ **Simplify** $\frac{32}{80}$. To simplify $\frac{32}{80}$, find a number that both 32 and 80 are divisible by. Both are divisible by 8 and 16. Then: $\frac{32}{80} = \frac{32 \div 8}{80 \div 8} = \frac{4}{10}$. 4 and 10 are divisible by 2, so: $\frac{4}{10} = \frac{2}{5}$ or $\frac{32}{80} = \frac{32 \div 16}{80 \div 16} = \frac{2}{5}$
Your Turn!	1) $\frac{2}{12}$ 2) $\frac{16}{62}$
	3) $\frac{7}{49}$ 4) $\frac{10}{32}$
	5) $\frac{9}{33}$ 6) $\frac{14}{16}$
	7) $\frac{25}{40}$ 8) $\frac{48}{80}$
	9) $\frac{10}{45}$ 10) $\frac{22}{44}$
	11) $\frac{15}{75}$ 12) $\frac{52}{169}$

bit.ly/3nOGNko

Topic	Using Number Lines to Present Decimal
Notes	✓ Decimal numbers have a whole number and a fractional part, which are separated by the decimal point. ✓ To indicate decimal numbers on the number line, you must divide the unit length between 0 and 1 into 10 identical parts. In between any 2 integers, for instance, 1 and 2, you will get 1.1, 1.2, 1.3, 1.4, 1.5, 1.6, 1.7, 1.8, and 1.9.
Example	**Find number 1.4 on the number line.** First, on the number line, you must jump to one number, after that, you must divide the unit length between 1 and 2 into 10 identical parts. Then, you must jump to the 4th part.

Your Turn!		
	1) 1.7	2) 5.6
	3) −1.8	4) −2.9
	5) 0.5	6) −1.3
	7) −4.8	8) −0.9
	9) −0.3	10) 3.2

Fraction, Decimals and Mixed Numbers

Topic	Repeating Decimals	
Notes	✓ The description for a decimal that repeats is a fractional number where one or more of the numbers after a decimal point keep repeating forever. ✓ A fractional depiction of $\frac{1}{6}$ is shown as 0.1666666 (the number 6 repeats forever) is an illustration of a decimal that repeats. ✓ It shows one must put down each of the fractions by utilizing a decimal. Divide its numerator by its denominator to get the fraction. Thus, $1 \div 6 = 0.1666666$	
Example	*How do you write $\frac{1}{9}$ as a decimal?* First, divide the numerator by the denominator. $1 \div 9 = 0.111 \ldots$ $\frac{1}{9}$ is approximately equal to 0.111 …. *How do you write $\frac{2}{3}$ as a decimal?* First, divide the numerator by the denominator. $2 \div 3 = 0.666 \ldots$ $\frac{2}{3}$ is approximately equal to 0.666 ….	$\begin{array}{r} 0.111 \\ 9)\overline{1.000} \\ -9 \\ \hline 10 \\ -9 \\ \hline 10 \\ -9 \\ \hline 1 \end{array}$ $\begin{array}{r} 0.666 \\ 3)\overline{2.000} \\ -1.8 \\ \hline 20 \\ -18 \\ \hline 20 \\ -18 \\ \hline 2 \end{array}$
Your Turn!	1) $\frac{1}{15}$	2) $\frac{1}{11}$
	3) $\frac{2}{15}$	4) $\frac{1}{36}$
	5) $\frac{1}{3}$	6) $\frac{4}{6}$
	7) $\frac{4}{15}$	8) $\frac{48}{90}$

Topic	Convert Between Fractions and Decimals
Notes	✓ The simplest method of converting fractions to decimals is by dividing their numerator by their denominator using a calculator. ✓ Firstly, write down the given decimal as a ratio ($\frac{p}{q}$), in which its denominator equals 1. ✓ Then, you must multiply its denominator and the numerator by multiples of 10 for each decimal point, so the decimal for the numerator ends up a whole number.
Example	*Write 0.25 as a fraction.* First, add 1 to the denominator of the decimal number. Then, you must multiply its denominator and the numerator by multiples of 100, for each decimal point. Then, simplify: $0.25 = \frac{0.25}{1} = \frac{0.25 \times 100}{1 \times 100} = \frac{25}{100} = \frac{1}{4}$ *Write $\frac{1}{2}$ as a decimal number.* Divide the numerator by the denominator: $1 \div 2 = 0.5$
Your Turn!	**Write decimal as a fraction.**

1) 0.75	2) 0.65
3) 0.22	4) 0.6
5) 0.20	6) 0.35

Write fraction as a decimal.

7) $\frac{7}{100}$	8) $\frac{27}{50}$
9) $\frac{28}{10}$	10) $\frac{4}{25}$
11) $\frac{3}{4}$	12) $\frac{1}{2}$

Fraction, Decimals and Mixed Numbers

Topic	**Unit Prices with Decimals and Fractions**
Notes	✓ Utilize multiplication for discovering the total price utilizing unit prices and amounts in fractions and decimals. ✓ You must divide the cost of a certain amount of units of an item by the number of units to discover the item's unit price. ✓ Unit rates are rates with a 1 in their denominator. ✓ If there is a rate, like something's cost per some amount of items, and the denominator's quantity isn't 1, then determine the unit rate or price per unit via a division operation: numerator divided via the denominator.
Example	*According to the given table:* *Sophia went to the store and bought $6\frac{1}{4}$ kilograms of the banana. How much did she spend?* | fruits	Per kilogram
Blueberries	$1.5
Raspberries	$2
Blackberries	$5
Banana	$5
Mango	$3 | Find the cost of the banana. Multiply the price per kilogram by the number of kilograms. $\$5 \times 6\frac{1}{4} = \$5 \times 6.25 = \$31.25$, So, she spends $31.25.
Your Turn!	1) The Price of each history book is $9. If the history book has a discount of 0.15, how much is the discount for 1 book?
	2) The Price of each dictionary book is $16. If the dictionary book has a discount of 0.25, how much is the total discount for 3 books?
	3) The Price of each encyclopedia book is $28. If you pay $\frac{3}{4}$ of the total amount for the encyclopedia book, what is its new cost for 5 volumes?
	4) The Price of each cookbook is $3. If you pay $\frac{5}{6}$ of the total amount for the cookbook, what is its new cost?
	5) The Price of each vegetable oil per pound is $7. If Emma buys 3.5 pounds of vegetable oil, what is the total cost?
	6) The Price of each peanut oil per pound is $3. If Williams buys 1.25 pounds of peanut oil, what is the total cost?

bit.ly/42fAif5
Find more at

www.EffortlessMath.com

Topic	Convert Between Decimals and Mixed Numbers
Notes	✓ If the decimal has a number on the left-hand side of the decimal point it signifies that there's a whole part as well as several pieces of a whole. ✓ With decimals, the numbers on the left-hand side of a decimal point stand for the whole part and any numbers on the right-hand side of a decimal point stand for the decimal or the fraction part. ✓ If you wish to convert any decimal into a mixed number, you have to keep the whole number the same and then convert its decimal portion.
Example	**Write 2.9 as a mixed fraction.** Add 1 to the denominator of the decimal number. Then, you must multiply its denominator and the numerator by multiples of 10. $2.9 = \frac{2.9}{1} = \frac{2.9 \times 10}{1 \times 10} = \frac{29}{10}$. Now write the improper fraction as a mixed fraction: $\frac{29}{10} = 2\frac{9}{10}$ **Write $3\frac{1}{4}$ as a decimal number.** Solution: Multiply the denominator and numerator until the denominator becomes a power of 10. Therefore, the integers in the mixed fractions are the numbers to the left of the decimal point, and the fractional numbers are the decimal numbers to the right of the decimal: $3\frac{1}{4} = 3\frac{1 \times 25}{4 \times 25} = 3\frac{25}{100} \rightarrow 3\frac{1}{4} = 3.25$
Your Turn!	**Write decimal as a mixed fraction.**

1) 2.75	2) 1.60
3) 5.88	4) 4.25

Write a mixed fraction as a decimal.

5) $4\frac{2}{5}$	6) $3\frac{8}{25}$
7) $1\frac{7}{100}$	8) $5\frac{13}{20}$

bit.ly/3YQdkZj
Find more at

Fraction, Decimals and Mixed Numbers

Topic	Convert Between Improper Fractions and Mixed Numbers
Notes	In order to translate an improper fraction into a mixed number: ✓ You divide its numerator by its denominator. The result is the whole number, plus the remainder is now the new fraction's numerator. ✓ The new fraction's denominator is the same as the original denominator. ✓ If no remainder is present, there's not a fraction and the resulting number is merely a whole number. $\frac{5}{2} = 2\frac{1}{2}$
Example	Write $2\frac{3}{8}$ as an improper fraction. First, multiply the whole number by the denominator, then add it with the numerator and write in the numerator. In this way, an improper fraction is obtained from a mixed fraction: $2\frac{3}{8} = \frac{(2\times 8)+3}{8} = \frac{19}{8}$ Write $\frac{37}{7}$ as a mixed fraction. First, divide the numerator by the denominator $37 \div 7$. The result is the whole number 5, plus the remainder is now the new fraction's numerator 5: $\frac{37}{7} = \frac{(5\times 7)+2}{7} = 5\frac{2}{7}$
Your Turn!	**Write fractions as an improper fraction.** 1) $7\frac{1}{3}$ 2) $2\frac{5}{8}$ 3) $2\frac{5}{16}$ 4) $6\frac{3}{7}$ 5) $3\frac{7}{8}$ 6) $5\frac{2}{5}$ **Write improper fraction as a mixed fraction.** 7) $\frac{12}{10}$ 8) $\frac{78}{25}$ 9) $\frac{49}{11}$ 10) $\frac{29}{13}$ 11) $\frac{74}{9}$ 12) $\frac{19}{6}$

bit.ly/3lgKWlf

Topic	Order of Decimals, Mixed Numbers and Fractions
Notes	✓ For a comparison of mixed numbers and decimals, you must change all these numbers into a decimal format. ✓ The lowest number must be placed first on the list, while the highest number must be the last one. The rest of the numbers must be put in between in ascending order. ✓ For instance, numbers that go from lowest to highest will be $2\frac{1}{2} = 2.5, 3.5, 5.85,$ and 7.5. ✓ They can also be written by the use of the less than symbol as $2.5 < 3.5 < 5.85$ and < 7.5.
Example	*Order each set of integers from greatest to least.* $1.3, \frac{11}{3}, 6\frac{7}{9}, 9.8$ The largest number is 9.8, and the smallest number is 1.3. Now compare the integers and order them from greatest to least: $$9.8 > 6\frac{7}{9} > \frac{11}{3} > 1.3$$

Your Turn!	**Order each set of rational numbers from greatest to least.**	
	1) $5\frac{3}{5}, 4.8, 5.3, 5\frac{1}{8}$	2) $7\frac{1}{4}, 4.5, 7\frac{1}{2}, 6.8$
	3) $1\frac{2}{9}, 2.6, 1\frac{1}{2}, 1.1$	4) $3.5, 6\frac{9}{10}, 4.3, 4\frac{1}{2}$
	5) $1.4, 1\frac{1}{5}, 2\frac{1}{5}, 1.5$	6) $\frac{3}{10}, 1.8, \frac{5}{6}, \frac{2}{5}$
	Order each set of rational numbers from least to greatest.	
	7) $5.3, 5\frac{2}{9}, 5.5, 5\frac{3}{5}$	8) $1.9, 1\frac{8}{9}, 1\frac{1}{2}, 2.2$
	9) $0.4, \frac{8}{9}, 1.3, 0.8$	10) $\frac{7}{10}, \frac{3}{6}, \frac{2}{7}, \frac{4}{5}$
	11) $0.3, 2.8, \frac{2}{2}, \frac{4}{9}$	12) $2.4, 1\frac{8}{10}, 2\frac{1}{2}, 2.7$

bit.ly/3ZSS1rs

Chapter 2: Answers

Using Number Lines to Represent Fractions

1) $\frac{7}{4}$ 4) $\frac{4}{3}$ 7) $\frac{3}{4}$

2) $\frac{9}{10}$ 5) $\frac{13}{7}$ 8) $\frac{21}{10}$

3) $\frac{6}{21}$ 6) $\frac{1}{2}$

Using Strip Diagrams to Represent Fractions

1) f   4) e   7) b

2) h   5) g   8) c

3) a   6) d

Word Problems of a Number's Fraction

1) 5   3) $\frac{1}{8}$ 4) $1\frac{1}{5}$

2) $1\frac{4}{5}$

Word Problems Involving Fractions of a Group

1) $\frac{1}{8}$ 4) $\frac{1}{9}$ 7) $\frac{1}{6}$

2) $\frac{1}{5}$ 5) $\frac{5}{11}$ 8) $\frac{3}{5}$

3) $\frac{1}{8}$ 6) $\frac{4}{9}$

Simplifying Fractions

1) $\frac{1}{6}$ 5) $\frac{3}{11}$ 9) $\frac{2}{9}$

2) $\frac{1}{2}$ 6) $\frac{7}{8}$ 10) $\frac{1}{2}$

3) $\frac{1}{7}$ 7) $\frac{5}{8}$ 11) $\frac{1}{5}$

4) $\frac{5}{16}$ 8) $\frac{3}{10}$ 12) $\frac{4}{13}$

Using Number Lines to Present Decimal

1) [number line showing 1.7 between 1 and 2]

2) [number line showing 5.6 between 5 and 6]

3)

4)

5)

6)

7)

8)

9)

10)

Repeating Decimals

1) $0.0666\cdots$ 4) $0.027777\cdots$ 7) $0.26666\cdots$

2) $0.090909\cdots$ 5) $0.3333\cdots$ 8) $0.53333\cdots$

3) $0.13333\cdots$ 6) $0.6666\cdots$

Convert Between Fractions and Decimals

1) $\frac{3}{4}$ 5) $\frac{1}{5}$ 9) 2.8

2) $\frac{13}{20}$ 6) $\frac{7}{20}$ 10) 0.16

3) $\frac{11}{50}$ 7) 0.07   11) 0.75

4) $\frac{3}{5}$ 8) 0.54   12) 0.5

Unit Prices with Decimals and Fractions

1) $1.35   3) $105   5) $24.5

2) $12   4) $2.5   6) $3.75

Fraction, Decimals and Mixed Numbers

Convert Between Decimals and Mixed Numbers

1) $2\frac{3}{4}$
2) $1\frac{3}{5}$
3) $5\frac{22}{25}$
4) $4\frac{1}{4}$
5) 4.4
6) 3.32
7) 1.07
8) 5.65

Convert Between Improper Fractions and Mixed Numbers

1) $\frac{22}{3}$
2) $\frac{21}{8}$
3) $\frac{37}{16}$
4) $\frac{45}{7}$
5) $\frac{31}{8}$
6) $\frac{27}{5}$
7) $1\frac{2}{10}$
8) $3\frac{3}{25}$
9) $4\frac{5}{11}$
10) $2\frac{3}{13}$
11) $8\frac{2}{9}$
12) $3\frac{1}{6}$

Order of Decimals, Mixed Numbers and Fractions

1) $5\frac{3}{5}, 5.3, 5\frac{1}{8}, 4.8$
2) $7\frac{1}{2}, 7\frac{1}{4}, 6.8, 4.5$
3) $2.6, 1\frac{1}{2}, 1\frac{2}{9}, 1.1$
4) $6\frac{9}{10}, 4\frac{1}{2}, 4.3, 3.5$
5) $2\frac{1}{5}, 1.5, 1.4, 1\frac{1}{5}$
6) $1.8, \frac{5}{6}, \frac{2}{5}, \frac{3}{10}$
7) $5\frac{2}{9}, 5.3, 5.5, 5\frac{3}{5}$
8) $1\frac{1}{2}, 1\frac{8}{9}, 1.9, 2.2$
9) $0.4, 0.8, \frac{8}{9}, 1.3$
10) $\frac{2}{7}, \frac{3}{6}, \frac{7}{10}, \frac{4}{5}$
11) $0.3, \frac{4}{9}, \frac{2}{2}, 2.8$
12) $1\frac{8}{10}, 2.4, 2\frac{1}{2}, 2.7$

CHAPTER 3
Rational Numbers

Math topics that you'll learn in this chapter:

☑ Using Number Lines to Represent Rational Numbers
☑ Using Number Lines to Order Rational Numbers
☑ Word Problems of Comparing and Ordering Rational Numbers
☑ Convert Rational Numbers to a Fraction

Rational Numbers

Topic	Using Number Lines to Represent Rational Numbers	
Notes	✓ There are both negative and positive rational numbers. All of the numbers higher than 0 are considered positive, while all of them lower than 0 are considered negative. ✓ A rational number is one you can write as a fraction of 2 integers. For instance, to represent $\frac{3}{4}$ on the number line; firstly, divide the line between 0 to 1 into four parts. Since $\frac{3}{4}$ is positive, place this number on the right-hand side of 0.	
Examples	**Graph $\frac{5}{10}$ on the number line.** Divide the distance between 0 and 1 by 10 (the denominator). Then jump to the fifth part (the numerator). **Graph -1.25 on the number line.** First, you must jump one number to the left. Afterward, the length between -1 and -2 is divided into 4 parts. So, the length of each part is $\frac{1}{4}$ or 0.25. Now, to find -0.25, count 1 tick mark to the left of -1.	
Your Turn!	1) -0.4	2) 1.6
	3) $-\frac{3}{5}$	4) $\frac{5}{7}$
	5) 0.2	6) -2.75
	7) $\frac{7}{15}$	8) $-\frac{3}{2}$

Topic	Using Number Lines to Order Rational Numbers
Notes	✓ Number lines make it possible for comparing and ordering negative rational numbers. ✓ The number line is divided into gaps, which signify the relationship between these numbers. ✓ Whenever one goes to the right-hand side of 0, all the numbers will be higher.
Examples	*Order this set of rational numbers from least to greatest. And utilize number lines.* $-0.25, -\frac{3}{4}, 1, \frac{1}{2}$ Locate the numbers on the line. The largest number is on the right side and the smallest number is on the left side. Then, compare the rational numbers and order them from least to greatest: $-\frac{3}{4} > -0.25 > \frac{1}{2} > 1$
Your Turn!	**Order each set of rational numbers from greatest to least.**

1) $-\frac{1}{8}, -\frac{3}{5}, -0.25$	2) $0.125, \frac{9}{7}, -1.25$
3) $\frac{1}{3}, 0.6, -\frac{1}{2}$	4) $1.2, -0.3, 0.1$

Compare rational numbers utilizing number lines.

5) $1.25, \frac{1}{4}, -1.125$	6) $-\frac{3}{10}, 0, -1.2$
7) $-\frac{4}{3}, -\frac{5}{9}, \frac{2}{3}$	8) $-0.4, 0.1, -0.7$

Topic	Word Problems of Ordering Rational Numbers
Notes	✓ You use word problems in order to learn a lesson better. ✓ For a word problem solution: • 1st step: review the problem, then determine what is being asked of you. • 2nd step: highlight the details of the problem • 3rd step: Specify the numbers that should be written in order. • 4th step: Compare which of the numbers is bigger and which is smaller. Sort the numbers accordingly.
Examples	*Bettie and Matt discovered they both have the same breed of cat, a Scottish Fold. Bettie said she gives her Scottish Fold, Bubba, 1.5 cups of cat food each day. Matt gives his Scottish Fold, Copper, $1\frac{2}{3}$ cups of cat food each day. Which Scottish Fold gets more cat food?* First, write 1.5 as a mixed number: $1.5 \rightarrow 1\frac{1}{2}$ And $1\frac{1}{2}$, or 1.5, is smaller than $1\frac{2}{3}$. So, Copper gets more cat food.
Your Turn!	1) There was a blizzard yesterday. Paul heard that it snowed 9.7 inches, and Janet heard that it snowed $9\frac{3}{5}$ inches. Who heard that it snowed less?
	2) Three gamers completed a game. They calculated each person's total time to compare their activity time. The total activity of gamer–1 is 4.2 hours, gamer–2 is $4\frac{1}{3}$ hours, and gamer–3 is 5.1 hours. Who finished the game faster?
	3) Estelle and her mother, are debating how many creams to add to their strawberry-nut bread. Estelle wants to add $\frac{4}{5}$ of a cup, and her mother wants to add 0.65 cups. Who wants to add more cream to the bread?
	4) Mason and Liam just hiked towards each other in a 2-mile walk. Mason hiked the distance in 1.1 hours, and Liam hiked it in $1\frac{5}{6}$ hours. Who has been on the road the most?

bit.ly/3ZNo7ov

Topic	Convert Rational Numbers to a Fraction
Notes	✓ Numbers written in the format of $\frac{a}{b}$, or any number that can be written in the format $\frac{a}{b}$, in which 'a' and 'b' are integers plus $b \neq 0$, are known as rational numbers. ✓ So, rational numbers are any number that can be expressed it as the quotient of 2 integers, with the condition being that its divisor isn't 0.
Example	**Write 0.7 in the form $\frac{a}{b}$, where a and b are integers.** 0.7 is 7 tenths. So, write 7 in the numerator and 10 in the denominator: $0.7 = \frac{7}{10}$ **Write -5 in the form $\frac{a}{b}$, where a and b are integers.** -5 is an integer. So, you can write -5 in the numerator and 1 in the denominator: $-5 = -\frac{5}{1}$

Your Turn!

1) 0.35	2) 93
3) 1.77	4) −3.33
5) −0.56	6) 2.007
7) −3	8) 0.15
9) 13	10) −27
11) 1.05	12) 101

bit.ly/3lgROPD

Chapter 3: Answers

Using Number Lines to Represent Rational Numbers

Using Number Lines to Order Rational Numbers

1) $-\frac{1}{8}, -0.25, -\frac{3}{5}$

2) $\frac{9}{7}, 0.125, -1.25$

3) $0.6, \frac{1}{3}, -\frac{1}{2}$

4) $1.2, 0.1, -0.3$

5)

6)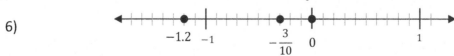

7)

8) [number line with points at −0.7, −0.4, 0.1; marks at −1, 0, 1]

Word Problems of Ordering Rational Numbers

1) Janet
2) Gamer−1
3) Estelle
4) Liam

Convert Rational Numbers to a Fraction

1) $\frac{7}{20}$

2) $\frac{93}{1}$

3) $\frac{177}{100}$

4) $-\frac{333}{100}$

5) $-\frac{14}{25}$

6) $\frac{2007}{1000}$

7) $-\frac{3}{1}$

8) $\frac{3}{20}$

9) $\frac{13}{1}$

10) $-\frac{27}{1}$

11) $\frac{21}{20}$

12) $\frac{101}{1}$

CHAPTER 4
Ratios and Proportions

Math topics that you'll learn in this chapter:

- ☑ Write a Ratio
- ☑ Ratio Tables
- ☑ Using a Fraction to Write down a Ratio
- ☑ Matching a Model with a Ratio
- ☑ Word Problems Involving Writing a Ratio
- ☑ Finding Equivalent Ratio
- ☑ Word Problems Involving Comparing Ratio
- ☑ Word Problems Involving Equivalent Ratio
- ☑ Similarity and Ratios
- ☑ Equivalent Rates
- ☑ Word Problems Involving Comparing Rates
- ☑ Word Problems Involving Rates and Ratios
- ☑ Make a Graph of Ratios and Rates

Topic	Write a Ratio
Notes	✓ Ratios compare 2 quantities. They show us the number of times one quantity greater than another. The numbers in ratios are known as terms. ✓ Special types of ratios are unit rates, rates, measurement conversions, and percentages.
Examples	*What is the ratio of circles to squares?* First, count the number of circles. Write it down, 2. Then, count the number of squares. Write it down, 7. So, write the ratio as: $2:7$
Your Turn!	**What is the ratio of the given in each group to each other?** 1) ⚪⚪ ■■■■ 2) ☆☆☆☆☆ ■■■ 3) ☆☆☆ ●●●●●● 4) ▢▢▢▢ ●● 5) ▢▢▢▢ ★★★★★★★★ 6) ▢ ★★★ 7) △△△△ ■■■■ △△ 8) ▢▢▢▢ ▲▲▲▲ ▢▢

Topic	Ratio Tables
Notes	✓ Ratio tables are simply tables utilized to show a relationship in between 2 separate quantities. ✓ Ratio tables help visualizing relationships between the 2 separate quantities. ✓ To compare ratio tables, you must utilize either division or multiplication.
Example	**Complete the ratio table.** Start with the first row, $4:3$. Then write the ratio as a fraction, $\frac{4}{3}$. After it, multiply the numerator and the denominator by the same number to find an equivalent ratio. $\frac{4}{3} = \frac{4\times3}{3\times3} = \frac{12}{9}$, $\frac{4}{3} = \frac{4\times7}{3\times7} = \frac{28}{21}$. Then write the answer in the table. | 4	3 | | 8 | 6 | | 12 | ☐ | | 16 | 18 | | ☐ | 21 |

Your Turn!

1)

7	2
21	6
35	☐
42	12
63	18

2)

3	5
6	10
☐	15
12	20
15	25

3)

1	4
☐	8
3	12
4	16
5	20

4)

☐	7
18	14
27	21
36	28
45	35

5)

10	3
50	15
100	30
150	☐
200	60

6)

5	6
☐	18
30	36
45	54
60	72

7)

2	1
6	3
10	5
14	7
18	☐

8)

4	☐
8	22
12	33
20	55
40	110

9)

2	9
4	18
6	27
8	36
☐	45

Ratios and Proportions

Topic	**Using a Fraction to Write down a Ratio**
Notes	✓ Ratios compare two amounts, showing the number of times greater one amount is than another amount. ✓ This discussion will cover part-to-part ratios, part-to-total ratios, methods for determining various kinds of ratios, ratios, and fractions, simplifying ratios, equivalent ratios, and ratios and percentages.
Example	***What is the ratio of stars to triangles? Write the ratio as a fraction.*** First, count the number of stars. Write it in the numerator, 4. Then, count the number of triangles. Write it in the denominator, 5. So, write the ratio as a fraction: $$\frac{4}{5}$$
Your Turn!	1) 2) 3) 4) 5) 6) 7) 8)

Topic	Matching a Model with a Ratio
Notes	✓ There are several methods of representing a ratio. ✓ The most common method of writing a ratio is by doing so as a fraction, $\frac{2}{11}$. ✓ You can also write it utilizing the word "to," as in "2 to 11." ✓ Lastly, write down this ratio utilizing a colon in between the 2 numbers, $2:11$.
Example	**Which model (A or B) shows $4:7$?** Count the number of shapes in each model, then compare it with the given ratio. Model (A) has 4 circles and 7 stars. It represents the ratio of 4 to 7. Model (B) has 3 triangles and 4 stars. It does not represent the ratio of 4 to 7.

Your Turn!	Which model shows which ratio?	
	1) $\frac{1}{4}$	a)
	2) $2:3$	b)
	3) $\frac{4}{6}$	c)
	4) $\frac{2}{5}$	d)
	5) 5 to 6	e)
	6) $7:2$	f)
	7) $\frac{7}{3}$	g)
	8) 5 to 4	h)

Ratios and Proportions

Topic	**Word Problems Involving Writing a Ratio**
Notes	✓ Ratios are a comparison of 2 numbers. ✓ A ratio can be written in several ways. You can write these using a colon (1: 5), utilizing the word "to" (1 to 5), or as a fraction: $\frac{1}{5}$.
Example	*A chef made 14 bowls of soup that contained onion and 28 bowls of soup that contain garlic. What is the ratio of the number of soup bowls with onion to the number of soup bowls with garlic?* First, write the numbers of bowls of onion soup and the numbers of bowls of garlic soup. Number of bowls of onion soup = 14 Number of bowls of garlic soup = 28 Then, write the ratio, 14: 28.
Your Turn!	**The table shows the number of sold museum tickets per age category on a recent weekend. Write the ratios in question.**

1) The ratio of 5 − 15 to 36 − 45?

2) The ratio of 26 − 35 to 36 − 45?

3) The ratio of 46 − 55 to 16 − 25?

4) The ratio of 36 − 45 to 26 − 35?

5) The ratio of 16 − 25 to 56 and up?

6) The ratio of 56 and up to 26 − 35?

Age category	Number of tickets sold
5 − 15	86
16 − 25	38
26 − 35	21
36 − 45	15
46 − 55	9
56 and up	3

Write the ratio.

7) There are 36 green crystals and 16 red crystals on Maria's dress. What is the ratio of the number of red crystals to the number of green crystals?

8) There are 18 classic novels and 24 adventure novels in Maria's library. What is the ratio of the number of classic novels to the number of adventure novels?

9) Ava read 5 of her letters and has 15 of them left. What is the ratio of the number of read letters to the number of unread letters?

bit.ly/3JhREzz

Topic	Finding Equivalent Ratio
Notes	✓ Ratios are a comparison of 2 quantities. ✓ An equivalent ratio is a ratio that is identical whenever you do a comparison. You can compare 2 or more ratios with one another to find out if they are identical or not. For instance, $1:3$ and $2:6$ are equivalent weight ratios. ✓ Equivalent ratios have an identical value. To figure out if 2 ratios are equivalent in weight, write them down as fractions. If these fractions are equal, then so are the ratios. $$\frac{1}{3} = \frac{2}{6} \rightarrow \frac{1}{3} = \frac{1}{3}$$
Example	**Are the ratios $2:8$ and $4:16$ equivalent?** Convert a ratio as a fraction, $\frac{2}{8}$ and $\frac{4}{16}$. And you can compare the fractions using a common denominator. The denominators are 8 and 16. You can use 16 as the common denominator since 16 is a multiple of 2 and 8. $\frac{2}{8} = \frac{2 \times 2}{8 \times 2} = \frac{4}{16}$. So, $\frac{2}{8}$ and $\frac{4}{16}$ are equal. Therefore, ratios $2:8$ and $4:16$ are equivalent.
Your Turn!	1) $2:3$ and $4:6$ 2) $7:3$ and $72:27$ 3) $1:2$ and $14:24$ 4) $9:5$ and $40:25$ 5) $4:9$ and $40:85$ 6) $1:5$ and $7:30$ 7) $7:11$ and $49:77$ 8) $1:6$ and $8:48$ 9) $3:8$ and $24:64$ 10) $6:12$ and $42:77$ 11) $5:2$ and $35:14$ 12) $5:9$ and $45:81$

bit.ly/3TjG4Z7

Find more at

Ratios and Proportions

Topic	Word Problems Involving Comparing Ratio
Notes	Comparison of ratios can be done using two different and simple methods. Let us examine both the methods below: ✓ *LCM* method of comparing ratios • First find the least common multiple (*LCM*) of the consequents and divide it by the consequents. • Multiply the quotient obtained with the ratios. ✓ Comparing ratios by cross multiplication method • Multiply the antecedent of the first ratio with the consequent of the second ratio and the consequent of the first ratio with the antecedent of the second ratio. For example - $8:9$ and $7:8$ according to this method we multiply the numbers. 8×8 and 9×7.
Example	*Megan and Jessika had smoothies for breakfast. Megan made her smoothie with 1 cup of melon and 4 cups of orange. Jessika made a giant smoothie with 3 cups of melon and 12 cups of orange. Did the smoothies have the same ratio of melon to orange?* The ratio of melon to oranges for Megan was $\frac{1}{4}$. The ratio of melon to oranges for Jessika was $\frac{3}{12}$. To simplify $\frac{3}{12}$ to $\frac{1}{4}$, the ratios are equal. $\frac{3}{12} = \frac{3 \div 3}{12 \div 3} = \frac{1}{4}$. So, the smoothies had the same ratio of melon to orange.
Your Turn!	1) Ava's recipe for apple pie calls for 4 cups of chopped apple and 7 cups of flour. Mia's recipe calls for 2 cups of chopped apple and 5 cups of flour. Whose recipe makes a stronger apple flavor?
	2) There are two alloys A and B, both made up of carbon and iron. The ratio between carbon and iron in alloy (A) is $2\frac{1}{5}:4$. And the ratio between carbon and iron in the alloy (B) is $1\frac{1}{4}:2$. In which alloy do we have more carbon?
	3) The price of 5 apples at the Quick market is $2.44. The price of 7 apples of the same type at Walmart is $3.20. Which place is the better buy?
	4) Rebecca works in a rehabilitation center. In the first month, she helped to rehabilitate 13 patients and 5 patients were discharged. In the second month, she helped to rehabilitate 26 patients and 8 patients were discharged. In which month was she more successful in discharging patients?

Topic	Word Problems Involving Equivalent Ratio
Notes	✓ When a word problem expresses a ratio, follow these steps to find an equivalent ratio that solves the problem: ✓ Step 1: Identify the ratio given in the word problem. ✓ Step 2: One of the two values involved in the ratio will have a given value. Identify this value. ✓ Step 3: Divide the given value in step 2 by the corresponding value in the ratio from step 1. ✓ Step 4: Construct the equivalent ratio to the given ratio by multiplying both numbers in the original ratio by the number found in step 3.
Example	*Are these ratios equivalent? 12 full-time employees for every 24 part-time employees, 3 full-time employees for every 6 part-time employees.* For comparison: First, write the ratios as fractions: $\frac{12}{24}$ and $\frac{3}{6}$. Then, you can compare the fractions by writing a proportion. $\frac{12}{24} = \frac{3}{6}$. To understand that there is an equal relationship, use cross multiplication: $12 \times 6 = 24 \times 3 \rightarrow 72 = 72$ So, the fractions are equivalent, which means the ratios are equivalent.
Your Turn!	1) Express ratios as a proportion. For 160 miles on 4 gallons of gas, how many miles can be driven on 1 gallon of gas?
	2) Bob has 16 red cards and 28 green cards. What is the ratio of Bob's red cards to his green cards?
	3) At a party, 9 soft drinks are required for every 15 guests. If there are 260 guests, how many soft drinks are required?
	4) In Jack's class, 8 of the students are tall and 18 are short. In Michael's class, 55 students are tall and 25 students are short. Are these ratios equivalent?
	5) A free study club has 66 members, of which 28 are males and the rest are females. What is the ratio of females to males?
	6) The ratio of boys to girls in a class is 5: 7. If there are 15 boys in the class, how many girls are in that class?

Topic	**Similarity and Ratios**
Notes	✓ Two figures are similar if they have the same shape. ✓ Two or more figures are similar if the corresponding angles are equal, and the corresponding sides are in proportion.
Example	***Two rectangles are similar. The first is 5 feet wide and 15 feet long. The second is 10 feet wide. What is the length of the second rectangle?*** Let's put x for the length of the second rectangle. Since the two rectangles are similar, their corresponding sides are in proportion. Write a proportion and solve for the missing number. $$\frac{5}{10} = \frac{15}{x} \rightarrow 5x = 10 \times 15 \rightarrow 5x = 150 \rightarrow x = \frac{150}{5} = 30$$ The length of the second rectangle is 30 feet.
Your Turn!	1) Two rectangles are similar. One is 6.5 meters by 9 meters. The longer side of the second rectangle is 45 meters. What is the other side of the second rectangle? _____ 2) Two rectangles are similar. The first is 9 feet wide and 30 feet long. The second is 12 feet wide. What is the length of the second rectangle? _____ 3) The following triangles are similar. What is the value of the unknown side? 4) Two rectangles are similar. The first is 7 inches wide and 27 inches long. The second is 81 inches in length. What is the width of the second rectangle? _____

Topic	Equivalent rates
Notes	✓ Equivalent ratios will yield identical values. ✓ To see if 2 ratios are equivalent, write them down as fractions. If these fractions are equal, then the ratios are equivalent. ✓ Equivalent ratios are ratios that are equal when compared. You can compare two or more ratios with one another in order to check if they're equivalent or not.
Example	**Complete the proportion and type in the blank box.** 3 oranges on 1 bowl = 21 oranges on ☐ bowls Write the ratios as fractions, $\frac{3}{1}$. Then, write an equivalent fraction with 21 as the numerator. $\frac{3}{1} = \frac{3 \times 7}{1 \times 7} = \frac{21}{7}$. So, 21 oranges on 7 bowls.
Your Turn!	1) $\frac{2}{9} = \frac{8}{x}, x =$ ____ 2) $\frac{5}{2} = \frac{10}{x}, x =$ ____
	3) $\frac{1}{5} = \frac{6}{x}, x =$ ____ 4) $\frac{6}{5} = \frac{24}{x}, x =$ ____
	5) $\frac{2}{11} = \frac{12}{x}, x =$ ____ 6) $\frac{6}{18} = \frac{30}{x}, x =$ ____
	7) $\frac{6}{4} = \frac{x}{20}, x =$ ____ 8) $\frac{4}{9} = \frac{24}{x}, x =$ ____
	9) $\frac{7}{4} = \frac{x}{8}, x =$ ____ 10) $\frac{6}{7} = \frac{36}{x}, x =$ ____
	11) $\frac{3}{13} = \frac{54}{x}, x =$ ____ 12) $\frac{6}{9} = \frac{54}{x}, x =$ ____

Topic	**Word Problems Involving Comparing Rates**
Notes	✓ Rates are a special type of ratio. They measure the amount one quantity or thing varies in relation to the other. ✓ Rate word problems involve problems that deal with rates, time, distances, and water or wind currents. ✓ Additional kinds of word problems utilizing systems of equations involve money word problems as well as age word problems.
Example	*Lucas's dog returns 18 ball throws per hour. William's dog returns 39 ball throws in 3 hours. Do the two dogs return the ball at the same rate?* Compare the return times per unit of time. Lucas's dog returns 18 ball throws per hour. Find the return times per unit of time (hour), $\frac{18 \div 1}{1 \div 1} = \frac{18}{1}$. William's dog returns 39 ball throws in 3 hours. Find the return times per unit of time (hour), $\frac{39 \div 3}{3 \div 3} = \frac{13}{1}$. 13 returns per unit time is less than 18 returns per unit time. So, Lucas's dog is faster than William's dog at returning the ball.
Your Turn!	1) James is buying some cereal from the store. He finds a box of 5 frosted flakes for $3.50. And a box of 15 honey bunches of oats for $9.00. Which brand is the better value?
	2) Which is the best value? 12 pens that cost $8 or 5 pens that cost $2.50
	3) Benjamin wants to learn to play the piano. His parents recommended two different music schools. Music school (A) charges $685 for 10 hours of lessons. Music school (B) offers 15 hours of lessons for $980. Which school offers the better deal?
	4) Which is the best value? 4 gallons of oil at $5.80 or 1.5 gallons of oil at $4.00

bit.ly/3ZSWv10

Topic	Word Problems Involving Rates and Ratios
Notes	✓ Rate word problems involve problems which deal with rates, time, distances, and water or wind currents. ✓ Additional kinds of word problems utilizing systems of equations involve money word problems as well as age word problems. ✓ To solve these types of word problems, follow these steps: • Identify the known ratio and the unknown ratio. • Set up the proportion. • Cross-multiply and solve. • Check the answer by plugging the result into the unknown ratio.
Example	*On weekday mornings, it takes William 45 minutes to hike 1.5 miles to his school. This Saturday, William will hike to the park to meet his friends. The park is 4 miles away from William's house. If he hikes at the same rate, how many minutes will it take William to get to the park?* It takes William 45 minutes to hike 1.5 miles. Write this as a rate, $\frac{45 \text{ minutes}}{1.5 \text{ miles}}$. Divide the numerator and denominator by 1.5 to find the unit rate, $\frac{45 \text{ minutes} \div 1.5}{1.5 \text{ miles} \div 1.5} = \frac{30 \text{ minutes}}{1 \text{ mile}}$. Now you need to find how many minutes it will take him to hike 4 miles at the same rate. Write a proportion, $\frac{30 \text{ minutes}}{1 \text{ mile}} = \frac{x \text{ minutes}}{4 \text{ miles}} \rightarrow 30 \times 4 = 1 \times x \rightarrow x = 120 \text{ minutes}$ It will take William 120 minutes to hike to the park.
Your Turn!	1) If books sell at 5 for $0.65, how many books can be bought for $1.95?
	2) If the rent of a room for 4 weeks is $450, how much rent is paid for 12 weeks?
	3) How far will a car travel in 6 hours if it travels 40 miles in 1 hour?
	4) A bus takes 1.5 hours to go 75 miles. How long will it take the bus to go 500 miles?
	5) A plane like a Boeing 747 uses approximately 1.2 gallons of fuel every second. Over a 1-and-a-half hour (per hour is 3,600 seconds) flight, how many gallons might it burn?
	6) Leo drew a square with a perimeter of 30 inches. Since the ratio of the side length of a square to the square's perimeter is always 1 to 4. What is the side length of the square that Leo drew?

Ratios and Proportions

Topic	**Make a Graph of Ratios and Rates**
Notes	✓ A ratio table shows a bunch of equivalent ratios. ✓ Find and organize equivalent ratios in a ratio table and generate a ratio table by using repeated addition or multiplication. ✓ To draw a ratio table, use equivalent ratios to create ordered pairs of the form (first quantity, second quantity) and plot these ordered pairs in a coordinate plane and draw a line, starting at (0,0), through the points.
Example	*An airplane leaves Chicago and flies at a constant speed. The airplane flies 155 miles in 15 minutes. Complete the table and make a graph.* The airplane flies 155 miles in 15 minutes, which can be written as a rate. Using this rate, complete the table to find distances, $\frac{155 \text{ miles}}{15 \text{ minutes}}$. $\frac{155 \, mi \times 2}{15 \, min \times 2} = \frac{310 \, mi}{30 \, min}$, $\frac{155 \, mi \times 3}{15 \, min \times 3} = \frac{465 \, mi}{45 \, min}$ and $\frac{155 \, mi \times 4}{15 \, min \times 4} = \frac{620 \, mi}{60 \, min}$ To graph the data, write the pairs of numbers in the table as (x, y) ordered pairs. $x =$ minutes and $y =$ miles. | minutes | 15 | 30 | 45 | 60 | |---|---|---|---|---| | miles fly | 155 | 310 | 465 | 620 | Points: (15,155), (30,310), (45,465), (60,620)

Your Turn!

1) To make the dipping sauce, Daniel uses 9 cups of sour cream for every 4 cups of yogurt.

Cups of sour cream	9	18	27	36
Cups of yogurt	4	—	—	—

2) Kyle runs to exercise. He always runs 2 miles lengths at a slow pace for every 0.25 mile length at a fast pace.

Slow lengths	2	4	6	8
Fast lengths	0.25	—	—	—

3) Eli makes beaded earrings to sell at craft fairs. She uses 8 yellow beads for every 4 purple beads.

Yellow beads	8	16	24	32
Purple beads	4	—	—	—

4) James is planting in his field. He is planting 1 row of strawberry plants for every 3 rows of raspberry plants.

Rows of strawberry plants	1	2	3	4
Rows of raspberry plants	3	—	—	—

bit.ly/42dME7E

www.EffortlessMath.com

Chapter 4: Answers

Write a Ratio

1) 2 ∶ 4
2) 5 ∶ 4
3) 3 ∶ 6
4) 4 ∶ 2
5) 5 ∶ 7
6) 1 ∶ 3
7) 6 ∶ 5
8) 8 ∶ 4

Ratio Tables

1) 10
2) 9
3) 2
4) 9
5) 45
6) 15
7) 9
8) 11
9) 10

Using a Fraction to Write down a Ratio

1) $\frac{8}{3}$
2) $\frac{7}{2}$
3) $\frac{1}{5}$
4) $\frac{4}{2}$
5) $\frac{1}{3}$
6) $\frac{5}{9}$
7) $\frac{3}{9}$
8) $\frac{7}{5}$

Matching a Model with a Ratio

1) g
2) d
3) h
4) b
5) c
6) a
7) f
8) e

Word Problems Involving Writing a Ratio

1) 86 ∶ 15
2) 21 ∶ 15
3) 9 ∶ 38
4) 15 ∶ 21
5) 38 ∶ 3
6) 3 ∶ 21
7) 16 ∶ 36
8) 18 ∶ 24
9) 5 ∶ 15

Finding Equivalent Ratio

1) Yes
2) No
3) No
4) No
5) No
6) No
7) Yes
8) Yes
9) Yes
10) No
11) Yes
12) Yes

Word Problems Involving Comparing Ratio

1) Ava's recipe
2) Alloy B
3) Walmart
4) In the first month

Word Problems Involving Equivalent Ratio

1) 40
2) $\frac{4}{7}$
3) 156
4) No
5) $\frac{19}{14}$
6) 21

Similarity and Ratios

1) 32.5
2) 40
3) 24
4) 21

Equivalent Rates

1) 36
2) 4
3) 30
4) 20
5) 66
6) 90
7) 30
8) 54
9) 14
10) 42
11) 234
12) 81

Word Problems Involving Comparing Rates

1) The honey bunches
2) 5 pens are less value
3) School (B)
4) 4 gallons of oil are less value

Word Problems Involving Rates and Ratios

1) 15
2) 1,350
3) 240
4) 10
5) 6,480
6) 7.5

Completing a Table and Make a Graph of Ratios and Rates

1) 8, 12, 16

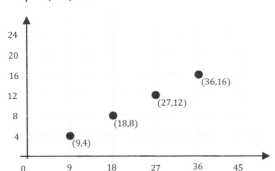

2) 0.5, 0.75, 1

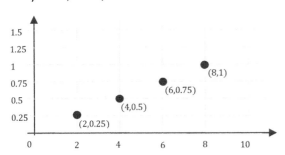

3) 8, 12, 16

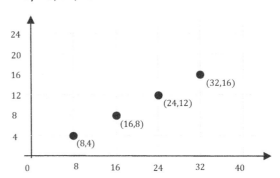

4) 6, 9, 12

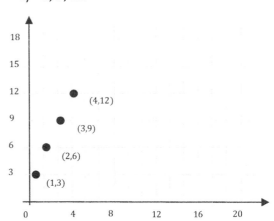

CHAPTER 5: Percentage

Math topics that you'll learn in this chapter:

- ☑ Representing Percentage
- ☑ Using Number Line to Graph Percentages
- ☑ Using Grid models to Represent Percent
- ☑ Using Strip Models to Explain Percent
- ☑ Using Grid Models to Solve Percentage Problems
- ☑ Using Strip Models to Solve Percentage Problems
- ☑ Word Problems of Determining Percentage of a Number
- ☑ Solving Percentage Word Problems
- ☑ Fractional and Decimal Percentages
- ☑ Using Grid Models to Convert Fractions to Percentages
- ☑ Word Problems: Comparing Percent and Fractions
- ☑ Word Problems: Conversion of Percent, Fractions, and Decimals
- ☑ Percent Problems

Percentage

Topic	Representing Percentage
Notes	✓ In math, a percentage is a number or the ratio that may be expressed as a fraction of 100. ✓ If you need to compute the percentage of a number, you divide it by the whole and then multiply this by 100. ✓ Therefore, a percentage means a part per hundred. One hundred percent implies per 100. ✓ Hence, 1% represents $\frac{1}{100}$ or one-hundredths, and 9 percent signifies $\frac{9}{100}$ or nine-hundredths.
Examples	*What percentage of the shape is shaded?* This shape has 100 parts, and 56 of the parts are shaded. Then write 56 out of 100 as a percentage: 56%
Your Turn!	**What percentage of the shape is shaded?** 1) 3)

Topic	Using Number Line to Graph Percentages
Notes	✓ To determine a percentage, you must divide its value by the total value and then you will multiply the result by 100. $Percentage\ formula = (\frac{Value}{Total\ value}) \times 100.$
Example	**Graph 60% on the number line.** Write the 60% as a fraction, which is $\frac{3}{5}$. Then divide 100 by the denominator of the fraction to find out how much each part represents, $100\% \div 5 = 20\%$. Label the number line, and now finds 3 parts or 60% on the number line. 0 20% 40% 60% 80% 100%

Your Turn!	1) 75%	2) 87.5%
	3) $66\frac{2}{3}\%$	4) 62.5%
	5) $42\frac{6}{7}\%$	6) 30%
	7) 50%	8) 37.5%
	9) 10%	10) $57\frac{1}{7}$

bit.ly/3liOPGs

Percentage

Topic	Using Grid Models to Represent Percent
Notes	✓ The percentage is the rate per 100. You may utilize 10×10 grids to represent a percentage. ✓ To transform a decimal into a percentage, multiply by 100 (simply move the decimal point two spaces to the right). ✓ To obtain a percentage of a number, such as 20 percent of 70, merely multiply. For instance, $\left(\frac{20}{100}\right)(70) = 0.2 \times 70 = 14$. ✓ With any computation, the percent value must be changed in a number in fractional format via removing the percentage symbol and dividing it by 100.
Example	**Show 54% on the grade and write as a fraction and decimal.** To display 54% in the grid shape, shade 54 of the 100 squares. To write as a decimal and fraction. The grid shows that 54% is equivalent to $\frac{54}{100}$. To write as a decimal: $54 \div 100 = 0.54$ To write as a fraction in the simplest form: divide the numerator and denominator by 2: $$\frac{54}{100} = \frac{54 \div 2}{100 \div 2} = \frac{27}{50}$$

Your Turn!	Show percentage on the grid and write as a fraction and decimal.	
	1) 16%	2) 44%
	3) 59%	4) 50%
	5) 25%	6) 80%

Topic	Using Strip Models to Explain Percent
Notes	✓ It's a rectangular model used to display numerical relationships. It can be used to represent fractions or to solve equations involving operations. Total number of cookies 96 cookies | 84 cookies Total number of cookies in each bag , , ... How many bags are needed?
Example	**Represent 25% using a strip model.** First, write 25% as a fraction. 25% means 25 parts out of 100, which is the same as $\frac{25}{100}$. Simplify the fraction to $\frac{1}{4}$. Now to draw the strip model according to the fraction, shade 1 part out of 4 total parts.

Your Turn!		
	1) 40%	a)
	2) 55%	b)
	3) 93.75%	c)
	4) 30%	d)
	5) 25%	e)
	6) 60%	f)
	7) 75%	g)
	8) 62.5%	h)

bit.ly/3lgrViS

Topic	Using Grid Models to Solve Percentage Problems
Notes	✓ A percentage compares a number to 100. ✓ So, the percentage of a number is a ratio between that number and 100.
Example	*Anne was experimenting on mice in the laboratory. During experiments, 45% of the mice died; actually, the number of mice that died was 9. Shade the grid to show the mice that died. How many mice were there in total?* The grid has 100 squares. Since 45% of the mice died, shade 45 of the 100 squares in the grid. The 45 shaded squares represent the 9 dead mice. However, the whole grid represents the total number of mice. So, find the number of dead mice that each row of squares represents. Since 4.5 shaded rows represent 9 dead mice, you can divide, $9 \div 4.5 = 2$. Each row represents 2 mice. Now, multiply 10 rows by 2 mice. $$10 \times 2 = 20$$ So, there were 20 mice in her experiment.
Your Turn!	1) In a box of muffins, 25 of the muffins have a nuts core. That is 50% of the muffins in the box. Shade the grid to show the percent of muffins that have a nuts core. How many muffins are in the box? 2) 8 of the 32 bears at the zoo were born in the wild. Shade the grid to show the fraction of the bears that were born in the wild. What percent of the bears were born in the wild? 3) In the library, there are 80 books on the shelves. 60% of those books are old. Shade the grid to show the percentage of books that are old, and how many books are old? 4) Maria bakes bread. 15% of them were burned and the number of burned bread pieces is 27. Shade the grid to show the burned bread, and how many loaves of breads were there in total?

Topic	Using Strip Models to Solve Percentage Problems
Notes	✓ For solving a problem, you must use a formula. $$Part \div whole = percentage$$
Example	**40% of the 60 dishes on the shelves have a blue flower print. How many of the dishes on the shelves have a blue flower print? Use a strip model to show.** The total percentage of dishes is 60 and the percentage of blue flower print dishes is 40%. Since 40% is $\frac{4}{10}$ of 100%, divide the strip model into 10 parts. Then divide 60 by 10 to find the number of each part of the percentage, $60 \div 10 = 6$. To find 40% of the blue flower print dishes, multiply the 4 parts of the strip model by 6 in each part, $4 \times 6 = 24$. So, the number of blue flower print dishes is equal to 24. 0% 10% 20% 30% 40% 50% 60% 70% 80% 90% 100% | 6 | 12 | 18 | 24 | 30 | 36 | 42 | 48 | 54 | 60 |
Your Turn!	1) Jones filled 20% of the 3 liters pot with water to cook the soup. How many liters of water did he put in the pot? Use strip model to show. 2) The Royals softball team played 75 games and won 45 of them. What percent of the games did they win? Use a strip model to show. 3) A cinema has 240 seats. 144 seats were sold for the current movie. What percent of seats are sold? Use a strip model to show. 4) Frank bought a new coat at a discount. He paid just $175, but its cost was $250. What percentage of the cost did he pay? Use a strip model to show. 5) An artist's color palette contained 560 grams of paint, which she used for 1 month, and now her color palette is down to 112 grams. What percentage of colors are left? Use a strip model to show. 6) Louis has 40 books from the library, and 30% of them are about the economy. How many of the books are about the economy? Use a strip model to show.

Topic	Word Problems of Determining Percentage of a Number
Notes	✓ Percentages have no dimension. Hence, they are called dimensionless numbers. If we say, 30% of a number, it means 30 percent of its whole. ✓ Problems involving percentages have three quantities to work with: the percent, the amount, and the base. • The percent has the percent symbol (%) or the word "percent." • The base is the whole amount. • The amount is the number that relates to the percentage. It is always part of the whole.
Example	*A veterinarian examined chickens in aviculture to see if they were infected with a virus. 36 out of 120 chickens were infected with the virus. What percentage of chickens were infected?* 36 is a part of the number 120. To find the percent of 36 out of 120, first, let x represents the percent. So, write a proportion for x, $\frac{36}{120} = \frac{x}{100} \rightarrow 36 \times 100 = 120x \rightarrow 3600 = 120x \rightarrow 3600 \div 120 = x \rightarrow 30 = x$. 30% of chickens were infected with the virus.
Your Turn!	1) There are 48 employees in the company. On a particular day, 34 were present. What percent showed up for work?
	2) There are 45 students in a class and 18 of them are girls. What percent of the students are girls?
	3) A shirt was originally priced at $68. It went on sale for $49.30. What was the percentage of the discount that the shirt received?
	4) A bank is offering simple interest on a savings account. If you deposit $9,800, you will earn $760 interest in six months. What percentage is the bank offering?
	5) Isabella has a new beaded necklace. 7 out of the 35 beads on the necklace are pink. What percentage of beads on Isabella's necklace are pink?
	6) There are 22 boys and 46 girls in the class. 11 students do not take the bus to school. What percentage of students do not take the bus to school?

Topic	Solving Percentage Word Problems
Notes	✓ Percent problems can be solved by writing equations. An equation uses an equal sign (=) to show that two mathematical expressions have the same value. ✓ Percents are fractions, and just like fractions, when finding a percent (or fraction, or portion) of another amount, you multiply. ✓ The percent of the base is the amount. *The Percentage of the Base is the Amount.* *Percent × Base = Amount*
Example	*A home appliance store has 70 employees. 20% of the employees work part-time. How many part-time employees does the home appliance store have?* To find 20% of 70. First, determine x instead of the unknown part. And write a proportion for x, $\frac{70}{x} = \frac{100}{20} \rightarrow 70 \times 20 = 100x \rightarrow 1400 = 100x \rightarrow 1400 \div 100 = x \rightarrow 14 = x$. The home appliance store has 14 part-time employees.
Your Turn!	1) A new car, valued at $34,000, depreciates at 9% per year. What is the value of the car one year after purchase?
	2) A metal bar weighs 24 ounces. 10% of the bar is gold. How many ounces of gold are in the bar?
	3) A crew is made up of 19 women; the rest are men. If 20% of the crew are women, how many people are in the crew?
	4) The price of a pair of shoes increases by 24% from $25. How much has the price increased?
	5) At a coffee shop, the price of a cup of coffee was $1.60. In the new year, there is a 15% price increase in the cost of coffee. What is the new price of a cup of coffee?
	6) 34% is cut from a 40 cm board. How much is the reduction in length?
	7) In a class, the number of new students is 35%. In total, there are 40 students. What is the number of new students?
	8) Students voted to appoint a new representative. 90% of the 50 votes were in favor of the new representative. How many votes were in favor?

Topic	Fractional and Decimal Percentages
Notes	✓ A percentage in mathematics is a number or ratio which can be represented as a fraction of 100. The symbol (%) is used to denote the percentage. ✓ Similarly, the percentage is sometimes denoted by the abbreviation 'pct.' For example, we can express 50 percent as 50% or 50 pct. ✓ Percentages are written as whole numbers, fractions, or decimals. For example, 5%, 20%, 0.8%, 0.35%, $\frac{5}{6}$%, etc. are all percentages.
Example	**Complete:** 62.5% of $80 =$ ☐ The whole is 80. And 62.5% is a part of 80. Let x represent the part. Then write a proportion for x and solve it, $\frac{x}{80} = \frac{62.5}{100} \to 100x = 62.5 \times 80 \to 100x = 5000 \to x = 5000 \div 100 \to x = 50$. So, 62.5% of 80 is 50. **Complete:** $12\frac{1}{2}\%$ of $150 =$ ☐ The whole is 150. And $12\frac{1}{2}\%$ is a part of 150, which is 12.5%. Let x represent the part. Then write a proportion for x and solve it, $\frac{x}{150} = \frac{12.5}{100} \to 100x = 12.5 \times 150 \to 100x = 1875 \to x = 1875 \div 100 \to x = 18.75$. So, $12\frac{1}{2}\%$ of 150 is 18.75.
Your Turn!	1) $18\frac{1}{4}\%$ of 40 2) 66% of 200 3) 15% of 464 4) $35\frac{1}{4}$ of 100 5) 45% of 120 6) $62\frac{1}{2}\%$ of 60 7) $40\frac{1}{2}\%$ of 90 8) 25% of 650

Topic	Using Grid Models to Convert Fractions to Percentages
Notes	✓ If the total is lower than 1 whole, you must use one 10×10 grid. ✓ If the total is larger than 1 whole, you must use more than a single grid. ✓ Here are 2 steps to change a fraction into a percentage: • According to the fraction, shade a fraction of the 100 squares in the grid. Multiply to find how many **squares** to shade: $\frac{3}{5}$ • The number of shaded squares out of a total of 100 squares determines the percent of the grid that is shaded: 60%
Example	Shade $\frac{2}{10}$ of the grid model and write the percentage. To display $\frac{2}{10}$ in the 100 squares of the grid model, multiply to find how many squares to shade: $\frac{2}{10} \times 100 = \frac{2}{10} \times \frac{100}{1} = \frac{200}{10} = 20$ Shade 20 of the 100 squares. Count the shaded squares, and you'll find there are 20 shaded squares out of a total of 100 squares. So, write 20%.
Your Turn!	According to the fraction shade, write the grid model as a percentage. 1) $\frac{6}{8}$ 2) $\frac{4}{5}$ 3) $\frac{13}{20}$ 4) $\frac{3}{4}$ 5) $\frac{9}{25}$ 6) $\frac{39}{50}$

bit.ly/3Th7tep

Topic	Word Problems: Comparing Percent and Fractions
Notes	✓ The percentage of the whole number is calculated by dividing the value by the total value and then multiplying by 100. The percentage is nothing but "per 100". $$Percentage = \left(\frac{Value}{Total\ Value}\right) \times 100$$ ✓ Follow the steps below to convert between a percentage and a fraction: • Step 1: Write the given percent divided by 100. That means $\frac{percent}{100}$. • Step 2: If the given number is not a whole number, then multiply and divide by 10 for every number after the decimal point. • Step 3: Simplify the fraction.
Example	*In the hotel, the manager wants to hire a crew that includes an equal number of women and men. After a week, 55% of the required number of women crew members have been hired, and $\frac{3}{4}$ of the required number of men. Which members of the crew have the largest now?* Firstly, write a fraction as a decimal. And then convert to a percentage, $\frac{3}{4} = 0.75 = 75\%$. Now compare the percentages, $75\% < 55\%$. Members of the men's crew are the largest now.
Your Turn!	1) Adams owns 66% of the restaurants in Houston. In Lincoln, Frank owns $\frac{4}{5}$ of the restaurants. Who owns a greater percentage of restaurants in his area?
	2) Last night, Carol drove 35% of the way to the next state. Then she rests for a while and today she drives $\frac{2}{5}$ of the way. Which day did she drive the most?
	3) Yesterday, Susan read 42% of her novel book and Beti read $\frac{3}{8}$ of her novel book. Who reads a greater percentage of her book?
	4) So far, Mason has completed 68% of his school project. Jacob has finished $\frac{6}{10}$ of his school project. Who has finished a greater percentage of his school project?

Topic	Word Problems: Conversion of Percent, Fractions, and Decimals
Notes	✓ A decimal is a different way to represent a fraction. Some decimals have whole number parts and fractional parts, while others have only fractional parts. Examples of decimals include 2.3, 0.85, and 0.012. ✓ Here is how to change a decimal to a percent: • Percent means per hundred, so multiply the decimal by 100. • Add a % sign.
Example	*Leo is helping his dad clean out the basement. He finds a bolt that is $\frac{3}{8}$ of a foot in diameter.* *Write $\frac{3}{8}$ of a foot as a decimal. And write $\frac{3}{8}$ of a foot as a percent.* To write as a decimal, divide 3 by 8, $3 \div 8 = 0.375$. To write as a percent, multiply $\frac{3}{8}$ by 100, $\frac{3}{8} \times 100 = \frac{3}{8} \times \frac{100}{1} = \frac{300}{8} = 37.5$. $\frac{3}{8}$ is equal to 0.375 and 37.5%.
Your Turn!	**Write as a fraction and decimal.**
	1) In a school, 65% of the students were taken on a trip.
	2) Jenny spent 29% of her money to buy a new bag.
	3) In a camp, 44% of the tents have blue fabrics.
	4) Farmer Johnson plants corn in 85% of his fields
	Write as a decimal and percent.
	5) One ounce is equal to $\frac{1}{20}$ of a pound.
	6) In a park, $\frac{7}{8}$ of the flowers are pink.
	7) Sarah used $\frac{9}{25}$ of her pen.
	8) Jack has traveled $\frac{7}{50}$ of the way to reach the city.

Topic	Percent Problems
Notes	✓ Percent is a ratio of a number and 100. It always has the same denominator, 100. The percent symbol is "%". ✓ Percent means "per 100". So, 20% is $\frac{20}{100}$. ✓ In each percent problem, we need to find the base, the part, or the percent. ✓ Use these equations to find each missing component in a percent problem: • Base = Part ÷ Percent • Part = Percent × Base • Percent = Part ÷ Base
Example	**80 is 50 percent of what number?** In this problem, we are looking for the base. Use this equation: $Base = Part \div Percent \rightarrow Base = 80 \div 50\% = 80 \div 0.50 = 160$ Then: 80 is 50 percent of 160. **25 is what percent of 400?** In this problem, we are looking for the percentage. Use this equation: $Percent = Part \div Base \rightarrow Percent = 25 \div 400 = 0.0625 = 6.25\%$. Then: 25 is 6.25 percent of 400.
Your Turn!	1) What is 10% of 160? _____ 2) What is 27% of 230? _____ 3) What is 45% of 45? _____ 4) What is 63% of 140? _____ 5) 70 is what percent of 200? ____% 6) 30 is what percent of 80? ____% 7) 17 is what percent of 68? ____% 8) 49 is what percent of 70? ____% 9) 30 is 20 percent of what number? 10) 70 is 40 percent of what number? 11) 15 is 75 percent of what number? 12) 44 is 25 percent of what number?

bit.ly/34Gy3FL

Chapter 5: Answers

Representing Percentage

1) 74%
2) 35%
3) 22%
4) 41%

Using Number Line to Graph Percentages

1)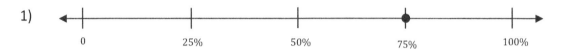

2)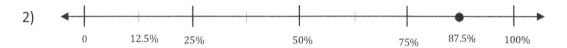

3)

4)

5)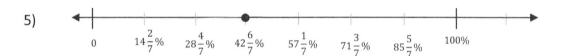

6)

7)

8)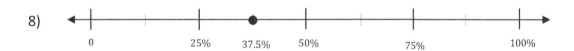

9)

10)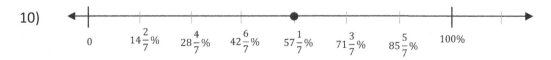

Using Grid models to Represent Percent

1) $\frac{4}{25}$, 0.16

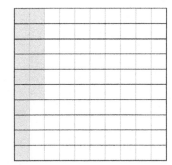

4) $\frac{1}{2}$, 0.5

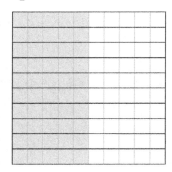

2) $\frac{11}{25}$, 0.44

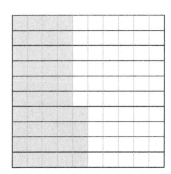

5) $\frac{1}{4}$, 0.25

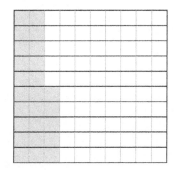

3) $\frac{59}{100}$, 0.59

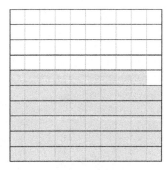

6) $\frac{4}{5}$, 0.8

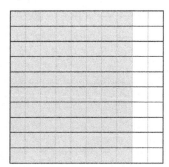

Using Strip Models to Explain Percent

1) c
2) f
3) g
4) a
5) h
6) e
7) d
8) b

Using Grid Models to Solve Percentage Problems

1) 50

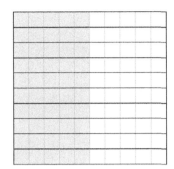

2) 25%

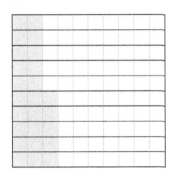

3) 48

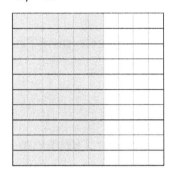

4) 180

Using Strip Models to Solve Percentage Problems

1) 0.6

0%	20%	40%	60%	80%	100%
0.6	1.2	1.8	2.4	3	

2) 60%

0%	20%	40%	60%	80%	100%
15	30	45	60	75	

3) 60%

0%	10%	20%	30%	40%	50%	60%	70%	80%	90%	100%
24	48	72	96	120	144	168	192	216	240	

4) 70%

0%	10%	20%	30%	40%	50%	60%	70%	80%	90%	100%
25	50	75	100	125	150	175	200	225	250	

5) 20%

0%	10%	20%	30%	40%	50%	60%	70%	80%	90%	100%
56	112	168	224	280	336	392	448	504	560	

6) 12

	0%	10%	20%	30%	40%	50%	60%	70%	80%	90%	100%
	4	8	12	16	20	24	28	32	36	40	

Word Problems of Determining Percentage of a Number

1) 70.83%   3) 27.5%   5) 20%
2) 40%   4) 8%   6) 16.18%

Solving Percentage Word Problems

1) 30,940   4) 6   7) 14
2) 2.4   5) 1.84   8) 45
3) 95   6) 13.6

Fractional and Decimal Percentages

1) 7.3   4) 35.25   7) 36.45
2) 132   5) 54   8) 162.5
3) 69.6   6) 37.5

Using Grid Models to Convert Fractions to Percentages

1) 75%
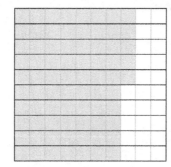

3) 65%
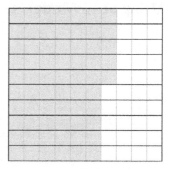

2) 80%
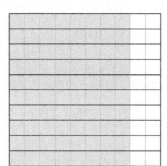

4) 75%
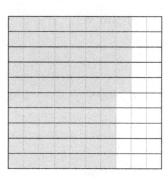

5) 36%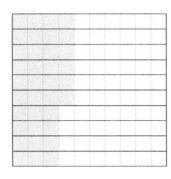

6) 78%

Word Problems: Comparing Percent and Fractions

1) Frank
2) Today
3) Susan
4) Mason

Word Problems: Converting of Percent, Fractions, and Decimals

1) $\frac{13}{20}$, 0.65
2) $\frac{29}{100}$, 0.29
3) $\frac{11}{25}$, 0.44
4) $\frac{17}{20}$, 0.85
5) 0.05, 5%
6) 0.875, 87.5%
7) 0.36, 36%
8) 0.14, 14%

Percent Problems

1) 16
2) 62.1
3) 20.25
4) 88.2
5) 35%
6) 37.5%
7) 25%
8) 70%
9) 150
10) 175
11) 20
12) 176

CHAPTER 6: Absolute Value

Math topics that you'll learn in this chapter:

- ☑ Absolute Value Definition
- ☑ Integers and Absolute Value
- ☑ Using Number Lines to Present Absolute Value
- ☑ Integer Inequalities Involving Absolute Values
- ☑ Word Problems of Absolute Value and Integers
- ☑ Absolute Value of Rational Numbers
- ☑ Absolute Values and Opposites of Rational Numbers

Absolute Value

Topic	Absolute Value Definition
Notes	✓ The absolute value of a number is its distance from 0 on a number line. ✓ Absolute value of a number is the non-negative value of the number, no matter its sign. As a result, the absolute value of any real number is always positive. Absolute value of $9 = 9$ Absolute value of $-9 = 9$
Example	**Find the absolute value of $\|-13\|$.** According to $13 \geq 0$, the absolute value of -13 is thirteen units away from 0. Thus, $\|-13\| = 13$. **Find the absolute value of $\|-3\|$.** According to $3 \geq 0$, the absolute value of -3 is placed three units away from 0. Thus, $\|-3\| = 3$.

Your Turn!

1) $|+73| = $ ___

2) $|-323| = $ ___

3) $|-19| = $ ___

4) $|-75| = $ ___

5) $|0| = $ ___

6) $|+90| = $ ___

7) $|-7| = $ ___

8) $|+30| = $ ___

9) $|+2| = $ ___

10) $|+170| = $ ___

11) $|+55| = $ ___

12) $|+11| = $ ___

Topic	Integers and Absolute Value
Notes	✓ The absolute value of a number is its distance from zero, in either direction, on the number line. ✓ The absolute value of an integer is the numerical value without its sign. (Negative or positive) ✓ The vertical bar is used for absolute value as in $\|x\|$. ✓ The absolute value of a number is never negative; because it only shows, "how far the number is from zero".
Example	*Calculate.* $\|13 - 5\| \times 3 =$ First, solve $\|13 - 5\|$, $\rightarrow \|13 - 5\| = \|8\|$, the absolute value of 8 is 8, $\|8\| = 8$, Then: $8 \times 3 = 24$ *Solve.* $\frac{\|-25\|}{5} \times \|2 - 9\| =$ First, find $\|-25\| \rightarrow$ the absolute value of -25 is 25. Then: $\|-25\| = 25$, $\frac{25}{5} \times \|2 - 9\| =$ Now, calculate $\|2 - 9\|$, $\rightarrow \|2 - 9\| = \|-7\|$, the absolute value of -7 is 7. $\|-7\| = 7$ Then: $\frac{25}{5} \times 7 = 5 \times 7 = 35$
Your Turn!	1) $\|-3\| + \|5 - 10\| =$ 2) $-1 + \|2 - 6\| + \|1 - 9\| =$ 3) $\|-6 + 6\| + \|2\| =$ 4) $\frac{\|-42\|}{6} \times \frac{\|-24\|}{4} =$ 5) $\|5\| + \|1 - 8\| =$ 6) $\frac{\|-10\|}{10} \times \frac{\|-36\|}{9} =$ 7) $\|12\| - \|9 - 12\| =$ 8) $\|1 \times (-4)\| \times \frac{\|-27\|}{9} =$ 9) $\|9 - 15\| + \|8 - 1\| =$ 10) $\|-5 \times 2\| \times \frac{\|-48\|}{8} =$ 11) $\|-7 + 11\| - \|-2 + 3\| =$ 12) $\frac{\|-54\|}{6} - \|-3 \times 6\| =$

Absolute Value

Topic	Using Number Lines to Present Absolute Value
Notes	✓ Absolute value is the distance between zero and a number. ✓ To find absolute value of 6 and −6, firstly, a number line is drawn. Then: • Write down the numbers going from 0 to 6 on the right-hand side of 0. • Write down the numbers from 0 to −6 on the left-hand side of 0. ✓ After that, start with zero and count the number of jumps from 0 to the given number. ✓ Therefore, the number of jumps is its absolute value, and this is always going to be positive.
Example	*Find the absolute value of |9|, and graph it on the number line.* According to $9 \geq 0$, the absolute value of a positive number is the distance from 0 to the right side from 0. Thus, $\|9\| = 9$.
Your Turn!	**Find the absolute value on the number line.**
	1) $\|-9\| =$ ___ 2) $\|-13\| =$ ___
	3) $\|+17\| =$ ___ 4) $\|-16\| =$ ___
	5) $\|+5\| =$ ___ 6) $\|+15\| =$ ___
	7) $\|-2\| =$ ___ 8) $\|-24\| =$ ___

bit.ly/3LppFjV

Topic	Integer Inequalities Involving Absolute Values
Notes	✓ An absolute value of any number is the distance it is from 0 on the number line. ✓ An easy example of an absolute value would be $\|10\|$. This signifies that it's ten spaces from 0. Therefore, the absolute value of it is also 10. ✓ An absolute value is either zero or positive.
Example	***Compare the absolute value of the numbers:*** $\|-5\|, \|1\|$ Simplify the absolute value, then decide which number is greatest, least or if they are equal. $\|-5\| = 5$ and $\|1\| = 1$. So, $5 > 1$ ***Compare the absolute value with the integer:*** $\|-3\|, 8$ Simplify the absolute value, then decide which number is greatest, least or if they are equal. $\|-3\| = 3$. So, $3 < 8$.

Your Turn! Compare.

1) $\|9\|, \|-1\|$	2) $\|9\|, -9$
3) $\|-10\|, \|-7\|$	4) $\|-11\|, \|8\|$
5) $-9, \|-18\|$	6) $0, \|-7\|$
7) $3, \|-3\|$	8) $\|5\|, \|-5\|$

bit.ly/3lgQITV

Absolute Value

Topic	**Word Problems of Absolute Value and Integers**
Notes	✓ In mathematics, word problems can be described as exercises where background details are presented by way of text, as opposed to using mathematical notation. ✓ For a word problem solution: • Review: Review the problem, then determine what is being asked of you. • Coordinate: After determining what you are being asked, isolate the information that has been provided. Now determine what you don't know. • Deduce: What strategy should be used to get any information that is missing? Will it require division, multiplication, subtraction, or addition?
Example	*A scientist uses a tracking device to study animal behavior. The table shows the elevations of a hawk and a sea dolphin at $12:00$ A.M.* *Which animal is farthest from the sea level?* | Animal	Elevation (ft.)
Hawk	45
Dolphin	−32 | The hawk's elevation is positive, so it is above sea level. The dolphin's elevation is negative, so it is below sea level. And to find which animal is farther from sea level, use absolute value. Hawk: $\lvert 45 \rvert = 45$ Dolphin: $\lvert -32 \rvert = 32$ Then, $45 > 32$. Thus, the hawk is 45 feet above sea level, while the dolphin is 32 feet below sea level. The hawk is farthest from sea level.
Your Turn!	1) A hiker starts hiking at the beginning of a trail that is 110 feet below sea level. She hikes to a location on the trail that is 390 feet above sea level and stops for some rest. How far did she hike?
	2) In the lab, Mike is measuring the temperature of different chemical liquids. The temperature of liquid−1 is −4, and that of liquid−2 is 8. Which liquid's temperature is closest to zero?
	3) Becky has two cats, Jake and Rob. She is worried because Jake keeps eating Rob's food. She asks their vet how much each cat's weight has changed since their last visit. The weight change for Jake is $4 \; oz$, and that for Rob is $-2 \; oz$. Which cat has changed the most?
	4) Bob's cottage is close to two cities. A path passes through a lake at the bottom of a small mountain. The other trail passes through a mountain peak. The elevation of the lake destination is $-350 \; ft$, and that of the mountain peak destination is $280 \; ft$, which is shown on the map. Which trail's destination is farther from sea level?

Topic	Absolute Value of Rational Numbers
Notes	✓ Absolute value of rational numbers means the distance of rational numbers from zero. Absolute values are always positive (distance cannot be negative!). ✓ A rational number is a number that you can write as a fraction of 2 integers. An integer can be either negative or positive.
Example	**Find the absolute value of** $-\frac{6}{5}$. The absolute value of rational numbers is the distance from zero and distance cannot be negative; thus, $\left|-\frac{6}{5}\right| = \frac{6}{5} = 1\frac{1}{5}$ **What is** $\|1.9\|$? The absolute value of rational numbers is the distance from zero and distance cannot be negative; thus, $\|1.9\| = 1.9$

Your Turn!	1) $|-4.96| = $ ___	2) $\left|\frac{-1}{9}\right| = $ ___
	3) $|53| = $ ___	4) $|1.163| = $ ___
	5) $\left|-1\frac{2}{7}\right| = $ ___	6) $\left|-\frac{9}{7}\right| = $ ___
	7) $\left|8\frac{1}{6}\right| = $ ___	8) $\left|\frac{2}{9}\right| = $ ___
	9) $|-0.8| = $ ___	10) $|3.8| = $ ___
	11) $\left|-1\frac{3}{20}\right| = $ ___	12) $\left|-\frac{9}{18}\right| = $ ___

Absolute Value

Topic	**Absolute Values and Opposites of Rational Numbers**
Notes	✓ A positive number's opposite will be negative, and a negative number's opposite is always positive. ✓ Absolute value is the distance of a number from 0. ✓ A rational number is written as a fraction of 2 integers. ✓ A rational number's opposite is either positive or negative.
Example	**What is the opposite of $-\frac{5}{8}$?** $-\frac{5}{8}$ is $\frac{5}{8}$ units to the left of 0. So, the opposite of $-\frac{5}{8}$ is $\frac{5}{8}$. **What is the absolute value of 0.45?** 0.45 is 0.45 units to the right of 0. So, the absolute value of 0.45 is 0.45.

Your Turn!

What is the opposite of the following rational numbers?

1) $0.11 =$ ___	2) $-9\frac{2}{5} =$ ___
3) $-\frac{7}{13} =$ ___	4) $-32.71 =$ ___
5) $\frac{1}{21} =$ ___	6) $9.1616\ldots =$ ___

Find the absolute value of the following rational numbers.

7) $|-0.2| =$ ___	8) $\left|6\frac{-6}{7}\right| =$ ___
9) $\left|\frac{-3}{8}\right| =$ ___	10) $|-5.22| =$ ___
11) $|-11.06| =$ ___	12) $\left|\frac{-1}{2}\right| =$ ___

Chapter 6: Answers

Absolute Value Definition

1) 73
2) 323
3) 19
4) 75
5) 0
6) 90
7) 7
8) 30
9) 2
10) 170
11) 55
12) 11

Integers and Absolute Value

1) 8
2) 11
3) 2
4) 42
5) 12
6) 4
7) 9
8) 12
9) 13
10) 60
11) 3
12) −9

Using Number Lines to Present Absolute Value

1)

2)

3)

4)

5)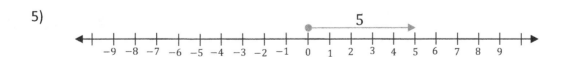

6)

7)

8)

Integer Inequalities Involving Absolute Values

1) $9 > 1$
2) $9 > -9$
3) $10 > 7$
4) $11 > 8$
5) $-9 < 18$
6) $0 < 7$
7) $3 = 3$
8) $5 = 5$

Word Problems of Absolute Value and Integers

1) 500
2) 1
3) Jake
4) lake destination

Absolute Value of Rational Numbers

1) 4.96
2) $\frac{1}{9}$
3) 53
4) 1.163
5) $1\frac{2}{7}$
6) $\frac{9}{7}$
7) $8\frac{1}{6}$
8) $\frac{2}{9}$
9) 0.8
10) 3.8
11) $1\frac{3}{20}$
12) $\frac{9}{18}$

Absolute Values and Opposites of Rational Numbers

1) -0.11
2) $9\frac{2}{5}$
3) $\frac{7}{13}$
4) 32.71
5) $-\frac{1}{21}$
6) $-9.1616\ldots$
7) 0.2
8) $6\frac{6}{7}$
9) $\frac{3}{8}$
10) 5.22
11) 11.06
12) $\frac{1}{2}$

Chapter 7: Expressions and Equations

Math topics that you'll learn in this chapter:

- ☑ Identifying Expressions and Equations
- ☑ Identify Equivalent Expressions
- ☑ Using Properties to Write Equivalent Expressions
- ☑ Using Strip Models to Identify Equivalent Expressions
- ☑ Using Algebra Tiles to Identify Equivalent Expressions
- ☑ Using Exponents to Write down Multiplication Expressions
- ☑ Using Exponents to Write Powers of Ten
- ☑ Prime Factorization with Exponents
- ☑ Identifying Errors Which Involving the Order of Operations
- ☑ Writing down Variable Expressions Involving Two Operations
- ☑ Using Area Models to Factor Variable Expressions
- ☑ Using Distributive Property to Factor Variable Expressions
- ☑ Using Distributive Property to Factor Numerical Expressions

Topic	Identifying Expressions and Equations
Notes	✓ Expressions are mathematical phrases that contain numbers, variables, or both. ✓ Expressions may additionally contain operations; however, they never have an equal sign. Equations are mathematical sentences showing that 2 expressions are equal. Equations will always have an equal sign. For instance, $3x + 13$ is the expression on the left-hand side, and it is equal to the expression 28 on the right-hand side. $$3x + 13 = 28$$
Example	**Determine if this is an expression or an equation.** $$(x + 7) \div 9$$ This is an expression, as it does not have an equal sign and only contains numbers and a variable, and operations without the equal sign.
Your Turn!	1) $(7 + 8) \div 5$ 2) $35 + 7w$ 3) $\dfrac{2}{3+p}$ 4) $y = 3f$ 5) $5 \times (7 - 3) = 20$ 6) $5 + w$ 7) $(c \times 11) + 2 = 8$ 8) $15 - 3 \times \dfrac{p}{5} = 0$ 9) $\dfrac{2}{x} \times 47$ 10) $x = 3u - 6$

Topic	Identify Equivalent Expressions
Notes	✓ Usually, if 2 things are equal, then they are called equivalent. ✓ In math, equivalent expressions are expressions that are the same, even if the expression doesn't look the same. However, if the values are placed into the expression, both expressions provide the same answer. For example, $3(x + 2)$ and $3x + 6$ are equivalent expressions since the value of both stays the same for any value of x.
Example	*Determine the equivalent expression below.* $$10k + 5k$$ Combine like terms to form the standard form: $$10k + 5k = 15k$$ So, the expression $10k + 5k$ is equivalent to $15k$. *Determine the equivalent expression below.* $$3u + ((u + 5u) \div 3u)$$ Combine like terms to form the standard form: $$3u + ((u + 5u) \div 3u) = 3u + (6u \div 3u) = 3u + 2$$ So, the expression $3u + ((u + 5u) \div 3u)$ is equivalent to $3u + 2$.
Your Turn!	**Write the equivalent of the following expressions.**

1) $7p + 2p + 8$	2) $25d - 17d + 3 - 3d$
3) $4(2x - 4)$	4) $(3 \div (8x - 2x)) - 6$
5) $11t - 7t + 3$	6) $10 - 10y - 25 + 13y$
7) $-3(3k - 6)$	8) $-2(-5g + 7g) + 5g$

Topic	Using Properties to Write Equivalent Expressions
Notes	✓ It's possible to write equivalent expressions via a combination of like terms. A like term is a term that has the same variables raised to the same powers. ✓ Properties are utilized to simplify algebraic expressions. ✓ You can use properties of operations to write equivalent expressions. Here are some common properties: | Commutative property of addition	$a + b = b + a$
Commutative property of multiplication	$a \times b = b \times a$
Associative property of addition	$(a + b) + c = a + (b + c)$
Associative property of multiplication	$(a \times b)c = a(b \times c)$
Distributive property	$a(b + c) = a \times b + a \times c$	
Example	**Complete and solve the expressions.** $7x \times 5 = 5 \times \boxed{} = ?$ According to the two expressions, the commutative property of multiplication shows changing the order of factors does not change the product. So, these expressions are equivalent if the missing factor is $7x$. And multiply $7x$ by 5, to solve the expression. Therefore, it will be: $7x \times 5 = 5 \times 7x = 35x$
Your Turn!	1) $9 + 13p + 8 = 13p + 8 + \cdots = ?$ 2) $9f \times 9 = 9 \times \cdots = ?$ 3) $6r + 1 + 2r = 6r + \cdots + 1 = ?$ 4) $6 \times (3 \times 2a) = (6 \times 3) \times \cdots = ?$ 5) $w(14 + 6) = 14 \times w + 6 \times \cdots = ?$ 6) $4g \times 11 = \cdots \times 4g = ?$ 7) $5s + (5s + 2) = (5s + \cdots) + 2 = ?$ 8) $(13t - 1) \times 3 = \cdots \times 3 - 1 \times 3 = ?$

Topic	Using Strip Models to Identify Equivalent Expressions
Notes	✓ Two expressions are equal if you can simplify them to the same third expression or if one of them can be written as the other one. ✓ One may additionally determine if 2 expressions are equivalent when values are substituted in for the variable and both yield the same answer.
Example	**What expression does this model represent?** | a	a	a	a	x	x	x	x	x	x | This model represents $a + a + a + a + x + x + x + x + x + x$. There are 4 times a and 6 times x in the model, which can be written as $4a$ and $6x$. $\overbrace{}^{4a}$ $\overbrace{}^{6x}$ | a	a	a	a	x	x	x	x	x	x | So, the total length of the model is $4a + 6x$.
Your Turn!	**Write an expression that represents the model.** 1) | n | n | n | n | n | n | n | d | d | d | 2) | x | x | x | x | x | x | n | n | n | n | n | n | 3) | e | j | j | 4) | $\frac{t}{a}$ | $\frac{t}{a}$ | $\frac{t}{a}$ | 3 | 3 | 5) | 1 | 1 | v | v | v | v | 6) | f | f | f | f | f | 2 | 2 | 2 | 2 | 2 | 2 | 2 | 2 | 2 | 7) | y | y | y | y | y | y | y | y | y | | z | z | z | z | 1 |

bit.ly/3YQKGan

Topic	**Using Algebra Tiles to Identify Equivalent Expressions**
Notes	✓ An algebra tile is a square or rectangular-shaped tile or a tile that signifies numbers and variables. ✓ For instance, you may utilize square tiles to signify numbers. Each of the square tiles equals one. Thus, you can represent four using four tiles. ✓ If both expressions have the same amount of rectangular variable tiles along with the same amount of positive or negative tiles, then these expressions are equivalent. ✓ If there's any difference between the number of rectangular variable tiles or square plus or minus 1 tile, then these expressions aren't equivalent.
Example	*These tiles represent the expression $2x + 6 + 3x$. Write the equivalent expression.* First, combine like terms. There are 5 of (x) tiles and 6 of (1) tiles in all. So, $5x + 6$ is the equivalent expression to the algebra tiles.
Your Turn!	**Write the equivalent of the following expressions, using algebra tiles.** 1) $3 + 2x + 1$ 2) $2x + 2 + 1x - 2$ 3) $-10 + 5x + 8$ 4) $-6x + 12 + 5x - 3$ 5) $3 + 5x + 7 - x$ 6) $2x + 3 + 6x$ 7) $2x + 2 - 2x - 2$ 8) $2x + 10 + 5x$

Topic	Using Exponents to Write down Multiplication Expressions
Notes	✓ Exponential expressions are merely a method of writing down powers in a short form. ✓ The base number shows which number gets multiplied. The exponent, a small number placed above and to the right-hand side of the base number, explains the number of times the base number gets multiplied. ✓ The exponent signifies the number of times the base is utilized as a factor. Thus, in the example of 64, it may be written as $4 \times 4 \times 4 = 4^3$, where 4 is the "base" and 3 is the "exponent". You will read this expression as "four to the third power".
Example	*Write the expression using an exponent.* $$9 \times 9 \times 9 \times 9 \times 9 \times 9 =?$$ Since 9 is used 6 times, the base is 9 and the exponent is repeat times, that is 6. $$9 \times 9 \times 9 \times 9 \times 9 \times 9 = 9^6$$ *Write the expression using an exponent.* $$7 \times 7 \times 7 =?$$ Since 7 is used 3 times, the base is 7 and the exponent is repeat times, that is 3. $$7 \times 7 \times 7 = 7^3$$
Your Turn!	1) $8 \times 8 \times 8 \times 8 =$ ___ 2) $7 \times 7 =$ ___ 3) $2 \times 2 \times 2 \times 2 \times 2 =$ ___ 4) $11 \times 11 \times 11 \times 11 \times 11 \times 11 \times 11 \times 11 =$ ___ 5) $3 \times 3 \times 3 \times 3 \times 3 =$ ___ 6) $1 \times 1 \times 1 \times 1 \times 1 \times 1 =$ ___ 7) $4 \times 4 \times 4 \times 4 \times 4 \times 4 \times 4 \times 4 \times 4 \times 4 =$ ___ 8) $13 \times 13 \times 13 \times 13 \times 13 \times 13 \times 13 \times 13 \times 13 =$ ___ 9) $10 \times 10 \times 10 =$ ___ 10) $5 \times 5 \times 5 =$ ___

bit.ly/3Jp7HeX

Topic	Using Exponents to Write Powers of Ten
Notes	✓ Power is a product of multiplying a number by itself. Generally, power is signified using a base number as well as an exponent. ✓ A base number shows the number that is getting multiplied. An exponent, a small number placed above and to the right-hand side of the base number, indicates the number of times the base number is multiplied. ✓ Whenever 10 is raised to a whole number exponent, its value will have a leftmost digit of 1 and all the other digits are 0. The exponent indicates the number of 0s that come after the 1. ✓ To determine a missing exponent, you must look at the right-hand side of an equation and count how many zeros are after the 1.
Example	*Find the exponent.* $$10 = 1,000,000$$ Since when 10 is raised to a whole number exponent, the value of the leftmost digit is 1 and all other digits are 0. The exponent tells you how many 0's come after the 1. So, count the number of 0s. There are 6 of them. Then, $10^6 = 1,000,000$. *Write the number as an exponent based on* **10**. $$1,000 = ?$$ Count the number of 0s. There are 3 of them. Then, $1,000 = 10^3$.

Your Turn!

Find the exponent.

1) 10 = 10,000,000,000	2) 10 = 10,000,000
3) 10 = 10,000	4) 10 = 1,000,000,000,000

Write the number as an exponent based on 10.

5) 10 = ___	6) 100 = ___
7) 1,000 = ___	8) 1 = ___

bit.ly/3ZVuLcm

Topic	Prime Factorization with Exponents
Notes	✓ A prime factorization shows how to write a number as the product of prime factors. ✓ Prime factorization is when you break down a number into the prime numbers which multiply to form by the original number.
Example	**Write the prime factorization of 45 with exponents.** Divide by prime factors, and the final quotient must be 1. $45 = 5 \times 9 \rightarrow 45 = 5 \times 3 \times 3$ The prime factorization of 45 is $5 \times 3 \times 3$. And write the repeated factor (3) with an exponent, as $3^2 \times 5$. **Write the prime factorization of 64 with exponents.** Divide by prime factors, and the final quotient must be 1. $64 = 2 \times 32 \rightarrow 64 = 2 \times 2 \times 16 \rightarrow 64 = 2 \times 2 \times 2 \times 8$ $\rightarrow 64 = 2 \times 2 \times 2 \times 2 \times 4$ $\rightarrow 64 = 2 \times 2 \times 2 \times 2 \times 2 \times 2$ The prime factorization of 64 is $2 \times 2 \times 2 \times 2 \times 2 \times 2$. Write the repeated factor (2) with an exponent, as 2^6.
Your Turn!	1) 256 = ___ 2) 420 = ___ 3) 75 = ___ 4) 54 = ___ 5) 196 = ___ 6) 27 = ___ 7) 1,225 = ___ 8) 144 = ___ 9) 40 = ___ 10) 63 = ___

Topic	**Identifying Errors Involving the Order of Operations**
Notes	✓ To assess an expression having multiple operations, one may follow the order of operations: • Do the operations inside the parentheses and the brackets. Begin with the operations inside the inner parentheses or brackets, calculating the expression from the inside out. • Calculate the exponents. • Multiply and divide from left to right. • Add and subtract from left to right
Example	**How can you simplify $6 \times 2 + (10 - 2) \div 2^2 + 3$?** First, perform operations inside parentheses $(10 - 2) = 8$. Second, calculate exponents, $2^2 = 4$. Thus, you have $6 \times 2 + 8 \div 4 + 3$ Third, multiply and divide from left to right, $6 \times 2 = 12$ and $8 \div 4 = 2$. Thus, $12 + 2 + 3$. You finally add from left to right, $12 + 2 + 3 = 17$. So, $6 \times 2 + (10 - 2) \div 2^2 + 3 = 17$
Your Turn!	**Which operation is true?**

1) $4 \times -2 + \frac{8}{2} = -8 + 4 = -4$	
2) $(2.6 + 1.4) \times 3^2 \div 2 = 4 \times 9 \div 2 = 36 \div 2 = 18$	
3) $2 \times \frac{4 \times 3}{2 + 4} + 5 - 1 = 2 \times 2 + 5 - 1 = 2 \times 7 - 1 = 2 \times 6 = 12$	
4) $8 \div 2^2 - 1 + 7 = 4^2 - 1 + 7 = 22$	

Tell which operation is to be done first. Then calculate

5) $15 \div \frac{2 \times 6}{2 + 2}$	6) $3^5 \div 9$
7) $\frac{2+5}{14} \times 6$	8) $21 \div 3 + 5$

bit.ly/3ZO3DMa

Topic	Writing down Variable Expressions Involving Two Operations
Notes	✓ Variables are letters whose values are unknown. ✓ For instance, x is the variable in the expression: $3x + 45$. ✓ The coefficient is a numerical value utilized along with a variable. For instance, 3 is the coefficient in the expression $3x + 45$. ✓ Whenever you write down a mathematical expression, find the keywords to assist you in identifying the operations. ✓ Utilize the keywords for converting the description into an expression, performing one operation at a time.
Example	*Write an expression for the sequence of operations described below.* ***Divide 8 by x, then add 16 to the result.*** See the keywords. Keywords are 'divide' and 'add'. Then use keywords to write an expression. Convert the first keyword: divide 8 by x, $\frac{8}{x}$. Then convert the second keyword: then add 16 to the result, $\frac{8}{x} + 16$. So, $\frac{8}{x} + 16$.
Your Turn!	1) Subtract 2 from y.
	2) Add 10 to b, then subtract c from the result.
	3) Add 13 to g, then divide p by the result.
	4) 3 divided by x.
	5) Multiply 12 by x, then add 4 to the result.
	6) Add y to 5.
	7) Multiply 7 by a, then add u to the result.
	8) Add 7 and a, then subtract 1 from the result.
	9) Multiply a by 3, then subtract 20 from the result.
	10) Subtract 3 from r, then divide 4 by the result.
	11) 2 multiplied by x.
	12) Divide 3 by f, then subtract 1 from the result.

Expressions and Equations

Topic	Using Area Models to Factor Variable Expressions
Notes	✓ The area model of solving multiplication and division problems is derived from the concept of finding the area of a rectangle. $$Area\ of\ a\ rectangle = Length \times Width$$ • First, find the terms of the missing factor: $16x + 4$ • Divide each term by the factor given to you in the model: $4(4x + 1)$ ✓ Factors are expressions where something is multiplied by something else.
Example	**Use the area model for factoring $45 + 27x$.** First, divide each term by the factor given in the model, $45 \div 9 = 5, 27 \div 9 = 3$. Then complete the model. Now, you can write $45 + 27x$ in factored form. The area model shows it is equal to the product of 9 and $5 + 3x$
Your Turn!	1) $55b + 35$ 2) $49 + 21k$ 3) $6j + 18$ 4) $14x + 56x$ 5) $48s + 12t$ 6) $7a + 23a$ 7) $12d + 27$ 8) $65 + 25d$

bit.ly/3ThPCUJ

Find more at

Topic	Using Distributive Property to Factor Variable Expressions
Notes	✓ Use these four steps: • Distribute or multiply the outer term to the inner terms. • Combine the like terms. • Place terms so the constants and variables are on the opposite sides of the equal sign. • Solve the equation and simplify if you need to.
Example	**Factor the expression, $5s - 15t$. Write a product with a whole number greater than 1.** First, find the greatest common factor (GCF) of $5s$ and $15t$. For finding the GCF that appears in both lists, list the factors of both numbers: The factors of 5: $1, 5$ The factors of 15: $1, 3, 5$ Divide each number by 5. And now use the distributive property to write an equivalent expression, $5s - 15t = 5 \times s - 5 \times 3t = 5(s - 3t)$
Your Turn!	**Using distributive property, factor the expressions.**

1) $40 + 20n$	2) $85c + 35n$
3) $60d + 12d$	4) $12s - 44$
5) $105 - 42z$	6) $11a + 33b$
7) $84r + 14r$	8) $13p + 7p$

Expressions and Equations

Topic	Using Distributive Property to Factor Numerical Expressions
Notes	✓ In order to factor a polynomial, first identify the greatest common factor of the monomial terms. ✓ Use the distributive property to rewrite the polynomial as the product of the GCF and the remaining parts of the polynomial. ✓ To "distribute" involves dividing something or giving a share or a part of something. Based on the rules of the distributive property, multiplying the sum of two or more addends by a number is going to give the exact same answer as multiplying each of the addends individually by the number and then adding the products together. $$a(b + c) = a \times b + a \times c$$
Example	*Using the distributive property, factor the expression, $24 + 20$.* First, find the greatest common factor (GCF) of 24 and 20. To find the GCF that appears in both lists, list the factors of both numbers: Factor of 24: 1, 2, 3, 4, 6, 8, 12, 24 Factor of 20: 1, 2, 4, 5, 10, 20 Divide each number by 4, and then use the distributive property to write an equivalent expression: $24 + 20 = 4 \times 6 + 4 \times 5 = 4(6 + 5)$
Your Turn!	**Using distributive property, factor the numerical expressions.**

1) $28 + 48$	2) $9 - 57$
3) $63 - 21$	4) $15 + 45$
5) $24 - 6$	6) $117 - 65$
7) $34 - 26$	8) $161 + 46$

Chapter 7: Answers

Identifying Expressions and Equations

1) Expression
2) Expression
3) Expression
4) Equation
5) Equation
6) Expression
7) Equation
8) Equation
9) Expression
10) Equation

Identify Equivalent Expressions

1) $9p + 8$
2) $5d + 3$
3) $8x - 16$
4) $\frac{1}{2x} - 6$
5) $4t+3$
6) $3y - 15$
7) $-9k + 18$
8) $1g$

Using Properties to Write Equivalent Expressions

1) $9 + 13p + 8 = 13p + 8 + 9 = 13p + 17$
2) $9f \times 9 = 9 \times 9f = 81f$
3) $6r + 1 + 2r = 6r + 2r + 1 = 8r + 1$
4) $6 \times (3 \times 2a) = (6 \times 3) \times 2a = 36a$
5) $w(14 + 6) = 14 \times w + 6 \times w = 20w$
6) $4g \times 11 = 11 \times 4g = 44g$
7) $5s + (5s + 2) = (5s + 5s) + 2 = 10s + 2$
8) $(13t - 1) \times 3 = 13t \times 3 - 1 \times 3 = 39t - 3$

Using Strip Models to Identify Equivalent Expressions

1) $7n + 3d$
2) $6x + 7n$
3) $e + 2j$
4) $3\frac{t}{a} + 6$
5) $2 + 4v$
6) $5f + 20$
7) $10y$
8) $4z + 1$

Using Algebra Tiles to Identify Equivalent Expressions

1) $2x + 4$
2) $3x$
3) $-2 + 5x$
4) $-x + 9$
5) $4x + 10$
6) $8x + 3$
7) 0
8) $7x + 10$

Expressions and Equations

Using Exponents to Write down Multiplication Expressions

1) 8^4
2) 7^2
3) 2^5
4) 11^8
5) 3^5
6) 1^6
7) 4^{10}
8) 13^9
9) 10^3
10) 5^3

Using Exponents to Write Powers of Ten

1) 10^{10}
2) 10^7
3) 10^4
4) 10^{12}
5) 10^1
6) 10^2
7) 10^3
8) 10^0

Prime Factorization with Exponents

1) 2^8
2) $2^2 \times 7 \times 5 \times 3$
3) $5^2 \times 3$
4) $3^3 \times 2$
5) $7^2 \times 2^2$
6) 3^3
7) $7^2 \times 5^2$
8) $2^4 \times 3^2$
9) $2^3 \times 5$
10) $3^2 \times 7$

Identifying Errors Involving the Order of Operations

1) True
2) True
3) False
4) False
5) $15 \div 3 = 5$
6) $243 \div 9 = 27$
7) $\frac{1}{2} \times 6 = 3$
8) $7 + 5 = 12$

Writing down Variable Expressions Involving Two Operations

1) $y - 2$
2) $(b + 10) - c$
3) $p \div (g + 13)$
4) $\frac{3}{x}$
5) $(12 \times x) + 4$
6) $5 + y$
7) $(7 \times a) + u$
8) $(7 + a) - 1$
9) $(a \times 3) - 20$
10) $4 \div (r - 3)$
11) $2x$
12) $(3 \div f) - 1$

Using Area Models to Factor Variable Expressions

1) $5(11b + 7)$
2) $7(7 + 3k)$
3) $6(j + 3)$
4) $7x(2 + 8)$
5) $12(4s + t)$
6) $a(7 + 23)$
7) $3(4d + 9)$
8) $5(13 + 5d)$

Using Distributive Property to Factor Variable Expressions

1) $20(2 + n)$
2) $5(17c + 7n)$
3) $12d(5 + 1)$
4) $4(3s - 11)$
5) $21(5 - 2z)$
6) $11(a + 3b)$
7) $14r(6 + 1)$
8) $p(13 + 7)$

Using Distributive Property to Factor Numerical Expressions

1) $4(7 + 12)$
2) $3(3 - 19)$
3) $21(3 - 1)$
4) $15(1 + 3)$
5) $6(4 - 1)$
6) $13(9 - 5)$
7) $2(17 - 13)$
8) $23(7 + 2)$

Chapter 8
Fundamentals of Computations

Math topics that you'll learn in this chapter:

- ☑ Additive and multiplicative relationships
- ☑ Properties of Addition
- ☑ Using Area Models and the Distributive Property to Multiply
- ☑ Reciprocals

Fundamentals of Computations

Topic	**Additive and Multiplicative Relationships**
Notes	✓ Whenever the additive identity is added to a number, it yields the original number. Likewise, when the multiplicative identity is multiplied by any number, it yields the original number. ✓ Additive relationships imply you must add the IDENTICAL number to any x-value to get the resultant y-value. ✓ Multiplicative relationships imply you must multiply any x-value by the IDENTICAL number to yield the subsequent y-value.
Example	*Which table shows an additive relationship?* Firstly, find the relationships of x and y in the tables. Table (a): $1 + 2 = 3$, $2 + 2 = 4$, $3 + 2 = 5$, $4 + 2 = 6$, then $x + 2 = y$. So, table (a) shows an additive relationship. In contrast, table (b): $1 \times 4 = 4$, $2 \times 4 = 8$, $3 \times 4 = 12$, $4 \times 2 = 8$, then $x \times 4 = y$. So, table (b) shows a multiplicative relationship. Table a: (x,y): $(1,3), (2,4), (3,5), (4,6)$ Table b: (x,y): $(1,4), (2,8), (3,12), (4,16)$
Your Turn!	**What relationship (additive/ multiplicative) do the following equations show?**

1) $a = 8 + b$

2) $y = x + 12$

3) $m = 3h$

4) $z = \frac{2}{9}k$

5)

x	1	2	3	4
y	3	6	9	12

6)

x	0	2	4	6
y	1	3	5	7

7)

x	0	5	10	15
y	4	9	14	19

x	0	2	4	6
y	0	6	12	18

Topic	Properties of Addition
Notes	✓ The four properties of addition: • Commutative property. • Associative property. • Distributive property. • Additive identity property. ✓ In mathematics, the associative and commutative properties are laws used for addition and multiplication that always exist.
Example	*Write the equivalent of the following expression according to the commutative property of addition.* $$3 + b = ?$$ The commutative property demonstrates that you can add numbers in any order and get the same sum. So, $3 + b = b + 3$. *Which property of addition is shown in the equation below?* $$x + (z + w) = (x + z) + w$$ If you add z and w (as a group), then add x to the result, which is equivalent to another expression that says if you add x and z (as a group), then add w to the result. So, this is the associative property of addition.

Your Turn!		
	1) $(w + f) + 9 = w + (f + 9)$	2) $t + 8 + s = s + t + 8$
	3) $2 = 2 + 0$	4) $a + b + 0 = b + a$
	5) $4 + 7 = 7 + 4$	6) $7 + (1 + 2) = (7 + 1) + 2$
	7) $5(a + b) = 5a + 5b$	8) $2(3 + 5) = 6 + 10$

Topic	Using Area Models and the Distributive Property to Multiply
Notes	✓ To multiply two-digit numbers, using the area model, follow the given steps: • Draw a 2 × 2 grid. • Write the terms of one of the multiplicands on the top of the grid. • On the left of the grid, write the terms of the other multiplicand. • Write the products of the number on the cells. • Finally, add all the partial products to get the final product. $1^{st}Cell + 2^{nd}Cell + 3^{rd}Cell + 4^{th}Cell = 2-digit\ number \times 2-digit\ number$
Example	**Use the area model to multiply, 155×15.** 155 is the first factor with three digits, while 15 is the second factor that has 2 digits. Then, draw the model. This area model shows the partial products: Now, add the partial products to find the product: $$155 \times 15 = 1,000 + 500 + 500 + 250 + 50 + 25$$ $$155 \times 15 = 2,325$$
Your Turn!	1) 123×222	2) $408(1 + 5d)$
	3) 35×35	4) $20s \times 19$
	5) $24(4a + 6)$	6) $13(5x + 7y)$
	7) $13 \times 31a$	8) $5(9 + 7g + 2)$

Topic	Reciprocals
Notes	✓ A number's reciprocal is 1 divided by the number. ✓ Reciprocals represent something that is inversely related on both sides. For instance, the reciprocal of the number 5's is 1 divided by 5 and thus written as $\frac{1}{5}$. ✓ Reciprocals also are a number taken to the power of -1. Therefore, $\frac{1}{7}$ is equivalent to 7 to the power of -1. ✓ Reciprocal is often simply represented as the inverse of a value or a number. Thus, whenever they are multiplied together, they end up equal to 1.
Example	**Write the reciprocal of $\frac{3}{21}$:** If you swap the numerator and the denominator, then the reciprocal of the numbers is obtained: $\frac{3}{21} \rightarrow \frac{21}{3} = 7$ **Write the reciprocal of 6:** First, place the whole number over the 1, as $\frac{6}{1}$. Then swap the numerator and the denominator. Next, the reciprocal of the numbers is obtained: $\frac{6}{1} \rightarrow \frac{1}{6}$

Your Turn!

1) $\frac{2}{3}$	2) -7
3) 13	4) $-\frac{5}{8}$
5) 1	6) -9
7) $\frac{2}{36}$	8) $\frac{3}{9}$

Chapter 8: Answers

Additive and multiplicative relationships

1) Additive
2) Additive
3) Multiplicative
4) Multiplicative
5) Multiplicative
6) Additive
7) Additive
8) Multiplicative

Properties of Addition

1) Associative
2) Commutative
3) Identity
4) Identity and Commutative
5) Commutative
6) Associative
7) Distributive
8) Distributive

Using Area Models and the Distributive Property to Multiply

1) 27,306

	200 +	20 +	2
100 +	20,000	2,000	200
20 +	4,000	400	40
3	600	60	6

2) $408 + 2040d$

	1 +	$5d$
400 +	400	$2,000d$
00 +	0	0
8	8	$40d$

3) 1,225

	30 +	5
30 +	900	150
5	150	25

4) $380s$

	10 +	9
$20s$ +	$200s$	$180s$
$0s$	$0s$	$0s$

5) $96a + 144$

	$4a$ +	6
20 +	$80a$	120
4	$16a$	24

6) $65x + 91y$

	$5x$ +	$7y$
10 +	$50x$	$70y$
3	$15x$	$21y$

7) $403a$

	$30a\ +$	$1a$
10	$300a$	$10a$
+		
3	$90a$	$3a$

8) $55 + 35g$

	$9\ +$	$7g\ +$	2
5	45	$35g$	10

Reciprocals

1) $\frac{3}{2}$

2) $-\frac{1}{7}$

3) $\frac{1}{13}$

4) $-\frac{8}{5}$

5) 1

6) $-\frac{1}{9}$

7) 18

8) 3

CHAPTER 9
Algebraic Operation of Integers

Math topics that you'll learn in this chapter:

- ☑ Using Number Lines to Add Two Negative Integers
- ☑ Using Number Lines to Add two Different Signs Integer
- ☑ Using Input/Output Tables to Add and Subtract Integers
- ☑ Using Number Lines to Subtract Integers
- ☑ Using Number Lines for Multiplication by a Negative Integer
- ☑ Adding and Subtracting Integers
- ☑ Multiplying and Dividing Integers
- ☑ Multiply Three or More Numbers
- ☑ Order of Operations

Algebraic Operation of Integers

Topic	Using Number Lines to Add Two Negative Integers
Notes	✓ You must utilize the concepts of positive and negative integers on a number line to add the provided integers. ✓ First, draw the number line. Next, find the place of the first integer on this number line. ✓ Afterward, if the second integer is positive, move over that number of spaces to the right-hand side from where the first integer is. If the second one is negative, move over that number of spaces to the left-hand side from the first integer's location.
Examples	**Draw the number line of $(-3) + (-9)$, and solve it.** Find -3 and from that, move 9 units to the left side. Then, see where the arrow ends. The arrow ends at -12.
Your Turn!	**Find the sum of two negative integers. Utilizing the number line.** 1) $(-13) + (-7) =?$ 2) $(-8) + (-18) =?$ 3) $(-3) + (-11) =?$ 4) $(-1) + (-5) =?$ **According to the number line find the sum of two negative integers.** 5) 6) 7) 8)

Topic	Using Number Lines to Add two Different Signs Integers
Notes	✓ One method of adding integers that have different signs is via ignoring the sign and finding the difference between these 2 integers. ✓ First, you ignore the sign and then figure out the difference between the 2 numbers. ✓ Next, subtract the bigger absolute value from the lesser one. ✓ Then, attach the larger integer sign.
Examples	**Draw the number line of $7 + (-2)$, and solve it.** Find 7 and from that move 2 units to the left side. Observe where the arrow ends. The arrow ends are at 5. Then, $7 + (-2) = 5$

Your Turn!

Find the sum integers with different signs. Utilizing the number line.

1) $3 + (-3) =$	2) $17 + (-5) =$
3) $9 + (-14) =$	4) $11 + (-2) =$

According to the number line find the sum integers with different signs.

5)

6)

7)

8)

bit.ly/3JLNYHE

Find more at

Algebraic Operation of Integers

Topic	Using Input/Output Tables to Add and Subtract Integers
Notes	✓ Input-output tables are tables that show the relationship between sets of numbers that consistently follow the same rule. ✓ Input is a number in the first column of the table and output is the resulting number or the solution to a mathematical equation. ✓ Input-output table: This is the literal table that has sets of numbers on it.
Examples	*Figure out the rule to complete the table:* To find the rule, start with the number in the IN column. Figure out what number to subtract/add to give the value shown in the OUT column. $$-14 + ? = -17 \rightarrow -17 + 14 \rightarrow ? = -3$$ The rule is to subtract 3, now use the rule to find the missing number: $$0 - 3 = -3$$ IN / OUT table: −14 / −17, −5 / −8, 0 / __, 4 / 1

Your Turn!

What is the rule for tables?

1)

IN	Out
−15	−2
−10	3
−5	8
0	13

2)

IN	Out
−18	−25
−7	−14
0	−7
3	−4

3)

IN	Out
10	6
5	1
0	−4
−5	−9

4)

IN	Out
−3	2
2	7
5	10
8	13

Figure out the rule to complete the table.

5)

IN	Out
−9	−17
−1	−9
	−3
18	10

6)

IN	Out
−6	
−4	−2
−2	0
0	2

7)

IN	Out
−16	−4
−13	−1
14	26
18	

8)

IN	Out
1	−7
	3
12	4
20	12

Topic	Using Number Lines to Subtract Integers
Notes	✓ One method of utilizing a number line for subtracting integers is by moving in the opposite direction for adding integers. ✓ Utilize a number line for the addition and subtraction of integers: • Add positive integers by moving towards the right on a number line. • Add negative integers by moving towards the left on a number line. ✓ Subtract integers by the addition of their opposite.
Examples	**Solve.** $-1 - 5 =?$ **And graph on the number line.** Subtracting a number is the same as adding its opposite. Since the expression is equal to $(-1) + (-5)$, start at -1 on the number line and move 5 units to the left side. Then: $-1 - 5 = -6$
Your Turn!	Find each difference. And graph on the number line.

1) $3 - 7 =$	2) $-23 - (-17) =$
3) $-7 - 9 =$	4) $17 - 13 =$
5) $25 - 16 =$	6) $(-16) - 11 =$
7) $5 - (-10) =$	8) $(-14) - (-5) =$

bit.ly/3TkgeUW

Algebraic Operation of Integers

Topic	**Using Number Lines for Multiplication by a Negative Integer**
Notes	✓ Whenever you multiply more than two negative numbers, utilize the Even-Odd Rule. ✓ Therefore, you must count the number of negative signs. If there is an even number of negatives, the result is positive; but if there are an odd number of negatives, the result is negative.
Examples	*Solve.* $2 \times -3 = ?$ *And graph on the number line.* To model 2×-3 on the number line, start at 0 and jump 3 units to the left side 2 times. See where the last jump ends. Thus, the final jump ends at -6. $$2 \times -3 = -6$$ *Solve.* $-3 \times -3 = ?$ *And graph on the number line.* Now use this formula: $(negative) \times (negative) = positive$. So, $-3 \times -3 = 3 \times 3$ Then, to model 3×3 on the number line, start at 0 and jump 3 units to the right side 3 times. See where the last jump ends. Thus, the final jump ends at 9. $$-3 \times -3 = 9$$
Your Turn!	**Find each product. And graph on the number line.**

1) $5 \times -2 =$	2) $6 \times 3 =$
3) $4 \times -1 =$	4) $-2 \times 3 =$
5) $4 \times 3 =$	6) $-5 \times -3 =$
7) $3 \times 3 =$	8) $4 \times -2 =$

bit.ly/3JMzhUA

Topic	Adding and Subtracting Integers
Notes	✓ Integers include zero, counting numbers, and the negative of the counting numbers. $\{\ldots, -3, -2, -1, 0, 1, 2, 3, \ldots\}$ ✓ Add a positive integer by moving to the right on the number line. (You will get a bigger number) ✓ Add a negative integer by moving to the left on the number line. (You will get a smaller number) ✓ Subtract an integer by adding its opposite.
Examples	**Solve.** $(-4) - (-9) = ?$ Keep the first number and convert the sign of the second number to its opposite. (Change subtraction into addition. Then: $(-4) + 9 = 5$ **Solve.** $6 + (5 - 10) = ?$ First, subtract the numbers in brackets, $5 - 10 = -5$. Then: $6 + (-5) = \rightarrow$ change addition into subtraction: $6 - 5 = 1$
Your Turn!	

1) $-7 + 16 =$	2) $(-3) - (17 + 4) =$
3) $9 - (19 - 2) =$	4) $22 - 13 =$
5) $-29 - 6 =$	6) $3 + (-7 + 9) =$
7) $(-18) + (25 - 14) =$	8) $(-1 + 9) + (-3 + 5) =$
9) $(6 - 15) - (-6 + 17) =$	10) $(-7 + 2) - (6 - 1) =$
11) $(-8 - 4) - (-1 - 14)$	12) $(-11) + (-8 + 6) =$

bit.ly/42fKvZc

Algebraic Operation of Integers

Topic	Multiplying and Dividing Integers
Notes	✓ Use the following rules for multiplying and dividing integers: • (negative) × (negative) = positive • (negative) ÷ (negative) = positive • (negative) × (positive) = negative • (negative) ÷ (positive) = negative • (positive) × (positive) = positive • (positive) ÷ (negative) = negative
Examples	**Solve.** $(9 - 19) \times (-3) =?$ First, subtract the numbers in parentheses, $9 - 19 = -10 \rightarrow (-10) \times (-3) =$ Now use this rule: (negative) × (negative) = positive $\rightarrow (-10) \times (-3) = 30$ **Solve.** $(7 - 3) \div (-4) =?$ First, subtract the numbers in parentheses, $7 - 3 = 4 \rightarrow (4) \div (-4) =$ Now use this rule: (positive) ÷ (negative) = negative $\rightarrow$ $(4) \div (-4) = -1$

Your Turn!

1) $8 \times (-6) =$	2) $36 \div 4 =$
3) $(-1) \times 7 =$	4) $(-35) \div (-5) =$
5) $(-5) \times (6 + 5) =$	6) $(12 - 3) \times (-1) =$
7) $(6 - 7) \times (-5) =$	8) $(-7 + 5) \times (-8 + 6) =$
9) $(-15) \times (-12 + 12) =$	10) $(-13 - 3) \div (9 - 7) =$
11) $(-18 - 31) \div (-7) =$	12) $(-9) \times (-6 + 11) =$

Topic	Multiply Three or More Numbers
Notes	✓ Whenever you need to multiply three or more numbers together, begin by multiplying any two of the factors. ✓ Then, multiply that product with another factor. ✓ If there are more than 3 numbers, keep on multiplying until you've multiplied every factor: • First, multiply the 1st and 2nd factors: • Next, multiply the new product by the 3rd factor:
Examples	**Multiply** $9 \times 2 \times 4 =?$ First, multiply 9 and 2: $9 \times 2 = 18$. Then, $18 \times 4 = 72$. So, $9 \times 2 \times 4 = 72$. **Multiply** $2 \times 12 \times 5 =?$ First, multiply 2 and 12: $2 \times 12 = 24$. Then, $24 \times 5 = 120$. So, $2 \times 12 \times 5 = 120$.

Your Turn!

1) $6 \times 5 \times 4 =$	2) $5 \times 9 \times 3 =$
3) $2 \times 7 \times 6 =$	4) $1 \times 9 \times 8 =$
5) $6 \times 9 \times 6 =$	6) $2 \times 4 \times 3 =$
7) $8 \times 12 \times 2 =$	8) $5 \times 11 \times 3 =$
9) $5 \times 5 \times 6 =$	10) $4 \times 0 \times 13 =$
11) $3 \times 6 \times 8 =$	12) $7 \times 2 \times 5 =$

bit.ly/42fuyID
Find more at

Topic	Order of Operations
Notes	✓ In Mathematics, "operations" are addition, subtraction, multiplication, division, exponentiation (written as b^n), and grouping. ✓ When there is more than one math operation in an expression, use PEMDAS: (to memorize this rule, remember the phrase "Please Excuse My Dear Aunt Sally".) • Parentheses • Exponents • Multiplication and Division (from left to right) • Addition and Subtraction (from left to right)
Examples	**Calculate.** $(13-5) \div (4^2 \div 4) = ?$ First, simplify inside parentheses: $(8) \div (16 \div 4) = (8) \div (4)$, Then: $(8) \div (4) = 2$ **Solve.** $(3 \times 5) - (11-5) = ?$ First, calculate within parentheses: $(3 \times 5) - (11-5) = (15) - (6)$, Then: $(15) - (6) = 9$
Your Turn!	**Evaluate each expression.**

1) $(5 \times 3) - 7 =$	2) $3 + (2 \times 5) =$
3) $(-9 \times 5) + 16 =$	4) $(7 \times 3^2) - (-5) =$
5) $(9 - 2) + (7 \times 4) =$	6) $(-19 + 5) + (6 \times 2) =$
7) $(64 \div 4) + (1 - 13) =$	8) $(-16 + 5) - (54 \div 9) =$
9) $(-2^4 + 1) + (54 \div 6) =$	10) $(28 \div 4) + (2 \times 6) =$
11) $2[(2 \times 7) + (9 \times 3)] =$	12) $-5[(10 \times 3) \div (2 \times 3)] =$

bit.ly/3FtC4jk

Chapter 9: Answers

Using Number Lines to Add Two Negative Integers

1) −20

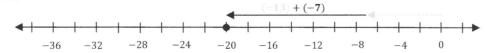

2) −26

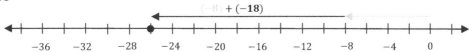

3) −14

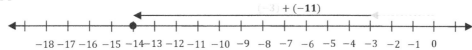

4) −6

5) $(-6) + (-5) = -11$ 7) $(-5) + (-12) = -17$

6) $(-1) + (-12) = -13$ 8) $(-9) + (-4) = -13$

Using Number Lines to Add two Different Signs Integer

1) 0

2) 12

3) −5

4) 9

5) $4 + (-11) = -7$ 7) $7 + (-3) = 4$

6) $8 + (-16) = -8$ 8) $4 + (-6) = -2$

Algebraic Operation of Integers

Using Input/Output Tables to Add and Subtract Integers

1) $IN + 13 = Out$
2) $IN - 7 = Out$
3) $IN - 4 = Out$
4) $IN + 5 = Out$
5) 5
6) -4
7) 30
8) 11

Using Number Lines to Subtract Integers

1) -4

2) -6

3) -16

4) 4

5) 9

6) -27

7) 15

8) -9

Using Number Lines for Multiplication by a Negative Integer

1) −10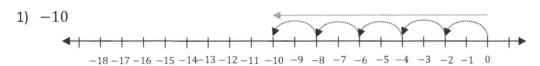

2) 18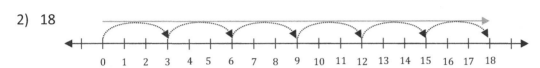

3) −4

4) −6

5) 12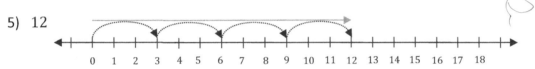

6) 15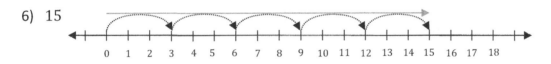

7) 9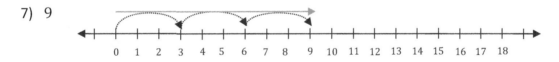

8) −8

Adding and Subtracting Integers

1) 9
2) −24
3) −8
4) 9
5) −35
6) 5
7) −7
8) 10
9) −20
10) −10
11) 3
12) −13

Algebraic Operation of Integers

Multiplying and Dividing Integers

1) −48
2) 9
3) −7
4) 7
5) −55
6) −9
7) 5
8) 4
9) 0
10) −8
11) 7
12) −45

Multiply Three or More Numbers

1) 120
2) 135
3) 84
4) 72
5) 324
6) 24
7) 192
8) 165
9) 150
10) 0
11) 144
12) 70

Order of Operations

1) 8
2) 13
3) −29
4) 68
5) 35
6) −2
7) 4
8) −17
9) -6
10) 19
11) 82
12) −25

CHAPTER 10
Operations of Fraction, Decimal, and Mixed numbers

Math topics that you'll learn in this chapter:

- ☑ Scaling Whole Numbers by Fractions
- ☑ Using Models to Divide Whole Numbers by Unit Fractions
- ☑ Dividing Fractions by Whole Numbers in Recipes
- ☑ Using Models to Multiply Two Fractions
- ☑ Multiplying and Dividing Fractions
- ☑ Word Problem for Explaining Fractions as Division
- ☑ Word Problem of Dividing Fractions
- ☑ Multiplication and Division of Decimals by Powers of Ten
- ☑ Estimate Products of Mixed Numbers
- ☑ Scaling by Fractions and Mixed Numbers
- ☑ Multiplying Mixed Numbers
- ☑ Dividing Mixed Numbers
- ☑ Word Problem of Multiplying Mixed Numbers
- ☑ Multiplying and Dividing Decimals
- ☑ Multiplying Three Rational Numbers, and Whole Numbers

Operations of Fraction, Decimal, and Mixed numbers

Topic	Scaling Whole Numbers by Fractions
Notes	✓ For scaling whole numbers by fractions, we must convert the number into an inverted format. ✓ If you know this concept, you can figure out if your answer is reasonable: • Whenever a fraction is multiplied by a fraction that is LESS THAN ONE WHOLE, its size gets scaled down. • Whenever a fraction is multiplied by a fraction that is LARGER THAN ONE WHOLE, its size gets scaled up.
Example	**Which expression is greater? 3 or $3 \times \frac{9}{4}$** Multiplying a whole number by a fraction greater than 1, the answer will be greater. Since, $\frac{9}{4}$ is greater than 1, multiplying by $\frac{9}{4}$ makes the value of the whole number greater. Then, $3 \times \frac{9}{4} > 3$. **Is this inequality correct? $5 \times \frac{2}{9} < 5$** Multiplying a whole number by a fraction less than 1, the answer will be less than the whole number. Since, $\frac{2}{9}$ is smaller than 1, multiplying by $\frac{2}{9}$ makes the value of the whole number smaller. Then, $5 \times \frac{2}{9} < 5$.
Your Turn!	1) $7 \;\square\; 4 \times \frac{10}{6}$ 2) $2 \;\square\; 1 \times \frac{7}{2}$ 3) $11 \;\square\; 9 \times \frac{7}{4}$ 4) $4 \;\square\; 4 \times \frac{2}{3}$ 5) $6 \;\square\; 6 \times \frac{3}{5}$ 6) $6 \;\square\; 5 \times \frac{8}{3}$ 7) $7 \;\square\; 11 \times \frac{1}{15}$ 8) $4 \;\square\; 2 \times \frac{7}{4}$

bit.ly/3FpzQ47

Topic	Using Models to Divide Whole Numbers by Unit Fractions
Notes	✓ A fraction is a number with a numerator and a denominator. ✓ For instance, this is the whole number 5 and a fraction of $\frac{2}{7}$ ✓ So, you wish to solve $5 \div \frac{2}{7} =?$ ✓ First, place the whole number over the 1 as $\frac{5}{1}$. ✓ Next, invert the 2 so it becomes the denominator and the 7 becomes the numerator, so it appears as $\frac{7}{2}$. ✓ Then multiply these numbers: $5 \times \frac{7}{2} = \frac{35}{2}$
Example	**Divide $4 \div \frac{1}{2}$. Use the models to help you.** First, model the whole number 4. Then model $\frac{1}{2}$ and see how many fraction pieces make up 4. To make 4 it takes 8 of the fraction pieces. So, $4 \div \frac{1}{2} = 8$.

Your Turn!		
	1) $4 \div \frac{1}{4}$	2) $1 \div \frac{4}{7}$
	3) $5 \div \frac{2}{5}$	4) $3 \div \frac{1}{3}$
	5) $4 \div \frac{2}{7}$	6) $6 \div \frac{3}{4}$
	7) $1 \div \frac{1}{6}$	8) $3 \div \frac{5}{6}$
	9) $2 \div \frac{3}{5}$	10) $5 \div \frac{5}{4}$

bit.ly/3LpdELv

Topic	**Dividing Fractions by Whole Numbers in Recipes**
Notes	✓ The first step you must do is to change the whole numbers to fractions. ✓ Firstly put 1 for the denominator of the whole number. Next, swap the numerator and denominator. ✓ Then, multiply the 2 numerators. Next, multiply the 2 denominators. Lastly, simplify the fractions if you need to.

Example	*What quantity of Sugar would you need to make a quarter recipe?* The recipe calls for $2\frac{1}{5}$ cups of sugar. To cut the recipe into quarters, divide $2\frac{1}{5}$ cups by 4. Write 4 as an improper fraction and convert $2\frac{1}{5}$ to an improper fraction, too, $\frac{11}{5} \div \frac{4}{1}$. You must turn this from a division problem into a multiplication problem by multiplying by the reciprocal. So, $\frac{11}{5} \div \frac{4}{1} = \frac{11}{5} \times \frac{1}{4} = \frac{11}{20}$. You would need $\frac{11}{20}$ of a cup of sugar.	**Strawberry cake**
		$2\frac{1}{5}$ cups sugar
		$3\frac{3}{5}$ cups flour
		$\frac{3}{5}$ cup mashed strawberry
		$1\frac{1}{3}$ cup milk
		$\frac{1}{3}$ cup vegetable oil
		$1\frac{1}{3}$ teaspoons vanilla
		$\frac{3}{5}$ teaspoon cinnamon
		1 teaspoon baking powder
		4 eggs

Your Turn! According to the recipes solve the word problems.

	Very cherry pie
1) What quantity of **cherries** would you need to make a third of the original very cherry pie recipe?	6 cups cherries
	$\frac{2}{5}$ cup sugar
2) What quantity of **flour** would you need to make a half very cherry pie recipe?	$\frac{1}{6}$ cup flour
	$2\frac{1}{5}$ teaspoons vanilla
3) What quantity of **pie crust** would you need to make half of the very cherry pie recipe?	$\frac{3}{8}$ teaspoon cinnamon
4) What quantity of **sugar** would you need to make a quarter very cherry pie recipe?	2 pie crust

bit.ly/42kny7e

Topic	**Using Models to Multiply Two Fractions**
Notes	✓ Use area models to show a visual depiction of the product of 2 fractions. • Draw a rectangle. The denominator in the first factor represents how many columns to draw, and the numerator represents how many columns to shade. • The denominator in the second factor represents how many rows to draw, and the numerator represents how many rows to shade. • The numerator for the product is the number of parts that were shaded twice. The denominator for the product is the number of total parts in the rectangle. • Simplify if necessary.
Example	**Use the model to find the product.** $\frac{1}{2} \times \frac{1}{4} =?$ The model has 2 columns and 4 rows. So, 1 out of 2 columns are shaded, representing the factor $\frac{1}{2}$. And 1 out of 4 rows are shaded, which represents the factor $\frac{1}{4}$. So, you can see there is 1 section with overlap. And for the denominator, the whole model has 2 columns and 4 rows. So, there are $2 \times 4 = 8$ sections in total. Thus, you have 1 section with an overlap out of 8 sections in total, $\frac{1}{8}$. Therefore, $\frac{1}{2} \times \frac{1}{4} = \frac{1}{8}$
Your Turn!	**Write the multiplication expression and solve.** 1) 2) 3) 4) **Multiply by model.** 5) $\frac{5}{6} \times \frac{1}{6} =?$ 6) $\frac{2}{5} \times \frac{3}{8} =?$ 7) $\frac{3}{8} \times \frac{1}{2} =?$ 8) $\frac{1}{3} \times \frac{1}{3} =$

Operations of Fraction, Decimal, and Mixed numbers

Topic	Multiplying and Dividing Fractions
Notes	✓ **Multiplying fractions:** multiply the top numbers and multiply the bottom numbers. Simplify if necessary. $\frac{a}{b} \times \frac{c}{d} = \frac{a \times c}{b \times d}$ ✓ **Dividing fractions:** Keep, Change, Flip ✓ Keep the first fraction, change the division sign to multiplication, and flip the numerator and denominator of the second fraction. Then, solve! $$\frac{a}{b} \div \frac{c}{d} = \frac{a}{b} \times \frac{d}{c} = \frac{a \times d}{b \times c}$$
Example	**Solve.** $\frac{1}{3} \div \frac{2}{9} =$ Keep the first fraction, change the division sign to multiplication, and flip the numerator and denominator of the second fraction. Then: $\frac{1}{3} \div \frac{2}{9} = \frac{1}{3} \times \frac{9}{2} = \frac{1 \times 9}{3 \times 2} = \frac{9}{6}$, simplify: $\frac{9}{6} = \frac{9 \div 3}{6 \div 3} = \frac{3}{2}$ **Calculate.** $\frac{8}{15} \times \frac{3}{4} =$ Multiply the top numbers and multiply the bottom numbers. $\frac{8}{15} \times \frac{3}{4} = \frac{8 \times 3}{15 \times 4} = \frac{24}{60}$, simplify: $\frac{24}{60} = \frac{24 \div 12}{60 \div 12} = \frac{2}{5}$
Your Turn!	**Find the products or quotients.**

1) $\frac{2}{9} \div \frac{4}{3} =$	2) $\frac{14}{5} \div \frac{28}{35} =$
3) $\frac{4}{3} \div \frac{2}{5} =$	4) $\frac{3}{12} \div \frac{1}{3} =$
5) $\frac{9}{25} \times \frac{5}{27} =$	6) $\frac{65}{72} \times \frac{12}{15} =$
7) $\frac{7}{9} \times \frac{5}{8} =$	8) $\frac{51}{100} \times \frac{15}{17} =$

Topic	Word Problem for Explaining Fractions as Division
Notes	✓ Here, you learn the simplest method of dividing fractions. You must follow 3 easy steps: ✓ Reverse the divisor into a reciprocal. ✓ Then the division sign must be changed to a multiplication sign. ✓ Then multiply.
Example	*Carmen sells pieces of cakes at the confectionery market. To make the pieces, she cuts a big* 3 *—pound block of cake into* 24 *pieces. How much does each piece of cake weigh? Write your answer as a proper fraction or mixed number.* Start by listing the information: The block of cake weighs 3 pounds. Carmen cuts the block of cake into 24 equal pieces. There are 3 pounds of a cake divided into 24 pieces $3 \div 24 = \frac{3}{24}$. simplify: $\frac{3}{24} = \frac{3 \div 3}{24 \div 3} = \frac{1}{8}$ So, each piece of cake weighs $\frac{1}{8}$ pounds.
Your Turn!	1) In a fish market, there are 8 gallons of water in the main tank. The water of this tank is shared between sixteen fish tanks. What fraction of a gallon of water is shared in each tank? 2) Adams shares his 15 —pack of football cards with his seven friends. What fraction of the pack of football cards does each friend receive? 3) Luci uses 8 laboratory tubes to do 35 tests. What fraction of tests have been performed with each tube? 4) Sara planted 9 of a packet of orchid flower seeds in eighteen equal rows. What fraction of the packet of orchid flower seeds does each row contain?

Topic	Word Problem of Dividing Fractions
Notes	✓ Step 1: Use keywords and phrases to identify the problem. In division, we look for phrases like "go into" or "get out of" that ask how much or how many of something can fit into something else. ✓ Step 2: When dividing fractions, the quickest and easiest way to solve them is to invert the second fraction and multiply instead of dividing. ✓ Step 3: Just multiply the numerators across and multiply the denominators across. If your problem involves mixed numbers, you will want to convert them to improper fractions first. ✓ Step 4: Simplify (reduce) the fraction if possible.
Example	*Karolina uses $\frac{3}{8}$ of a jar of peach jam to make six muffins. What fraction of the jar of peach jam does each muffin contain?* Divide the total amount of used peach jam by the number of muffins, $\frac{3}{8} \div 6$. Write 6 as an improper fraction, $\frac{3}{8} \div \frac{6}{1}$. Then, turn this from a division problem into a multiplication problem by multiplying by the reciprocal, and simplifying the product: $$\frac{3}{8} \times \frac{1}{6} = \frac{3 \times 1}{8 \times 6} = \frac{3}{48} = \frac{1}{16}$$
Your Turn!	**Solve, and simplify your answer.** 1) Workmen used $\frac{3}{4}$ of the paving pallet to pave the inner path of the park. They used $\frac{1}{12}$ of a pallet for each step. How many steps did they build? 2) A factory uses $\frac{3}{8}$ of a barrel of oatmeal in each batch of biscuits. The factory used $\frac{1}{16}$ of a barrel of oatmeal yesterday. How many batches of biscuits did the factory make? 3) Martha bought some potatoes and $\frac{1}{2}$ of a gallon of oil to fry the potatoes. She used $\frac{1}{20}$ gallon of oil per kilogram of potatoes. In the end, all the purchased oil was used up. How many kilograms of potatoes did Martha buy? 4) A restaurant put a bottle of pepper sauce at each table. They divided $\frac{1}{4}$ of a kilogram of pepper sauce evenly to put $\frac{1}{32}$ of a kilogram in each dish. How many bottles of pepper sauce did they fill?

Topic	Multiplication and Division of Decimals by Powers of Ten
Notes	✓ In order to multiply using the power of 10, merely move the decimal toward the right of the identical number of spaces as the exponent or as the number of zeros. ✓ Determining ten times as many are identical to multiplying by 10 (if you are using positive numbers); to multiply any whole number via 10, put a zero after the final digit in this number. ✓ In order to divide any multiple of 10 by 10, take out the last zero digit (in the ones place) from the number.
Example	**Divide:** $7.8 \div 10 = ?$ First, count the zeros in 10. And there is 1 zero in 10. Then, move the decimal point 1 place to the left in 7.8. So, $7.8 \rightarrow 0.78$ $$7.8 \div 10 = 0.78$$ **Multiply:** $1000 \times 0.053 = ?$ First, count the zeros in 1000. And there are 3 zeros in 1000. Then, move the decimal point 3 places to the right in 0.053. So, $0.053 \rightarrow 053.0$. $$1000 \times 0.053 = 53$$
Your Turn!	**Multiply.** 1) $0.708 \times 1,000 =$ 2) $17.5 \times 100 =$ 3) $0.5 \times 10,000 =$ 4) $10 \times 1.83 =$ **Divide.** 5) $16.8 \div 10 =$ 6) $15 \div 100 =$ 7) $75.5 \div 10 =$ 8) $95.2 \div 1,000 =$

Operations of Fraction, Decimal, and Mixed numbers

Topic	Estimate Products of Mixed Numbers
Notes	✓ Mixed numbers are whole numbers, along with a proper fraction represented together. It usually signifies a number in between any 2 whole numbers. ✓ To approximate the product, you must round a mixed number to the closest whole number, after that you multiply. The resulting product is an estimate.
Example	*Estimate the multiplication by rounding the first factor to the nearest whole number and the second factor to the nearest hundred.* $9 \times 111\frac{1}{7} = ?$ 9 rounded to the nearest ten is 10. $111\frac{1}{7}$ rounded to the nearest one is 100. Then: $10 \times 100 = 1,000$ *Estimate the result by rounding each number to the nearest whole number.* $13\frac{3}{5} \times 25\frac{1}{4} = ?$ $13\frac{3}{5}$ rounded to the nearest whole number is 14. $25\frac{1}{4}$ rounded to the nearest whole number is 25. Then: $14 \times 25 = 350$
Your Turn!	**Estimate the multiplication by rounding the first factor to the nearest whole number and the second factor to the nearest ten.** 1) $2\frac{3}{5} \times 41\frac{1}{5} = ?$ 2) $7\frac{8}{10} \times 18\frac{1}{5} = ?$ 3) $6\frac{5}{7} \times 33\frac{1}{8} = ?$ 4) $4\frac{1}{9} \times 13\frac{1}{2} = ?$ **Estimate the multiplication by rounding each number to the nearest whole number.** 5) $18\frac{1}{2} \times 43\frac{4}{5} = ?$ 6) $21\frac{1}{25} \times 1\frac{3}{4} = ?$ 7) $3\frac{1}{5} \times 14\frac{7}{8} = ?$ 8) $\frac{5}{8} \times 1\frac{6}{10} = ?$

Topic	Scaling by Fractions and Mixed Numbers
Notes	✓ Rules for scaling: • Whenever a fraction gets multiplied by a number SMALLER THAN ONE WHOLE, its size gets scaled down. • Whenever a fraction is multiplied via a number LARGER THAN ONE WHOLE, its size gets scaled up. ✓ When you know this concept, you can find out if your answer is reasonable.
Example	**Which expression is greater or least?** $2 \times 3\frac{1}{2}$ ☐ 5 First, calculate: $2 \times 3\frac{1}{2} = 2 \times \frac{7}{2} = \frac{14}{2} = 7$. According to, 7 is greater than 5. Then, $2 \times 3\frac{1}{2}$s greater than 5. **Which expression is greater or least?** $3 \times 3\frac{1}{3}$ ☐ 10 First, calculate: $3 \times 3\frac{1}{3} = 3 \times \frac{10}{3} = \frac{30}{3} = 10$. According to, 10 is equal to 10. Then, $3 \times 3\frac{1}{3}$ is equal to 10.
Your Turn!	**Which expression is greater or least?** 1) 15 ☐ $5 \times 3\frac{1}{2}$ 2) 7 ☐ $4 \times 1\frac{2}{3}$ 3) 6 ☐ $2 \times 2\frac{2}{7}$ 4) 5 ☐ $4 \times 1\frac{1}{9}$ 5) 12 ☐ $9 \times 1\frac{2}{4}$ 6) 5 ☐ $6 \times \frac{1}{2}$ 7) 5 ☐ $4 \times 1\frac{3}{9}$ 8) 8 ☐ $7 \times 1\frac{5}{6}$

Operations of Fraction, Decimal, and Mixed numbers

Topic	Multiplying Mixed Numbers
Notes	✓ Use the following steps for multiplying mixed numbers: ✓ Convert the mixed numbers into fractions. $a\frac{c}{b} = a + \frac{c}{b} = \frac{ab+c}{b}$ ✓ Multiply fractions. $\frac{a}{b} \times \frac{c}{d} = \frac{a \times c}{b \times d}$ ✓ Write your answer in lowest terms. ✓ If the answer is an improper fraction (numerator is bigger than denominator), convert it into a mixed number.
Example	**Multiply.** $5\frac{2}{5} \times 2\frac{5}{6} = ?$ Converting mixed numbers into fractions, $5\frac{2}{5} \times 2\frac{5}{6} = \frac{27}{5} \times \frac{17}{6}$ Apply the fractions rule for multiplication: $\frac{27}{5} \times \frac{17}{6} = \frac{27 \times 17}{5 \times 6} = \frac{459}{30} = 15\frac{3}{10}$ **Find the product.** $1\frac{1}{4} \times 2\frac{3}{8} = ?$ Convert mixed numbers to fractions: $1\frac{1}{4} = \frac{5}{4}$ and $2\frac{3}{8} = \frac{19}{8}$. Multiply two fractions: $\frac{5}{4} \times \frac{19}{8} = \frac{5 \times 19}{4 \times 8} = \frac{95}{32} = 2\frac{31}{32}$
Your Turn!	1) $1\frac{1}{2} \times 2\frac{3}{5} =$ 2) $2\frac{1}{9} \times 5\frac{1}{2} =$ 3) $1\frac{3}{4} \times 9\frac{3}{5} =$ 4) $3\frac{1}{5} \times 4\frac{1}{2} =$ 5) $4\frac{1}{2} \times 1\frac{5}{9} =$ 6) $6\frac{9}{10} \times 3\frac{1}{7} =$ 7) $1\frac{2}{7} \times 3\frac{1}{3} =$ 8) $7\frac{9}{8} \times 1\frac{1}{4} =$ 9) $2\frac{1}{3} \times 5\frac{1}{2} =$ 10) $2\frac{9}{5} \times 5\frac{1}{3} =$

Topic	Dividing Mixed Numbers
Notes	✓ Use the following steps for dividing mixed numbers: ✓ Convert the mixed numbers into fractions. $a\frac{c}{b} = a + \frac{c}{b} = \frac{ab+c}{b}$ ✓ Divide fractions: Keep, Change, Flip: Keep the first fraction, change the division sign to multiplication, and flip the numerator and denominator of the second fraction. Then, solve! $\frac{a}{b} \div \frac{c}{d} = \frac{a}{b} \times \frac{d}{c} = \frac{a \times d}{b \times c}$ ✓ Write your answer in lowest terms. ✓ If the answer is an improper fraction (numerator is bigger than denominator), convert it into a mixed number.
Example	**Solve.** $2\frac{1}{2} \div 1\frac{1}{5}$ Convert mixed numbers to fractions, then solve: $2\frac{1}{2} \div 1\frac{1}{5} = \frac{5}{2} \div \frac{6}{5} = \frac{5}{2} \times \frac{5}{6} = \frac{25}{12} = 2\frac{1}{12}$ **Solve.** $1\frac{4}{5} \div 2\frac{2}{3}$ Converting mixed numbers to fractions: $1\frac{4}{5} \div 2\frac{2}{3} = \frac{9}{5} \div \frac{8}{3}$ Keep, Change, Flip: $\frac{9}{5} \div \frac{8}{3} = \frac{9}{5} \times \frac{3}{8} = \frac{9 \times 3}{5 \times 8} = \frac{27}{40}$
Your Turn!	1) $1\frac{1}{3} \div 2\frac{2}{3} =$ 2) $2\frac{2}{3} \div 2\frac{3}{8} =$
	3) $2\frac{1}{3} \div \frac{1}{2} =$ 4) $1\frac{1}{2} \div 2\frac{2}{5} =$
	5) $5\frac{1}{5} \div 3\frac{1}{2} =$ 6) $4\frac{2}{7} \div \frac{1}{4} =$
	7) $3\frac{2}{7} \div 1\frac{1}{5} =$ 8) $2\frac{1}{2} \div 1\frac{1}{6} =$
	9) $4\frac{1}{5} \div 3\frac{2}{3} =$ 10) $1\frac{1}{6} \div 2\frac{1}{3} =$

Operations of Fraction, Decimal, and Mixed numbers

Topic	Word Problem of Multiplying Mixed Numbers
Notes	✓ Mixed numbers have a whole number as well as a fraction. ✓ For multiplying mixed numbers: • Write down the number as an improper fraction. • Write mixed numbers as an improper fraction. ✓ Multiply the numerators, then multiply the denominators. ✓ Simplify the product.
Example	*Sara planted an apple tree and an orange tree. The apple tree Is 8 feet tall. The orange tree is $2\frac{3}{4}$ times as tall as the apple tree. How tall is Sara's orange tree?* Since the apple tree is $2\frac{3}{4}$ times 8 feet tall. Multiply $2\frac{3}{4}$ in 8: $2\frac{3}{4} \times 8 = ?$, $2\frac{3}{4} = \frac{(2\times 4)+3}{4} = \frac{11}{4}$. And write 8 as an improper fraction too. Then, multiply the numerators and the denominators, $\frac{11}{4} \times \frac{8}{1} = \frac{88}{4}$. Now, simplify and write as a mixed number: $\frac{22}{1} = 22$ The apple tree is 22 feet tall.
Your Turn!	**Solve, simplify your answer, and write it as a fraction or as a whole or mixed number.**
	1) Kevin collected $1\frac{1}{6}$ pounds of his notebooks for the recycling drive. John collected $2\frac{1}{4}$ times as many notebooks as Kevin. How many pounds of notebooks did John collect?
	2) A house is $12\frac{1}{2}$ yards wide. Its length is $3\frac{2}{5}$ times as long as it is wide. How long is the length house?
	3) Last weekend, Ciara spent $1\frac{1}{5}$ hours watching movies. Bridgette watched movies for 3 times as many hours as Ciara did. How many hours did Bridgette spend watching movies?
	4) Daniel owns $5\frac{3}{5}$ acres of farmland. He grows corn on $\frac{2}{5}$ of the land. On how many acres of land does Daniel grow corn?

bit.ly/3Lv9aDc

Topic	Multiplying and Dividing Decimals
Notes	For multiplying decimal: ✓ Ignore the decimal point and set up and multiply the numbers as you do with whole numbers. ✓ Count the total number of decimal places in both factors. ✓ Place the decimal point in the product. For dividing decimals: ✓ If the divisor is not a whole number, move the decimal point to the right to make it a whole number. Do the same for the dividend. ✓ Divide similar to whole numbers.
Example	**Find the quotient.** $1.50 \div 0.3 =?$ The divisor is not a whole number. Multiply it by 10 to get 3: → $0.3 \times 10 = 3$ Do the same for the dividend to get 15. → $1.50 \times 10 = 15$ Now, divide $15 \div 3 = 5$. The answer is 5. **Find the product.** $0.6 \times 0.29 =?$ Set up and multiply the numbers as you do with whole numbers. Line up the numbers: $\begin{array}{r}6\\ \times 29\end{array}$ → Start with the ones place then continue with other digits → $\begin{array}{r}6\\ \times 29\\ \hline 174\end{array}$. Count the total number of decimal places in both factors. There are three decimal's digits. Then: $0.6 \times 0.29 = 0.174$
Your Turn!	1) $1.3 \times 0.2 =$ 2) $0.1 \times 8.4 =$
	3) $2.4 \div 0.3 =$ 4) $12.2 \times 3.20 =$
	5) $0.1 \times 1.4 =$ 6) $24.8 \div 0.4 =$
	7) $2.4 \div 1.2 =$ 8) $1.51 \times 2.2 =$
	9) $8.5 \div 0.2 =$ 10) $5.2 \times 3.1 =$
	11) $3.9 \times 0.8 =$ 12) $36.6 \div 1.2 =$

bit.ly/3B1ODzt

Operations of Fraction, Decimal, and Mixed numbers

Topic	**Multiplying Three Rational Numbers, and Whole Numbers**
Notes	✓ Write down the mixed numbers as well as the whole numbers in the form of improper fractions. ✓ Afterwards, multiply the numerators as well as multiply the denominators. ✓ Simplify the product.
Example	**Multiply** $5\frac{2}{3} \times 3 \times \frac{3}{4} = ?$ Converting mixed numbers to fractions, $5\frac{2}{3} = \frac{17}{3}$. And write 3 as an improper fraction, $\frac{3}{1}$. Then, apply the fractions formula for multiplication. First, multiply 1st factor by 2nd factor. After that multiply the new and 3rd factor: $\frac{17}{3} \times \frac{3}{1} \times \frac{3}{4} = \frac{51}{3} \times \frac{3}{4} = \frac{153}{12}$. Simplify the product: $\frac{153}{12} = \frac{51}{4} = 12\frac{3}{4}$
Your Turn!	Multiply, simplify your answer and write it as a fraction or as a whole or mixed number. 1) $1\frac{1}{5} \times 2 \times \frac{1}{4} =$ 2) $4\frac{2}{3} \times \frac{1}{2} \times \frac{4}{5} =$ 3) $4 \times \frac{2}{5} \times 2\frac{1}{3} =$ 4) $5\frac{1}{5} \times 3\frac{3}{4} \times 2\frac{1}{2} =$ 5) $1\frac{1}{2} \times 2\frac{3}{7} \times 7 =$ 6) $\frac{3}{4} \times 1\frac{3}{4} \times 1\frac{3}{5} =$ 7) $1\frac{3}{4} \times 1\frac{3}{5} \times 2 =$ 8) $5 \times 1\frac{2}{7} \times 3\frac{1}{5} =$

bit.ly/3JqxTpg

Chapter 10: Answers

Scaling Whole Numbers by Fractions

1) >
2) <
3) <
4) >
5) >
6) <
7) >
8) >

Using Models to Divide Whole Numbers by Unit Fractions

1) 16

2) $\frac{7}{4} = 1\frac{3}{4}$

3) $\frac{25}{2} = 12\frac{1}{2}$

4) 9

5) 14

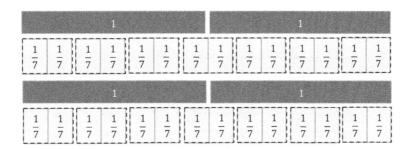

6) 8

7) 6

8) $\frac{18}{5} = 3\frac{3}{5}$

9) $\frac{10}{3} = 3\frac{1}{3}$

10) 4

Dividing Fractions by Whole Numbers in Recipes

1) 2
2) $\frac{1}{12}$
3) 1
4) $\frac{1}{10}$

Using Models to Multiply Two Fractions

1) $\frac{1}{4} \times \frac{3}{5} = \frac{3}{20}$
2) $\frac{2}{5} \times \frac{4}{6} = \frac{8}{30} = \frac{4}{15}$
3) $\frac{1}{2} \times \frac{1}{3} = \frac{1}{6}$
4) $\frac{4}{5} \times \frac{2}{3} = \frac{8}{15}$
5) $\frac{5}{36}$

6) $\frac{6}{40} = \frac{3}{20}$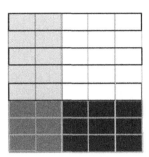

7) $\frac{3}{16}$

8) $\frac{1}{9}$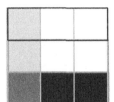

Multiplying and Dividing Fractions

1) $\frac{1}{6}$
2) $3\frac{1}{2}$
3) $3\frac{1}{3}$
4) $\frac{3}{4}$
5) $\frac{1}{15}$
6) $\frac{13}{18}$
7) $\frac{35}{72}$
8) $\frac{9}{20}$

Word Problem for Explaining Fractions as Division

1) $\frac{1}{2}$
2) $\frac{15}{7} = 2\frac{1}{7}$
3) $\frac{35}{8} = 4\frac{3}{8}$
4) $\frac{9}{18} = \frac{1}{2}$

Word Problem of Dividing Fractions

1) 9
2) 6
3) 10
4) 8

Operations of Fraction, Decimal, and Mixed numbers

Multiplication and Division of Decimals by Powers of Ten

1) 708
2) 1,750
3) 5,000
4) 18.3
5) 1.68
6) 0.15
7) 7.55
8) 0.0952

Estimate Products of Mixed Numbers

1) $3 \times 40 = 120$
2) $8 \times 20 = 160$
3) $7 \times 30 = 210$
4) $4 \times 10 = 40$
5) $19 \times 44 = 836$
6) $21 \times 2 = 42$
7) $3 \times 15 = 45$
8) $1 \times 2 = 2$

Scaling by Fractions and Mixed Numbers

1) <
2) >
3) >
4) >
5) <
6) >
7) <
8) <

Multiplying Mixed Numbers

1) $3\frac{9}{10}$
2) $11\frac{11}{18}$
3) $16\frac{4}{5}$
4) $14\frac{2}{5}$
5) 7
6) $37\frac{16}{35}$
7) $4\frac{3}{7}$
8) $10\frac{5}{32}$
9) $9\frac{1}{6}$
10) $20\frac{4}{15}$

Dividing Mixed Numbers

1) $\frac{1}{2}$
2) $1\frac{7}{57}$
3) $4\frac{2}{3}$
4) $\frac{15}{24}$
5) $1\frac{17}{35}$
6) $17\frac{1}{7}$
7) $2\frac{31}{42}$
8) $2\frac{1}{7}$
9) $1\frac{8}{55}$
10) $\frac{1}{2}$

Word Problem of Multiplying Mixed Numbers

1) $2\frac{5}{8}$
2) $42\frac{1}{2}$
3) $3\frac{3}{5}$
4) $2\frac{6}{25}$

Multiplying and Dividing Decimals

1) 0.26
2) 0.084
3) 8
4) 39.04
5) 0.014
6) 9.92
7) 2
8) 3.322
9) 42.5
10) 16.12
11) 3.12
12) 3.05

Multiplying Three Rational Numbers, and Whole Numbers

1) $\frac{3}{5}$
2) $1\frac{13}{15}$
3) $3\frac{11}{15}$
4) $48\frac{3}{4}$
5) $25\frac{1}{2}$
6) $2\frac{1}{10}$
7) $5\frac{3}{5}$
8) $20\frac{4}{7}$

CHAPTER 11
Variables and Equations

Math topics that you'll learn in this chapter:

- ☑ Independent and Dependent Variables in Tables and Graphs
- ☑ Independent and Dependent Variables in Word Problems
- ☑ Using Algebra Tiles to Model and Solve Equations
- ☑ Using Diagrams to Model and Solve Equations
- ☑ Evaluating One Variable

Topic	Independent and Dependent Variables in Tables and Graphs
Notes	✓ An independent variable is the one being controlled in the equation, and a dependent variable is one that changes because of that control. ✓ In the majority of data tables, the independent variable is going to be in the left-hand column and the dependent variable(s) are going to be in the right-hand column of a table. ✓ The "independent" variable is put onto the x-axis and a "dependent" variable is put onto the y-axis.
Example	*The table shows the relationship between the pounds of berry cake, p, and the total cost, c, In a bakery store. Which of the variables is independent and which is dependent? write the relationship between the dependent variable and the independent.* | p	c
1	$15
2	$30
3	$45
4	$60 | According to the table, the number of pounds, p, of berry cake does not depend on the total cost. So, p is the independent variable. On the other side, the total cost, c, depends on how many pounds of berry cake. So, c is the dependent variable. Now, according to table: $1 \times 15 = 15$, $2 \times 15 = 30$, and ... So, $p \times 15 = c$. The dependent variable, c, is 15 times the independent variable, p.
Your Turn!	Determine independent and dependent variables. write the relationship between the dependent and the independent variable. 1) Ava drives a car. The graph shows the relationship between the time, t, in hours and distances, d, in kilometers. 2) During summer, Elli practices running for the same number of hours each week. The table shows the relationship between the number of weeks that Elli goes to running practice, w, and the total number of hours that she practices, h. | w	h
1	1.5
2	3
3	4.5
4	6 | 3) There are phone plan charges for data usage. The graph shows the relationship between the number of gigabytes of data uses, d, and the total cost of the data, c, in dollars.

Topic	Independent and Dependent Variables in Word Problems
Notes	✓ When you go to a restaurant, the price of your order will determine how much taxes you pay. • $C =$ the price of your order, $T =$ tax amount due ✓ Which of these variables are independent and which are dependent? ✓ Begin by discovering the dependent variable. ✓ Because the tax amount you owe is dependent on your order price, Thus, the tax amount (T) is a dependent variable. ✓ Since the order price isn't dependent on how much the taxes are, Hence, the order price (C) is an independent variable.
Example	*Karen is baking cakes to sell at her bakery. The number of cups of flour she needs to use will affect how many the number of cakes she makes.* *c =The number of cakes she makes.* *s =The cups of flour she needs to use.* *Which of the variables is independent and which is dependent?* Since the number of cakes depends on how many cups of flour to use, the number of cakes is the dependent variable. So, *c* is the dependent variable. And since the number of cups of flour she needs to use does not depend on how many cakes she makes; the cups of flour are the independent variable. So, *s* is the independent variable.
Your Turn!	**Determine independent and dependent variables.**
	1) Maureen manages the farm which produces many corns. The more workers employed in the farm, the more bags of corn it produces. $w =$ The number of workers employed on the farm. $b =$ The number of bags of corn it produces.
	2) Kevin sorts the shelves of a fruit shop. The more shelves the store has, the more fruit packages can be sorted. $s =$ The number of shelves in the store $p =$ The number of packages
	3) Olivia is picking strawberries in the garden. The more time she spends in the garden, the more strawberries she picks. $s =$ The number of strawberries s she picks $t =$ Time of picking
	4) Charlotte runs for a few hours every morning. The more water she carries with her, the longer she can run. $w =$ The amount of water she carries $t =$ Time of running

bit.ly/44u1BDu

Topic	**Using Algebra Tiles to Model and Solve Equations**
Notes	✓ How to model and solve the given equations using algebra tiles? • Step 1: First we must model the given equation using the tiles. • Step 2: Solve means finding the value of the variable. For that, we need to isolate the variable.
Example	***Show the equation $x - 1 = 6$, by using the algebra tiles.*** Left side of the equation represent $x - 1$, which means 1 –tile of x and 1 –tiles of -1. And the right of the equation represents 6, which means 6 –tile of 1. Now, to solve the equation, to remove the tiles on the left side, should add two tiles, 1, to the left and right side. Then simplify tiles of -1 in 1 on the left side but the tiles on the right side add together. Then only the x tile remins on the left. So, the model shows $x = 7$.
Your Turn!	**Calculate the equation.** 1) [tiles: 2x + 3 = 2 + ...] 2) [tiles] 3) [tiles] 4) [tiles] 5) [tiles] 6) [tiles]

Topic	Using Diagrams to Model and Solve Equations
Notes	✓ Solve a system of linear equations VIA graphing: • Graph the $1st$ equation. • Graph the $2nd$ equation on the same rectangular coordinate system. • Ascertain if the lines are parallel, intersect, or are the same line. • Find the answer to the system. • Check the resolution for both equations.
Example	**Graph the diagram that represents the equation, $w - 9 = 7$.** The equation says that if you have a number, w, and subtract 9 from it, it is equal to 7. Or if you have a number, w, it is equal to the sum of 7 and 9, $w = 7 + 9$. So, w is included in 7 and 9. And graph this. Now, solve for w. $w = 7 + 9 \rightarrow w = 16$.

Your Turn!	1) $d + 5 = 3$	2) $b - 4 = 6$
	3) $3f = 9$	4) $\frac{k}{2} = 8$
	5) $2x + 5 = 19$	6) $\frac{a}{4} = -12$
	7) $h - 6 = 11$	8) $4p = 24$

Topic	Evaluating One Variable
Notes	✓ To evaluate one variable expressions, find the variable and substitute a number for that variable. ✓ Perform the arithmetic operations.
Example	**Calculate this expression for $x = 2$. $8 + 2x$** First, substitute 2 for x. Then: $8 + 2x = 8 + 2(2)$ Now, use order of operation to find the answer: $8 + 2(2) = 8 + 4 = 12$ **Evaluate this expression for $x = -1$. $4x - 8$** First, substitute -1 for x. Then: $4x - 8 = 4(-1) - 8$ Now, use order of operation to find the answer: $4(-1) - 8 = -4 - 8 = -12$
Your Turn!	Evaluate each expression using the value given. 1) $x = -3 \rightarrow -1 - 4x =$ ___ 2) $x = -6 \rightarrow -10x - 5 =$ ___ 3) $x = -1 \rightarrow 20x - 5 =$ ___ 4) $x = -12 \rightarrow 20 - 3x =$ ___ 5) $x = -5 \rightarrow 22 + 2x =$ ___ 6) $x = -4 \rightarrow 5 + x =$ ___ 7) $x = 9 \rightarrow 10x + 30 =$ ___ 8) $x = 8 \rightarrow 5x - 3 =$ ___ 9) $x = 5 \rightarrow 10 - 4x =$ ___ 10) $x = 1 \rightarrow 2x - 4 =$ ___ 11) $x = 2 \rightarrow x + 8 =$ ___ 12) $x = 7 \rightarrow 11 - x =$ ___

bit.ly/3ppujQZ

Chapter 11: Answers

Independent and Dependent Variables in Tables and Graphs

1) $t \times 90 = d$, $t =$ independent, $d =$ dependent
2) $w \times 1.5 = h$, $w =$ independent, $h =$ dependent
3) $d \times 4 = c$, $d =$ independent, $c =$ dependent

Independent and Dependent Variables in Word Problems

1) $w =$ independent, $b =$ dependent
2) $s =$ independent, $p =$ dependent
3) $s =$ independent, $t =$ dependent
4) $w =$ independent, t = dependent

Using Algebra Tiles to Model and Solve Equations

1) $2x + 3 = 5 \rightarrow x = 1$
2) $x + 6 = 3 \rightarrow x = -3$
3) $x + 4 = -5 \rightarrow x = -9$
4) $2x + 2 = 6 \rightarrow x = 2$
5) $3x - 1 = 11 \rightarrow x = 4$
6) $x - 3 = 5 \rightarrow x = 8$

Using Diagrams to Model and Solve Equations

1)

| 5 | d |

3

2)

| 4 | 6 |

b

3)

| f | f | f |

9

4)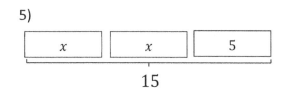

5)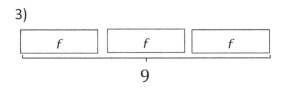

6)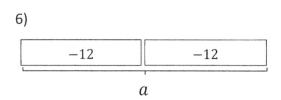

7)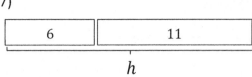

8)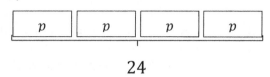

Evaluating One Variable

1) 11
2) 55
3) −25
4) 56

5) 12
6) 1
7) 120
8) 37

9) −10
10) -2
11) 10
12) 4

CHAPTER 12
One-Step Operations

Math topics that you'll learn in this chapter:

- ☑ One–Step Adding and Subtracting of Decimals and Fractions
- ☑ One–Step Multiplying and Dividing of Decimals and Fractions
- ☑ Graphing One-Step Multiplication and Division Equations
- ☑ Graphing One-Step Inequalities with Rational Numbers
- ☑ One-Step Equations
- ☑ Matching Word Problems with the One-Step Equation
- ☑ Word Problems of the One-Step Equation

One-Step Operations

Topic	**One-Step Adding and Subtracting of Decimals and Fractions**
Notes	✓ The subtraction and addition properties of equality state one is able to subtract or add a value from both sides of an equation with no change in the meaning of an equation. The key is that you must do the identical thing to both sides of an equation. ✓ In order to add 2 decimal numbers with opposite signs, discover their differences. The sign of the solution will be identical to the sign of the bigger number. ✓ Do not forget whenever adding decimals to line up the decimal points.
Example	**Solve the equation for y, $y - \frac{1}{9} = 3$. Write your answer as a fraction or as a whole or mixed number.** First add $\frac{1}{9}$ to both sides. Then write 3 as a fraction. $$y - \frac{1}{9} = 9 \rightarrow y - \frac{1}{9} + \frac{1}{9} = 3 + \frac{1}{9} \rightarrow y = \frac{27}{9} + \frac{1}{9} \rightarrow y = \frac{28}{9}$$ Then convert the answer as a mixed number, $y = 3\frac{1}{9}$. **Solve the equation for x, $x + 4.5 = 9$. Write your answer as a fraction or as a whole or mixed number.** First, use the inverse operation to undo the operations in the equation, to get the variable x alone on the side of the equation. Then subtract 4.5 from both sides. $$x + 745 = 9 \rightarrow x + 4.5 - 4.5 = 9 - 4.5 \rightarrow x = 4.5$$ So, x is equal to 4.5.
Your Turn!	1) $3 + x = \frac{3}{5}$ 2) $r = 5 + 1.5$ 3) $h - \frac{4}{5} = 1.6$ 4) $2 + \frac{1}{6} = p$ 5) $u + \frac{1}{5} = 5$ 6) $\frac{5}{2} - \frac{3}{5} = n$ 7) $t - 7.6 = 4.4$ 8) $d + 5.8 = 9$

bit.ly/3DcDrBe

Topic	One-Step Multiplying and Dividing of Decimals and Fractions
Notes	✓ One-step equations are equations requiring merely a single step to solve. Only one operation is needed to resolve or isolate the variable. ✓ You can convert a fraction to a decimal using division: Divide its numerator by its denominator.
Example	**Solve the equation for q, $q \div \frac{1}{5} = 4$. Write your answer as a fraction or as a whole or mixed number.** Use inverse the operation to get the variable q alone on the side of the equation. Therefore, multiply $\frac{1}{3}$ by both sides. $$q \div \frac{1}{5} = 4 \rightarrow q \div \frac{1}{5} \times \frac{1}{5} = 4 \times \frac{1}{5} \rightarrow q = \frac{4}{1} \times \frac{1}{5} \rightarrow q = \frac{4}{5}$$ So, $q = 2\frac{2}{3}$. **Solve the equation for e, $e \times 2.5 = 10$. Write your answer as a fraction or as a whole or mixed number.** Use inverse the operation to get the variable e alone on the side of the equation. Therefore, divide 2.5 by both sides. $$e \times 2.5 = 10 \rightarrow e \times 2.5 \div 2.5 = 10 \div 2.5 \rightarrow e = 4$$ So, e is equal to 4.

Your Turn!		
	1) $r \div 5 = \frac{5}{7}$	2) $m \times \frac{3}{4} = 2$
	3) $y \div 2.5 = 5$	4) $7 \div \frac{7}{9} = f$
	5) $x \times \frac{2}{3} = \frac{1}{6}$	6) $t \div \frac{8}{6} = \frac{9}{10}$
	7) $3 \times 1.5 = w$	8) $d \times 2 = 6.5$

bit.ly/3JZ8AvN

One-Step Operations

Topic	Graphing One-Step Multiplication and Division Equations
Notes	✓ There are four methods of solving one-step equations: • If you add the same number to both sides of an equation, both sides stay equal. • If you subtract the same number from both sides of an equation, both sides stay equal. • If you divide both sides of an equation by the same number, both sides stay equal. • If you multiply both sides of an equation by the same number, both sides stay equal.
Example	**Solve the equation. And graph the solution, $\frac{x}{4} = \frac{3}{4}$.** First, solve the equation, using inverse operations for x. And since x is divided by 4 in this equation, then its inverse is multiplied by 4 on both sides, $\frac{x}{4} \times 4 = \frac{3}{4} \times 4 \rightarrow x = 3$. Now graph $x = 3$ on the number line. **Solve the equation. And graph the solution, $9x = 36$.** First, solve the equation, using inverse operations for x. And since x is multiplied by 9 in this equation, then its inverse is divided by 9 on both sides, $\frac{9x}{9} = \frac{36}{9} \rightarrow x = 4$. Now, graph $x = 4$ on the number line.
Your Turn!	1) $13b = -65$ 2) $-4w = 32$
	3) $-\frac{a}{5} = 1$ 4) $\frac{k}{3} = 2$
	5) $\frac{z}{6} = -2$ 6) $3d = 24$
	7) $\frac{4}{n} = 2$ 8) $6v = 30$

bit.ly/3PSy7dT

Find more at

Topic	Graphing One-Step Inequalities with Rational Numbers
Notes	✓ Whenever you're graphing an inequality on a number line, you must pick between utilizing a filled-in or open circle. ✓ Utilize a filled-in circle whenever an inequality shows ≤ or ≥. $x \geq -1$ (number line from −2 to 6 with filled circle at −1, shaded right) ✓ Utilize an open circle whenever an inequality shows < or >. $x > -1$ (number line from −2 to 6 with open circle at −1, shaded right) ✓ You must utilize inverse operations for solving these problems.
Example	**Solve the inequality. And graph the solution, $\frac{y}{4} \geq -\frac{1}{2}$.** First, solve the inequality, using inverse operations for y. And since y is divided by 4 in this inequality, then its inverse is multiplied by 4 on both sides to find the solution, $\frac{y}{4} \times 4 \geq -\frac{1}{2} \times 4 \rightarrow y \geq -2$. Now graph $y \geq -2$ on the number line. The inequality $y \geq -2$ means that y can be any number greater than or equal to -2. So, draw a filled-in circle on -2. Then, draw a line on the right of the filled-in circle. (number line from −8 to 3 with filled circle at −2, shaded right)
Your Turn!	1) $-\frac{x}{2} \leq -4$ 2) $-3k > 18$ 3) $-\frac{t}{6} \geq -1$ 4) $4m < 28$ 5) $\frac{z}{2} > -2.5$ 6) $-4a \leq 12$ 7) $\frac{y}{3} > -3$ 8) $3w \geq 15$

bit.ly/3QfB8Ft

One-Step Operations

Topic	One–Step Equations
Notes	✓ The values of two expressions on both sides of an equation are equal. Example: $ax = b$. In this equation, ax is equal to b. ✓ Solving an equation means finding the value of the variable. ✓ You only need to perform one Math operation to solve the one-step equations. ✓ To solve a one-step equation, find the inverse (opposite) operation is being performed. ✓ The inverse operations are: • Addition and subtraction • Multiplication and division
Example	**Solve this equation for x. $6x = 18 \rightarrow x = ?$** Here, the operation is multiplication (variable x is multiplied by 6) and its inverse operation is division. To solve this equation, divide both sides of equation by 6: $6x = 18 \rightarrow \frac{6x}{6} = \frac{18}{6} \rightarrow x = 3$
Your Turn!	1) $x + 5 = 7 \rightarrow x = $ ___ 2) $25 - x = -12 \rightarrow x = $ ___ 3) $5 = 11 - x \rightarrow x = $ ___ 4) $-4 + x = 27 \rightarrow x = $ ___ 5) $-3 = 7 + x \rightarrow x = $ ___ 6) $-19 - x = -7 \rightarrow x = $ ___ 7) $x - 15 = -7 \rightarrow x = $ ___ 8) $35 - x = 9 \rightarrow x = $ ___ 9) $-15 = x + 3 \rightarrow x = $ ___ 10) $-25 - x = 11 \rightarrow x = $ ___ 11) $17 + x = -8 \rightarrow x = $ ___ 12) $45 + x = 17 \rightarrow x = $ ___

bit.ly/37Jq0tK

Topic	Matching Word Problems with the One-Step Equation
Notes	✓ One-step equations are algebraic equations that can be solved in just a single step. ✓ The equation has been resolved whenever you have the variable by itself, and there are not any numbers in front of it, on 1 side of the equal sign.
Example	*A recipe for cookies calls for 5 cups of flour. Olivia has already put in 3 cups. How many more cups does she need to put in? Write the equation for it, then solve it.* First look for words and phrases in the sentences that tell you what equation will model it. The total of flour is 5 cups. Already there are 3 cups. How many more cups need is x. And modeled by the add equation $x + 3 = 5$. Now solve it, $x = 2$. She needs 2 cups more.
Your Turn!	**Write the one-step equation for the word problem. Then solve.** 1) A hotel has a parking lot with enough space for 78 cars. There are 29 cars in the parking lot right now. How many more cars can park in the lot?
	2) Kate has $23. E-book downloads cost $2 each. How many E-books can she download and still have $3 left?
	3) If the weight of five bags of grain is 85 pounds, find the weight of one bag of grain?
	4) After using 4 cucumbers for a salad, Johnny has 13 cucumbers in the basket. How many cucumbers did he have before used the salad?
	5) In an examination, Mia ran 20 miles more than Emma. Mia ran 53 miles. How many miles did Emma run?
	6) For a trip, Daniel gave her brother $18.30 to buy some groceries. This covered $\frac{2}{9}$ of the cost. How much did the trip cost?

Topic	Word Problems of the One-Step Equation
Notes	✓ Equations are mathematical sentences showing that 2 expressions are identical. ✓ To obtain the solution for one-step equations, utilize inverse operations. It's vital not to forget that whatever is done to one side of this equation, is additionally done to the other one. • Addition ↔ Subtraction • Multiplication ↔ Division
Example	*Jessika gets to feed the dolphins! The dolphin trainer gives Jessika a bucket of fish to divide evenly among 9 dolphins. Each dolphin gets 5 fish. Which equation can you use to find the number of fish f in the bucket?* There are 9 dolphins, and there are 5 fish per dolphin. To find the total number of fish in the bucket you can display by an equation using division. Total number of fishes $\quad \frac{f}{9} = 5 \quad$ Number of fishes per dolphin Number of dolphins And solve this equation: $\frac{f}{9} = 5 \rightarrow f = 5 \times 9 = 45$
Your Turn!	1) How many packs of chips (p) can you buy for \$65 if one package costs \$5?
	2) At a cafe, frank and his six friends decided to divide the bill evenly. If each person paid, \$21 then what was the total bill (b)?
	3) Maria is practicing baking skills and bakes apple-pies with sugar powder. After baking the apple-pies, 11 of them will burn. In total she baked 58 apple-pies. How many apple-pies (a) are completely baked?
	4) If the weight of a package is multiplied by $\frac{4}{9}$ the result is 43.75 pounds. Find the weight (w) of the package?
	5) Sarah bought muffins in boxes of 15. The cost of a box is \$45. What is the price (p) of each muffin?
	6) Liam has \$32 to spend at the amusement park. The ticket to each game is \$4 and the rides cost to the amusement park \$12. How many tickets (t) can he buy?

bit.ly/3XUde3L

Chapter 12: Answers

One–Step Adding and Subtracting of Decimals and Fractions

1) $x = -2\frac{2}{5}$
2) $r = 6.5$
3) $h = 2\frac{2}{5}$
4) $p = 2\frac{1}{6}$
5) $u = 4\frac{4}{5}$
6) $n = 1\frac{9}{10}$
7) $t = 12$
8) $d = 3.2$

One–Step Multiplying and Dividing of Decimals and Fractions

1) $r = 3\frac{4}{7}$
2) $m = 2\frac{2}{3}$
3) $y = 12.5$
4) $f = 9$
5) $x = \frac{1}{4}$
6) $t = 1\frac{1}{5}$
7) $w = 4.5$
8) $d = 3.25$

Graphing One-Step Multiplication and Division Equations

1) $b = -5$

2) $w = -8$

3) $a = -5$

4) $k = 6$

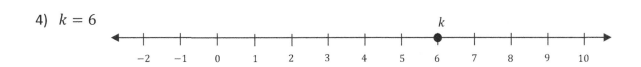

5) $z = -12$

6) $d = 8$
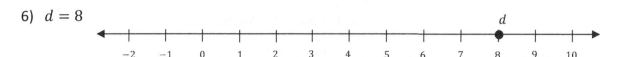

7) $n = 2$

8) $v = 5$

Graphing One-Step Inequalities with Rational Numbers

1) $x \leq 8$
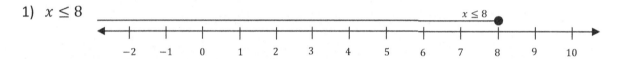

2) $k > -6$
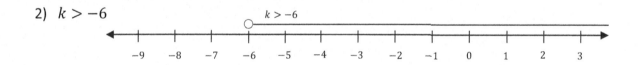

3) $t \geq 6$

4) $m < 7$
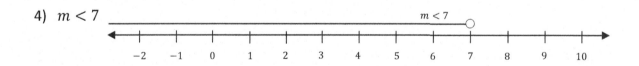

5) $z > -5$
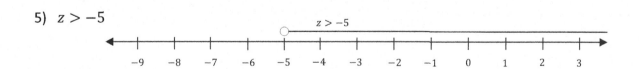

6) $a \leq -3$
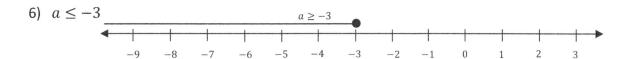

7) $y > -9$

8) $w \geq 5$

One-Step Equations

1) $x = 2$
2) $x = 37$
3) $X = 6$
4) $x = 31$
5) $x = -10$
6) $x = -12$
7) $x = 8$
8) $x = 26$
9) $x = -18$
10) $x = -36$
11) $x - -25$
12) $x = -28$

Matching Word Problems with the One-Step Equation

1) $x + 29 = 78 \to x = 49$
2) $2x + 3 = 23 \to x = 10$
3) $5x = 85 \to x = 17$
4) $x - 4 = 13 \to x = 17$
5) $x + 20 = 53 \to x = 33$
6) $\frac{2}{9}x = 18.30 \to x = 82.35$

Word Problems of the One-Step Equation

1) $5p = 65 \to p = 13$
2) $\frac{b}{7} = 21 \to b = 3$
3) $a + 11 = 58 \to a = 47$
4) $w \cdot \frac{4}{9} = 16 \to w = 36$
5) $15p = 45 \to p = 3$
6) $4t + 12 = 32 \to t = 5$

CHAPTER 13
Two-Variable Equation

Math topics that you'll learn in this chapter:

- ☑ Using a Table to Write down a Two-Variable Equation
- ☑ Complete a Table and Graph a Two-Variable Equation
- ☑ Evaluating Two Variables
- ☑ Solving Word problems by Finding Two-Variable Equation

Two-Variable Equation

Topic	Using a Table to Write down a Two-Variable Equation
Notes	✓ To write down a 2–variable equation from the given table. ✓ Firstly, you must look for the **proper** rule and after that, you just write it down on the table. ✓ In each of the table rows, the number appearing in the y column is 8 more than the one appearing in the x column. The equation is written thusly: $$y = x + 8$$ | x	y | |---|---| | 3 | 11 | | 4 | 12 | | 5 | 13 | | 6 | 14 |
Example	**Write the equation that represents the table.** First, determine the output and input columns. The left column, w, is input and the right column, h, is output. And can see relationships between w and h. Then find the rule that produces the number in the h column from the number in the w column in each row of the table, $1 + 3 = 4$, $2 + 3 = 5$, $3 + 3 = 5$, $4 + 3 = 7$. Write the equation like this, $w + 3 = h$. | w	h | |---|---| | 1 | 3 | | 2 | 5 | | 3 | 6 | | 4 | 7 |
Your Turn!	**Complete the equation.**

1) $j = \underline{\quad} \times k$

k	j
2	1
3	1.5
4	2
5	2.5

2) $m = u + \underline{\quad}$

u	m
1	6
2	7
3	8
4	9

3) $s = t - \underline{\quad}$

t	s
4	0
6	2
8	4
10	6

4) $l = \underline{\quad} \times q$

q	l
0	0
4	1
6	1.5
8	2

5) $b = a - \underline{\quad}$

a	b
5	−2
6	−1
7	0
8	1

6) $y = \underline{\quad} \times x$

x	y
4	14
5	20
6	24
7	28

Topic	Complete a Table and Graph a Two-Variable Equation
Notes	✓ Use the equation to finish the table: • Firstly, utilize the equation to finish the table. To figure out each y-value. • Then, graph the equation. Begin by writing these values in the table as ordered pairs. • Draw a line that passes through these points.
Example	***Complete the table by using the equation and graph the equation, $y = x + 3$.*** | x	0	2	4 | |---|---|---|---| | y | 3 | 5 | 5 | To find the y-value, put the value of x into the equation and calculate y. Now, graph the equation, by writing the values in the table as ordered pairs, $(0, 3), (2, 5), (4, 7)$. Then, draw a line that passes through determined points.
Your Turn!	**Complete the table and graph the equation.** 1) $y = x$ | x | 0 | 1 | 3 | 5 | |---|---|---|---|---| | y | | | | | 2) $y = x + 3$ | x | 0 | 1 | 2 | 3 | |---|---|---|---|---| | y | | | | | 3) $y = \frac{1}{3}x$ | x | 0 | 1 | 3 | 4 | |---|---|---|---|---| | y | | | | | 4) $y = 2x$ | x | 1 | 2 | 3 | 4 | |---|---|---|---|---| | y | | | | |

bit.ly/3OfT4OE

Topic	Evaluating Two Variables
Notes	✓ To evaluate an algebraic expression, substitute a number for each variable. ✓ Perform the arithmetic operations to find the value of the expression.
Example	**Evaluate this expression for $x = -2$ and $y = 2$. $(5x + 2y)$** Substitute -2 for x, and 2 for y. Then: $5x + 2y = 5(-2) + 2(2) = -10 + 4 = -6$ **Find the value of this expression $-2(3a - 5b)$, when $a = -3$ and $b = 7$.** Substitute -3 for a, and 7 for b. Then: $-2(3a - 5b) = -2(3(-3) - 5(7)) = -2(-9 - 35) = -2(-44) = 88$
Your Turn!	**Evaluate each expression using the values given.**

1) $x = 3, y = 2$
   $2x + 7y = $ _____

2) $a = 4, b = 7$
   $3a - 5b = $ _____

3) $x = 1, y = -6$
   $3x - 2y + 8 = $ _____

4) $a = -4, b = 1$
   $-5a + 2b + 6 = $ _____

5) $x = -2, y = -5$
   $-4x + 10 - 8y = $ _____

6) $x = 3, y = -3$
   $-2x + 7 - 5y = $ _____

7) $x = -1, y = 7$
   $-9x - 9y = $ _____

8) $a = -5, b = -5$
   $-2a - 3 - 8b = $ _____

Topic	Solving Word problems by Finding Two-Variable Equation
Notes	✓ To solve word problems, we need to write a set of equations that represent the problem mathematically. ✓ Problem-solving strategy: • Read the whole question. What are we asked to solve? • Assign variables to the unknown quantity, for example, x and y. • Translate the words into algebraic expressions by rewriting the given information in terms of the variable. • Set up an equation or system of equations to solve for the variable. $$y = mx + b$$ • Solve the equation algebraically using substitution. • Check the solution.
Example	*A store has 29 permanent employees. It hires some temporary employees during busy times of the year. Let t represent the number of temporary employees and w represent the total number of employees. Find the value of w when $t = 8$.* First, look for relationships between the number of temporary employees, t, and the total number of employees, w. In this relationship, t is the input, and w is the output. So, find w by adding 29 to t. Write the relationship as an equation, $w = t + 29$. Then, substitute 8 for t in the equation to find the w. $$w = t + 29 \rightarrow w = 8 + 29 \rightarrow w = 37$$ When $t = 8$, $w = 37$.
Your Turn!	1) Car manufacturing produces 29 new cars each month. Let m represent the number of months and c represent the total number of cars produced. Find the number of cars when $m = 5$.
	2) Jenny rides the train for 5 minutes every day. d represents the number of days and m represents the total number of minutes Jenny spends on the train. After a month how much time will she spend on the train?
	3) Jessica has 65 biscuits in her kitchen. In the afternoon, she has several guests who eat 3 biscuit. Let b represent the number of biscuits left, and g represent the number of guests. Find the number of biscuits left when $g = 14$.
	4) There are 12 cakes in a pack. Let p represent the number of packs and c represent the number of cakes. Find the number of cakes when $p = 5$.

Chapter 13: Answers

Using a Table to Write down a Two-Variable Equation

1) $j = \frac{1}{2} \times k$

2) $m = u + 5$

3) $s = t - 4$

4) $l = \frac{1}{4} \times q$

5) $b = a - 7$

6) $y = 4 \times x$

Complete a Table and Graph a Two-Variable Equation

1)

x	0	1	3	5
y	0	1	3	5

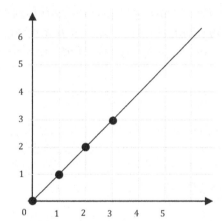

3)

x	0	1	3	4
y	0	$\frac{1}{3}$	1	$1\frac{1}{3}$

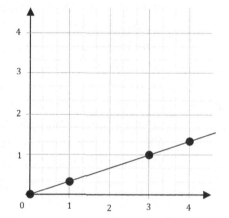

2)

x	0	1	2	3
y	3	4	5	6

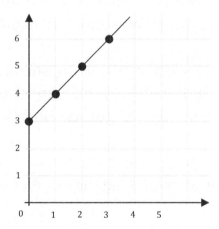

4)

x	1	2	3	4
y	2	4	6	8

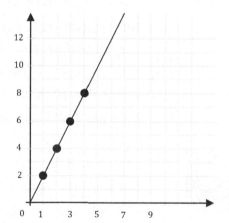

Evaluating Two Variables

1) 20
2) −23
3) 23
4) 28
5) 58
6) 16
7) −54
8) 47

Solving Word problems by Finding Two-Variable Equation

1) $c = 145$
2) $m = 150$
3) $b = 23$
4) $c = 60$

CHAPTER
14 Inequalities

Math topics that you'll learn in this chapter:

- ☑ Write Inequalities from Number Lines
- ☑ Graphing Single–Variable Inequalities
- ☑ One-Step Inequalities
- ☑ Word Problems Involving One-step Inequalities

Inequalities

Topic	Write Inequalities from Number Lines
Notes	✓ In order to plot an inequality, like $x > 2$, on a number line, firstly draw a circle over the number (e.g., 2). ✓ Next, if the sign includes equal to ($\geq$ or $\leq$), fill in that circle. If the sign doesn't include equal to ($>$ or $<$), don't fill in the circle. ✓ Lastly, draw a line starting from the circle in the direction of the numbers which allows the inequality to be true. $2 < x \leq 9$
Example	**What inequality does this number line show?** *Solution:* To write an inequality, the filled-in circle located on 4 shows that x can be equal to 4. And the line to the right indicates that x can be any number more than 4. Since x can be any number equal and more than 4, the inequality is $x \geq 4$.
Your Turn!	1) 2) 3) 4) 5) 6)

Topic	Graphing Single–Variable Inequalities
Notes	✓ An inequality compares two expressions using an inequality sign. ✓ Inequality signs are: "less than" $<$, "greater than" $>$, "less than or equal to" $\leq$, and "greater than or equal to" $\geq$. ✓ To graph a single–variable inequality, find the value of the inequality on the number line. ✓ For less than ($<$) or greater than ($>$) draw an open circle on the value of the variable. If there is an equal sign too, then use a filled circle. ✓ Draw an arrow to the right for greater or to the left for less than.
Example	**Draw a graph for this inequality.** $x > 3$ Since the variable is greater than 3, then we need to find 3 in the number line and draw an open circle on it. Then, draw an arrow to the right.
Your Turn!	**Draw a graph for this inequality.** 1) $x \leq -5$ 2) $x > 0$ 3) $x < 4$ 4) $x > -6$ 5) $x \geq 2$ 6) $x \leq 5$

Inequalities

Topic	One–Step Inequalities
Notes	✓ An inequality compares two expressions using an inequality sign. ✓ Inequality signs are: "less than" <, "greater than" >, "less than or equal to" ≤, and "greater than or equal to" ≥. ✓ You only need to perform one Math operation to solve the one-step inequalities. ✓ To solve one-step inequalities, find the inverse (opposite) operation is being performed. ✓ For dividing or multiplying both sides by negative numbers, flip the direction of the inequality sign.
Example	**Solve.** $3x \leq 15$ 3 is multiplied to x. Divide both sides by 3. Then: $3x \leq 15 \to \frac{3x}{3} \leq \frac{15}{3} \to x \leq 5$ **Solve.** $-2x \leq 6$ -2 is multiplied to x. Divide both sides by -2. Remember when dividing or multiplying both sides of an inequality by negative numbers, flip the direction of the inequality sign. Then: $-2x \leq 6 \to \frac{-2x}{-2} \geq \frac{6}{-2} \to x \geq -3$
Your Turn!	**Solve each inequality.**

1) $x - 5 \geq 4$	2) $-x - 3 > -6$
3) $3x \leq 36$	4) $6x \leq 12$
5) $4x < -3$	6) $-2x - 3 < 17$
7) $x + 6 \geq -5$	8) $x + 1 > 8$

Topic	Word Problems Involving One-step Inequalities
Notes	One-step inequalities are solved by dividing the same number into both sides of the equation or by multiplying the reciprocal coefficient of the term with a variable on both sides of the equation. ✓ First, search for clues in the form of keywords and phrases. Finding them helps you understand which operation and inequality symbols to use. ✓ Carefully read the text to understand what you are asked to solve. ✓ Write a number sentence then solve it in a single step.
Example	*Tyrone went to the grocery to buy 3 ice creams. He spent less than $9 in all to buy the ice cream. Let x represent how much each ice cream costs. This inequality describes the problem, $3x < 9$. Solve the inequality with algebra tiles. What is the price of each ice cream less than?* The expression $3x$ represents the total cost of the ice creams. That needs to be less than 9. The left side of the inequality is $3x$. So, the left side of your answer should have 3, x –tiles. The right side of the inequality is 9. So, the right side of your answer should have 9, 1 –tiles. And to solve the inequality for x, divide each side into 3 equal groups. Thus: The solution to the inequality is $x < 9$. So, each ice cream cost less than $5.
Your Turn!	1) Kate sells muffins in boxes of 6. Depending on the type of muffins, a box can cost at most $36. Let x represent how much each muffin cost. This inequality describes the problem, $6x \leq 36$. Solve the inequality. And what is the price of each muffin at most?
	2) A local restaurant has a parking lot with enough space for 38 cars. There are 15 cars in the parking lot right now. Let x represent how many more cars can park in the lot. This inequality describes the problem, $x + 15 \leq 38$. Solve the inequality. And how many more cars can park in the lot?
	3) Daniel had $28 to spend at the museum. If the admission to the museum in each section is $3 and the rides cost the museum $7. Let x represent how many times Daniel can go to different sections. Write the inequality for it and solve it. So, what is the greatest number of sections that Daniel can go to?
	4) Maria has $25. MP3 downloads cost $0.75 each. How many songs can she download and still have $3 left to spend? Write the inequality for it and solve it.

Chapter 14: Answers

Write Inequalities from Number Lines

1) $x < -1$
2) $-9 \leq x \leq -2$
3) $-1 \leq x < 8$
4) $-6 < x < 0$
5) $5 \leq x$
6) $-5 < x$

Graphing Single–Variable Inequalities

1) $x \leq -5$

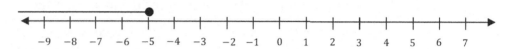

2) $x > 0$

3) $x < 4$

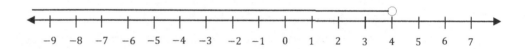

4) $x > -6$

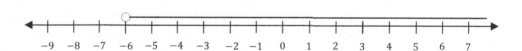

5) $x \geq 2$

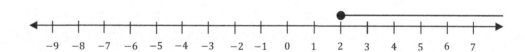

6) $x \leq 5$

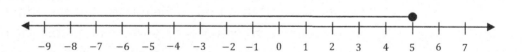

One-Step Inequalities

1) $x \geq 9$
2) $x < 3$
3) $x \leq 12$
4) $x \leq 2$
5) $x < -\frac{3}{4}$
6) $x > -10$
7) $x \geq -11$
8) $x > 7$

Word Problems Involving One-step Inequalities

1) $x \leq 6$, Each muffin costs at most $6.

2) $x \leq 23$, It can park up to 23 cars in the lot.

3) $3x + 7 \leq 28 \rightarrow x \leq 7$, can go to different sections up to 6 times.

4) $\frac{3}{4}x + 3 \leq 15 \rightarrow x \leq 16$, she can download 24 songs.

Chapter 15: Measurement System

Math topics that you'll learn in this chapter:

- ☑ Mixed Customary Units Operations
- ☑ Mixed Numbers and Fractions Customary Unit Conversions
- ☑ Using Proportions to Convert Traditional and Metric Units
- ☑ Compare the Temperatures Above and Below Zero

Topic	**Mixed Customary Units Operations**
Notes	✓ In mathematics, the traditional system may be described as a set of weights and measures utilized for measuring length, weight, capacity, and temperature. Lengths and distances in the traditional system will be measured in inches, feet, yards, and miles. ✓ In order to convert between traditional units, use these rules: • In order to convert from a bigger unit to a lesser smaller unit, you multiply. • In order to convert from a lesser unit to a bigger unit, you divide.
Example	*Compare. Select $>$, $<$, or $=$ to make the sentence true.* $13,505$ *yards* ☐ 8 *miles* 200 *yards* First, convert both sides to the smallest unit (yards). Since the left side is the yards unit. And now, the right side needs to convert to the yards. Convert 8 miles to yards, $8 \times 1,760 = 14,080$. Then, add 200 yards, $14,080 + 200 = 14,280$. So, 13,505 is smaller than 14,280. *Convert.* $3,780$ *pounds* $=$ ... *tons* ... *pounds* Since each ton is 2,000 pounds. So, divide, $\frac{3,780}{2,000} = 1\frac{1,780}{2,000}$. There are 1 tons, with 1,780 pounds left over. $3,780 = 1t\ 1,780\ yd$
Your Turn!	**Compare.** 1) 7 quarts 1 pint ☐ 13 pint 2) $11,315 ft$ ☐ $2mi\ 555yd$ 3) $3.5 kg$ ☐ $3,500,000 mg$ 4) 30 feet ☐ 1 meter **Convert.** 5) $6\ inche = \_\_\_ feet$ 6) $0.65\ kg = \_\_\_ g$ 7) $35\ cm = \_\_\_ mm$ 8) $26400 ft = \_\_\_ mi$ **Add and subtract.** 9) $2,010\ lb + 798\ lb = ... T ... lb$ 10) $2\ lb\ 8\ oz + 1\ lb\ 10\ oz = ... lb ... oz$ 11) $5\ cm\ 4mm - 3\ cm\ 8\ mm = ... cm ... mm$ 12) $2\ mi\ 860\ yd - 1\ mi\ 200\ yd = ... mi ... yd$

Topic	**Mixed Numbers and Fractions Customary Unit Conversions**
Notes	✓ Unit conversions express the identical property as a different unit of measurement. ✓ Whenever you need to do a conversion, the proper conversion factor to an equal value must be utilized. ✓ For instance, to convert inches to feet, the proper conversion value is 12 inches equal 1 foot. To convert minutes to hours, the appropriate conversion value is 60 minutes equals 1 hour.
Example	*Convert. Simplify and write as a fraction or whole or mixed number.* ☐ Inches $= \frac{1}{6}$ of a foot. To find out how many inches are in $\frac{1}{4}$ of a foot, multiply a larger unit by a smaller unit and cancel common factors: $$\frac{1}{6} \times 12 = \frac{1}{6} \times \frac{12}{1} = \frac{1 \times 2}{1 \times 1} = 2$$ So, 2 Inches $= \frac{1}{6}$ of a foot.
Your Turn!	**Convert. Simplify and write as a fraction or whole or mixed number.** 1) $5yd = \underline{\quad} in$ 2) $\underline{\quad} ounce = \frac{1}{10} lb$ 3) $5,000 lb = \underline{\quad} t$ 4) $12 \; quarts = \underline{\quad} gallon$ 5) $\underline{\quad} ft = \frac{3}{5} mi$ 6) $\underline{\quad} mi = 660 yd$ 7) $0.093 L = \underline{\quad} ml$ 8) $35 fl\; oz = \underline{\quad} cup$

bit.ly/3JV76TI

Measurement System

Topic	Using Proportions to Convert Traditional and Metric Units
Notes	✓ It's possible to convert any measuring unit to a different kind by multiplying it via a quite special ratio (or ratios) that equals one. You may form these special ratios from the conversion factors. ✓ For instance, $1 ft = 12\ in$ are a conversion factor and the ratios $\frac{1ft}{12in}$ and $\frac{12in}{1ft}$ can be written from it, in which both equal 1.
Example	*Write proportion to convert 8 inches to feet.* Solution: Write a unit rate that shows the relation between feet and per inch. Then, write another rate with the numbers in the problem. To match the unit rate, the unit is in numerator the same form and in the denominator as well, $\frac{1\ feet}{12\ inches} = \frac{?\ feet}{8\ inches}$. And use this proportion to convert. To get from 12 to 8, divide by $\frac{3}{2}$. $$\frac{1\ feet \div \frac{3}{2}}{12\ inches \div \frac{3}{2}} = \frac{\frac{2}{3}\ feet}{8\ inches}$$ So, $8\ inches = \frac{2}{3}\ feet$.
Your Turn!	**Write proportion to convert traditional and metric units.**

1) 18 inches to yards	2) 3.5 mile to feet
3) 28.03 kilogram to gram	4) 770 yard to mile
5) 1,320 feet to mile	6) 45 quarts to cups
7) 38 pints to quarts	8) 70 meters to kilometers
9) 350 milligrams to gram	10) 1.5 cups to pints
11) 28 quarts to gallons	12) 15 yard to feet

Find more at bit.ly/43mjVgg

Topic	Compare the Temperatures Above and Below Zero
Notes	✓ You can show the temperature changes via a number line. ✓ A number line has negative numbers to the left of 0 as well as positive numbers to the right of 0. That signifies the numbers beyond the right-hand side are always larger than the ones on the left-hand side. ✓ For the conditions of the temperature, the ones that are the coldest (the lower number) are on the left-hand side, as well as the warmest temperatures (the higher numbers) are on the right-hand side.
Example	*At $3:00$ AM the temperature was -5 degrees Celsius. At $3:00$ PM the temperature was 3 degrees Celsius. Did the temperature rise or fall?* 18 degrees Celsius is warmer than 9 degrees Celsius. So, the temperature rose. *The temperature in Chicago was $15°F$. The temperature in Houston was $11°F$. Was Chicago hotter or colder than Houston?* 15 degrees Fahrenheit is hotter than 11 degrees Fahrenheit. So, Chicago was hotter than Houston.
Your Turn!	1) There are low temperatures (in Celsius) for five days in summer: | Wednesday	Thursday	Friday	Saturday	Sunday
---	---	---	---	---
2	0	-1	-11	-4	 Arrange them in order from coldest to warmest. 2) On the first day of autumn, the high temperature in Sophia's city was 23 degrees below zero (in°C), and the second day the high temperature was 17 degrees below zero (in°C). Which day was hotter? 3) The lowest temperature ever recorded on Nick's country last year was 5°C. The lowest temperature on Karen's country was around minus 29°C. Which is the coldest? Write an inequality. 4) Jake recorded a temperature of 29 degrees Celsius, and Emma recorded a temperature of 35 degrees Celsius. Did Jake record a temperature that was warmer or cooler?

Chapter 15: Answers

Mixed Customary Units Operations (6.4.H)

1) >
2) <
3) =
4) <
5) $0.5 ft$
6) $650 g$
7) $350 mm$
8) $5 mi$
9) $1T\ 808 lb$
10) $4lb\ 2oz$
11) $9cm\ 2mm$
12) $3mi\ 1060yd$

Mixed Numbers and Fractions Customary Unit Conversions (6.4.H)

1) $180 in$
2) $1\frac{3}{5} oz$
3) $2\frac{1}{2} t$
4) $3 gal$
5) $3,168 ft$
6) $\frac{3}{8} mi$
7) $93 ml$
8) $4\frac{3}{8} c$

Using Proportions to Convert Traditional and Metric Units (6.4.H)

1) $\frac{1yd}{36in} = \frac{0.5yd}{18in}$
2) $\frac{1mi}{5.280ft} = \frac{3.5mi}{18,480ft}$
3) $\frac{1kg}{1000g} = \frac{28.03kg}{28,030g}$
4) $\frac{1mi}{1,760yd} = \frac{0.4375mi}{700yd}$
5) $\frac{1mi}{5,2810ft} = \frac{0.25mi}{1,320ft}$
6) $\frac{1qt}{4c} = \frac{45qt}{180c}$
7) $\frac{1qt}{2pt} = \frac{19qt}{38pt}$
8) $\frac{1km}{1000m} = \frac{0.07km}{70m}$
9) $\frac{1g}{1000mg} = \frac{0.35g}{3550mg}$
10) $\frac{1pt}{2c} = \frac{0.75pt}{1.5c}$
11) $\frac{1gal}{4qt} = \frac{7gal}{28qt}$
12) $\frac{1yd}{3ft} = \frac{15yd}{45ft}$

Compare the Temperatures Above and Below Zero (6.4.H)

1) $-11 < -4 < -1 < 0 < 2$
2) Second day
3) Karen's country, $-29 < 5$
4) cooler

CHAPTER 16
Geometry and Solid Figures

Math topics that you'll learn in this chapter:

- ☑ Triangles
- ☑ Triangle Inequality
- ☑ Relationships Between Sides and Angles in a Triangle
- ☑ Definition of the Area of a Triangle
- ☑ Polygons
- ☑ Cubes
- ☑ Rectangle Prisms
- ☑ Definition of the Area of a Parallelogram
- ☑ Word Problems Involving Area of Quadrilaterals and Triangles
- ☑ Definition of the Area of a Trapezoid
- ☑ Finding Area of Compound Figures
- ☑ Finding Area Between Two Rectangles
- ☑ Finding Area Between Two Triangles
- ☑ Volume of Cubes and Rectangular Prisms: Word Problems

Geometry and Solid Figures

Topic	Triangles
Notes	✓ In any triangle, the sum of all angles is 180 degrees. ✓ Area of a triangle $= \frac{1}{2}(base \times height)$
Example	**What is the area of this triangles?** Use the area formula: Area $= \frac{1}{2}(base \times height)$ $base = 18$ and $height = 7$, Then: $$Area = \frac{1}{2}(18 \times 7) = \frac{1}{2}(126) = 63$$

Your Turn!

Find the measure of the unknown angle in each triangle.

1) 74°, 85°, ?°

2) 60°, 45°, ?°

3) 60°, 90°, ?°

4) 50°, 50°, ?°

Find the area of each triangle.

5) 11 cm, 8 cm, 19 cm

6) 18 in, 10, 21 in

7) 9 m, 5 m

8) 3 ft, 8 ft

Topic	Triangle Inequality
Notes	✓ If the sum of any of the two sides is greater than the $3rd$, then the difference between any of the two sides is going to be less than the $3rd$. ✓ The sum of any of the two sides must be higher than the $3rd$ side. ✓ The side which is opposite to a bigger angle will be the longest side of the triangle. ✓ To figure out if the 3 side lengths are a triangle, utilize the triangle inequality theorem, which declares that the sum of 2 sides of a triangle must be larger than the $3rd$ side. Thus, you must add together each combination of the 2 sides to find out if it is larger than the $3rd$ side.
Example	**Can the sides of a triangle have the given lengths?** **Lengths of a triangle: $6, 12$ and 4** If $0 \leq a \leq b \leq c$, and $a + b > c$, then a, b, and c are the side of a triangle. Therefore, put the 3 numbers in order from smallest to largest, $a = 4$, $b = 6$, $c = 12$. Now, $4 + 6$ is smaller than 12 and this statement, $a + b > c$ is not true for these lengths, $4 + 6 \ngtr 12$. So, these are not the side lengths of a triangle.
Your Turn!	**Which lengths of the given sides represent a triangle?**

1) $a = 4, b = 7, c = 5$	2) $a = 7, b = 10, c = 17$
3) $a = 3, b = 5, c = 9$	4) $a = 10, b = 7, c = 9$
5) $a = 5, b = 6, c = 13$	6) $a = 8, b = 8, c = 8$
7) $a = 2, b = 3, c = 4$	8) $a = 2, b = 8, c = 11$

bit.ly/44Nof9m

Geometry and Solid Figures

Topic	Relationships Between Sides and Angles in a Triangle
Notes	✓ Angle-Side Relationships: With triangles, the biggest side is opposite the biggest angle and vice versa and the smallest side is opposite the tiniest angle and vice versa. ✓ Isosceles triangle: A triangle that has 2 equal side lengths. The opposite angles of these congruent sides are similarly equal. ✓ In any triangle, the sum of the lengths of any 2 sides are more than the length of the 3rd side.
Example	**Find the smallest angle of △ ABC.** Since $15 < 26 < 30$, $\overline{BA} < \overline{BC} < \overline{AC}$. And, their opposite angles are in the same order, from smallest to largest: $\angle C < \angle A < \angle B$ So, the smallest angle is $\angle A$.
Your Turn!	**Find the required side of the triangle.** 1) Smallest side (triangle MKL: M=65°, K=90°, L=25°) 2) Smallest side (triangle HIG: H=20°, I=130°, G=30°) 3) Largest side (triangle DEF: D=30°, E=65°, F=85°) 4) Largest side (triangle CAB: C=42°, A=60°, B=78°) **Find the required angle of the triangle.** 5) Smallest angle (triangle PRQ: PR=3 in, PQ=9 in, RQ=7 in) 6) Smallest angle (triangle WXV: WX=10 cm, WV=8 cm, XV=13 cm) 7) Largest angle (triangle NOM: NM=10 cm, NO=6 cm, OM=8 cm) 8) Largest angle (triangle SUT: SU=19 ft, UT=13 ft, ST=8 ft)

bit.ly/3rtWeW3

Topic	Definition of the Area of a Triangle
Notes	✓ The area of a triangle: $A = \frac{1}{2}(b \times h)$ square units. When b and h are the base and height of the triangle, correspondingly. ✓ The area of a triangle is described as the total space inhabited by the 3 sides of a triangle in a 2−dimensional plane. The basic formula for the area of a triangle is equal to half the product of its base and height, i.e., $A = \frac{1}{2} \times b \times h$.
Example	*What is the area of the triangle?* To find the area of a triangle, multiply, the base by the height, then multiply $\frac{1}{2}$ by the result. So, the area of the triangle is 35 in^2. $Area = base \times height \times \frac{1}{2} \to A = \frac{1}{2}(b \times h) \to A = \frac{1}{2}(6 \times 12) = 35$
Your Turn!	1) 5 ft, 12 ft, 9 ft 2) 12 in, 7 in, 22 in 3) 25 m, 14 m, 28 m 4) 5 cm, 3 cm, 8 cm 5) 3 cm, 5 cm, 2 cm 6) 7 ft, 11 ft, 9 ft 7) 9 yd, 6 yd, 3 yd 8) 53 mm, 46 mm, 50 mm

Topic	Polygons
Notes	✓ The perimeter of a square = 4 × side = 4s ✓ The perimeter of a rectangle = 2(width + length) ✓ The perimeter of trapezoid = a + b + c + d ✓ The perimeter of a regular hexagon = 6a ✓ The perimeter of a parallelogram = 2(l + w)
Example	**Find the perimeter of following trapezoid.** The perimeter of a trapezoid = a + b + c + d The perimeter of the trapezoid = 5 + 9 + 9 + 13 = 36 ft
Your Turn!	**Find the perimeter or circumference of each shape.** 1) Parallelogram with sides 10 cm, 12 cm, 10 cm, 12 cm 2) Rectangle 9 ft by 6 ft 3) Square with side 5 in 4) Regular hexagon with side 4 mm 5) Trapezoid with sides 4.5 yd, 3 yd, 5 yd, 3 yd 6) Quadrilateral with sides 8.5 m, 4 m, 8 m, 3 m

Topic	Cubes
Notes	✓ A cube is a three-dimensional solid object bounded by six square sides. ✓ Volume is the measure of the amount of space inside of a solid figure, like a cube, ball, cylinder, or pyramid. ✓ The volume of a cube = $(one\ side)^3$ ✓ The surface area of a cube = $6 \times (one\ side)^2$
Example	**Find the volume and surface area of this cube.** 7 cm Use volume formula: $volume = (one\ side)^3$ Then: $volume = (one\ side)^3 = (7)^3 = 343\ cm^3$ Use surface area formula: $surface\ area\ of\ a\ cube: 6(one\ side)^2 = 6(7)^2 = 6(49) = 294\ cm^2$
Your Turn!	**Find the volume of these cube.** 1) 3 cm 2) 6 ft 3) 5 in 4) 9 miles **Find the surface area of this cube.** 5) 2 yd 6) 10 km 7) 4 mm 8) 11 m

Geometry and Solid Figures

Topic	Rectangular Prisms
Notes	✓ A rectangular prism is a solid 3-dimensional object with six rectangular faces. ✓ The volume of a Rectangular prism = $Length \times Width \times Height$ $$Volume = l \times w \times h$$ $$Surface\ area = 2 \times (wh + lw + lh)$$
Example	**Find the volume and surface area of this rectangular prism.** Use volume formula: $Volume = l \times w \times h$ Then: $Volume = 9 \times 5 \times 6 = 270\ m^3$ Use surface area formula: $Surface\ area = 2 \times (wh + lw + lh)$ Then: $Surface\ area = 2 \times ((5 \times 6) + (9 \times 5) + (9 \times 6))$ $= 2 \times (30 + 45 + 54) = 2 \times (129) = 258\ m^2$
Your Turn!	**Find the volume of each Rectangular Prism.** 1) 8 cm, 7 cm, 4 cm 2) 9 m, 4 m, 3 m 3) 7 mm, 8 mm, 1 mm 4) 12 ft, 2 ft, 3 ft **Find the surface area of each Rectangular Prism.** 5) 10 yd, 8 m, 3 m 6) 8 m, 5 m, 4 m 7) 4 km, 5 km, 1 km 8) 6 in, 1 in, 2 in

Topic	Definition of the Area of a Parallelogram
Notes	✓ The formula for determining the area of a parallelogram is base times height. This means $A = bh$, the same as the formula for the area of a rectangle. ✓ Parallelograms are quadrilaterals having 2 pairs of parallel sides. he opposite sides of the parallelogram are identical in length, and the opposite angles are identical in measure. Likewise, the interior angles on the same side of the transversal are supplementary. ✓ The sum of all the interior angles equals 360 degrees. $\overline{AB} \parallel \overline{DC}, \overline{AD} \parallel \overline{BC}$ $\angle A = \angle C, \angle B = \angle D$
Example	**What is the area of the parallelogram?** To find the area of a parallelogram, multiply, the base by the height. So, the area of a parallelogram is $54\ cm^2$. $Area = base \times height \to A = b \times h \to A = 5 \times 8 = 40$
Your Turn!	1) 10 cm, 6 cm, 13 cm 2) 4 in, 2.5 in, 4 in 3) 6 in, 5 in, 9 in 4) 13 ft, 9 ft, 20 ft 5) 8 cm, 6 cm, 9 cm 6) 10 m, 8 m, 10 m 7) 15 yd, 5 yd, 12 yd 8) 5 mm, 3 mm, 5 mm

Topic	Word Problems Involving Area of Quadrilaterals and Triangles
Notes	✓ You can solve word problems by becoming a detective and searching for clues in the form of keywords and phrases. ✓ Finding them helps you understand which operation to use. ✓ Carefully read the text to understand what you are asked to solve in the problem. ✓ Write a number sentence then solve it in a single step.
Example	*Olivia likes to plant different flowers in her garden. She has a garden plot that is shaped like a square. Each side of the garden plot is 12 feet long. What is the area of the garden?* To determine the area of the garden. First, write an equation to find the area of the square, $A = S^2$. And the side is $12\ ft$. So, solve the equation: $$A = S^2 \rightarrow A = 12^2 \rightarrow A = 144$$ Thus, this garden has $144\ ft^2$ areas.
Your Turn!	1) A trapezoid has an area of $30\ cm^2$ and its height is $5\ cm$ and one base is $8\ cm$. What is the other base length?
	2) There is a chess board, that is shaped like a square, and its sides are 9 inches long. What is the area of the chess board?
	3) If a triangle has an area of $58\ ft^2$ and the length of the base is $16\ ft$, find the height?
	4) If a trapezoid has an area of $90\ m^2$ and its one base is $18\ m$ and other base is $12\ m$, find the length of the height?
	5) An advertising company made a banner for a construction company. The banner is shaped like a triangle with an area of 85 square feet. The banner is 17 feet tall. What is the length of the banner's base?
	6) The area of a parallelogram is $1,680\ ft^2$ and its height is $35\ ft$. what is the base length?
	7) The base of a parallelogram is 15 yards long, and its height is 7 yards. What is the area of the parallelogram?
	8) A triangle has an area of 45.5 square inches and a height of 7 inches. What is the length of the triangle's base?

Topic	Definition of the Area of a Trapezoid
Notes	✓ To determine the area of a trapezoid, multiply the sum of the bases (the parallel sides) by the height (the perpendicular distance between the bases), and after that divide by 2. ✓ Trapezoid Area Formula: Based on the trapezoid area formula, the area of a trapezoid is equal to half the product of the height and the sum of the two bases. Area=$\frac{1}{2}$×(Sum of parallel sides)×(perpendicular distance in between the parallel sides). $$A = \frac{1}{2} \times (\overline{AB} + \overline{DC}) \times (d)$$
Example	**What is the area of the trapezoid?** To find the area of a trapezoid, add the parallel sides, then multiply $\frac{1}{2}$ and the distance in between the parallel sides by the result. $$\frac{1}{2} \times (5 + 9) \times 4 = 28$$ So, the area of the trapezoid is in^2.
Your Turn!	1) 5 cm, 4 cm, 8 cm 2) 3 ft, 2.5 ft, 5 ft 3) 10 m, 8 m, 13 m 4) 2 cm, 2 cm, 5 cm 5) 15 in, 7 in, 8 in 6) 11 ft, 5 ft, 5 ft 7) 11 yd, 7 yd, 13 yd 8) 18 cm, 9 cm, 9 cm

Finding Area of Compound Figures

Notes

- To figure out the area of compound shapes you must divide the compound shape into basic shapes, then figure out the area of each of the basic shapes, and then they are added together.
- To figure out the area of irregular shapes, firstly, you must divide the irregular shape into regular shapes you are able to recognize like circles, rectangles, squares, triangles, etc. Afterward, figure out the area of these individual shapes and then add them to determine an area of irregular shapes.

Example

What is the area of this figure?

Divide the figure into rectangle and triangle, and rename the shapes, A and B. Then calculate each rectangle. Area of rectangle A, $11 \times 5 = 55\ cm^2$. Area of triangle B, $\frac{1}{2}(8-5) \times (11-4) = 10.5\ cm^2$

Now, add the areas of two shapes A and B, $55 + 10.5 = 65.5\ cm^2$. So, the area is 65.5 square centimeters.

Your Turn!

1) (4 in top, 2 in, 7 in right, 9 in bottom)

2) (7 m, 3 m, 3 m, 6 m, 5 m, 2 m, 2 m, 8 m)

3) (4 in, 12 in, 3 in, 19 in)

4) (3 ft, 7 ft, 15 ft, 3 ft, 5 ft, 22 ft, 3 ft)

5) (9 ft, 3 ft, 7 ft, 11 ft, 9 ft)

6) (4 yd, 4 yd, 5 yd, 3 yd, 1 yd, 7 yd)

Topic	Finding Area Between Two Rectangles
Notes	✓ The area of a rectangle is provided by the formula: $A = l \times w$ ✓ Step 1: Distinguish the length (l) and width (w) of the larger rectangle. Next, determine the area of the larger rectangle via utilizing the formula $A_B = l_B \times w_B$. ✓ Step 2: Distinguish the length (l) and width (w) of the lesser rectangle. Next, discover the area of the lesser rectangle via utilizing the formula $A_S = l_S \times w_S$. ✓ Step 3: Locate the area between the two rectangles by subtracting the area of the lesser rectangle from the area of the bigger rectangle.
Example	**What is the area of the shaded region?** First, find the area of the rectangle and square. Then subtract the area of the inner square from the area of the outer rectangle. The area of the inner square is, $2 \times 6 = 12 \ m^2$. The area of the outer rectangle is, $10 \times 10 = 100 \ m^2$. To find the shaded area, $100 - 12 = 88 \ m^2$. So, the area of the shaded region is 95 square meters.
Your Turn!	1) 22 yd, 12 yd, 3 yd, 5 yd 2) 15 yd, 15 yd, 9 yd, 9 yd 3) 21 in, 15 in, 15 in, 3 in 4) 7.5 in, 5 in, 1 in, 5 in 5) 5 ft, 11 ft, 3 ft, 3 ft 6) 6 m, 2.5 m, 3 m, 2 m

Topic	**Finding Area Between Two Triangles**
Notes	✓ $Area = \frac{1}{2} \times b \times h$, in which b is the length of the base of the triangle, and h is the height/altitude of the triangle. ✓ To locate the area of the shaded region, subtract the area of the inner shape from the area of the outer shape. Begin by discovering the area of the inner shape. Locate the base and height of the inner triangle
Example	**What is the area of the shaded region?** First, find the area of each triangle. Then subtract the area of the inner triangle from the area of the outer triangle. The area of the inner triangle, $\frac{1}{2} \times 3 \times 3 = 4.5\ ft^2$. The area of the outer triangle, $\frac{1}{2} \times 20 \times 11 = 90\ ft^2$. To find the shaded area, $90 - 4.5 = 85.5\ ft^2$. So, the area of the shaded region is 71 square feet.
Your Turn!	1) 2 in, 6 in, 4 in, 6 in 2) 4 m, 2 m, 1 m, 8.5 m 3) 7 ft, 4 ft, 3 ft, 15 ft 4) 15 m, 3 yd, 13 yd, 28 m 5) 19 mm, 10 mm, 8 mm, 13 mm 6) 18 in, 10 in, 5 in, 7 in

Topic	Volume of Cubes and Rectangular Prisms: Word Problems
Notes	✓ You can solve word problems by becoming a detective and searching for clues in the form of keywords and phrases. ✓ Finding them helps you understand which operation to use. ✓ Carefully read the text to understand what you are asked to solve in the problem. ✓ Write a number sentence then solve it in a single step.
Example	***Meg bought a new pink dress for her sister's birthday party. She returned home with a box that was 20 inches long, 12 inches wide, and 5 inches tall. What is the volume of the clothes box?*** To find out the volume of the clothes box, V, is, utilize the formula for the volume of a rectangular prism. $V = lwh$. Solve for V. $V = 20 \times 12 \times 5 \rightarrow V = 1,200\ in^3$ The clothes box is 1,200 cubic inches.
Your Turn!	1) There is the rectangular prism box for packing fruits that has a volume of 12,900 cubic centimeters. The prism has a width of 25 centimeters and a height of 12 centimeters. What is the length of the box? 2) Employees of a company, to make happy the cancer children. They prepared some gifts such as toys and colored pencils and a cute notebook. They display the gifts in a glass case shaped like a rectangular prism. It has a length of 32 inches, a height of 15 inches, and a volume of 7,200 cubic inches. What is the width of the prism? 3) There is a cube prism that has a volume of 2,197 cubic centimeters. The prism has a width of 13 centimeters. What is the length and height of the prism? 4) After visiting the zoo, Irma got her very own pet parrot. Irma bought a birdhouse shaped like a rectangular prism for her parrot to live in. The birdhouse is 33 inches long, 20 inches wide, and 45 inches tall. What is the volume of the birdhouse?

Chapter 16: Answers

Triangles

1) 21°
2) 75°
3) 30°
4) 80°
5) 76cm^2
6) 105in^2
7) 22.5m^2
8) 12ft^2

Triangle Inequality

1) It is a triangle.
2) It is a triangle.
3) It is not a triangle.
4) It is a triangle.
5) It is not a triangle.
6) It is a triangle.
7) It is a triangle.
8) It is not a triangle.

Relationships Between Sides and Angles in a Triangle

1) $\overline{MK}$ is the smallest.
2) $\overline{IG}$ is the smallest.
3) $\overline{DE}$ is the largest.
4) $\overline{CA}$ is the largest.
5) ∠Q is the smallest.
6) ∠X is the Smallest.
7) ∠O is the largest.
8) ∠T is the largest.

Definition of the Area of a Triangle

1) 22.5ft^2
2) 77in^2
3) 175m^2
4) 12cm^2
5) 3cm^2
6) 38.5ft^2
7) 9yd^2
8) 1,150mm^2

Polygons

1) 44cm
2) 30ft
3) 20in
4) 24mm
5) 15.5yd
6) 23.5m

Cubes

1) 27cm^3
2) 216ft^3
3) 125in^3
4) 729mi^3
5) 24yd^2
6) 600km^2
7) 96mm^2
8) 726m^2

Rectangle Prisms

1) 224cm^3
2) 108m^3
3) 56mm^3
4) 72ft^3
5) 268yd^2
6) 184m^2
7) 58km^2
8) 40in^2

www.EffortlessMath.com

Definition of the Area of a Parallelogram

1) $78\ cm^2$
2) $10\ in^2$
3) $45\ in^2$
4) $180\ ft^2$
5) $54\ cm^2$
6) $80\ m^2$
7) $60\ yd^2$
8) $15\ mm^2$

Word Problems Involving Area of Quadrilaterals and Triangles

1) $4\ cm$
2) $81\ in^2$
3) $7.25\ ft$
4) $6\ m$
5) $10\ ft$
6) $48\ ft$
7) $105\ yd^2$
8) $13\ in$

Definition of the Area of a Trapezoid

1) $26\ cm^2$
2) $10\ ft^2$
3) $92\ m^2$
4) $7\ cm^2$
5) $80.5\ in^2$
6) $40\ ft^2$
7) $84\ yd^2$
8) $121.5\ cm^2$

Finding Area of Compound Figures

1) $40.5\ in^2$
2) $37\ m^2$
3) $60.5\ in^2$
4) $110\ ft^2$
5) $127\ ft^2$
6) $23\ yd^2$

Finding Area Between Two Rectangles

1) $249\ yd^2$
2) $144\ yd^2$
3) $270\ in^2$
4) $32.5\ in^2$
5) $46\ ft^2$
6) $9\ m^2$

Finding Area Between Two Triangles

1) $14\ in^2$
2) $16\ m^2$
3) $46.5\ ft^2$
4) $190.5\ yd^2$
5) $83.5\ mm^2$
6) $72.5\ in^2$

Volume of Cubes and Rectangular Prisms: Word Problems

1) $43\ cm$
2) $15\ in$
3) $13\ cm$
4) $29{,}700\ in^3$

CHAPTER 17 Coordinate Plane

Math topics that you'll learn in this chapter:

- ☑ Objects on a Coordinate Plane
- ☑ Understanding Quadrants
- ☑ Coordinate Planes as Maps

Coordinate Plane

Topic	Objects on a Coordinate Plane
Notes	✓ Coordinate planes are created via a horizontal number line known as an x-axis along with a vertical number line known as a y-axis. ✓ Each of the axis lines crosses the other one at zero. The point at which these axis lines converge is known as its origin. ✓ An ordered pair (x, y) illustrates the location of a point on a coordinate plane. The 1st number is known as an x-coordinate and the 2nd number is known as a y-coordinate. $A = (0,3), B = (4,1)$ $C = (2,-2), D = (-3,-1)$
Example	*What is the y-coordinate of point A?* Draw a line perpendicular to the y-coordinate from point A. This position on the y-axis is 1 units above the origin. All y-coordinate above the origin are positive. So, the y-coordinate of point A is 1.
Your Turn!	According to the coordinate plane, determine the requested coordinates. 1) y − coordinate of point G 2) x −coordinate of point D 3) y − coordinate of point D 4) x −coordinate of point C 5) x −coordinate of point E 6) y − coordinate of point F 7) x −coordinate of point G 8) y −coordinate of point A

bit.ly/44r9466

Find more at

Topic	Understanding Quadrants	
Notes	✓ Quadrants are the area enclosed by the x and y axes; therefore, a graph has 4 quadrants. ✓ To describe, the 2−dimensional Cartesian plane gets divided by the x and y axes into 4 quadrants. Beginning at the top right-hand corner is *Quadrant I* and then moving counterclockwise you find *Quadrants II* through *IV*.	Coordinate plane showing Quadrant II (top left), Quadrant I (top right), Quadrant III (bottom left), Quadrant IV (bottom right), with axes labeled from −4 to 4.
Example	**Which shape is in Quadrant IV?** *Quadrant IV* is the bottom left quadrant. So, ⬠ is in *Quadrant IV*.	Coordinate plane with a square at approximately (−2, 2), a circle at (3, 3), a heart at (−1, −2), and a pentagon at (4, −4).
Your Turn!	1) Which shape is in *Quadrant III*?	Coordinate plane with a hexagon at approximately (−3, 3), a circle at (2, 1), a diamond at (3, −2), and a star at (−2, −3).
	2) Which shape is in *Quadrant I*?	
	3) Which shape is in *Quadrant IV*?	
	4) Which shape is in *Quadrant II*?	

Topic	**Coordinate Planes as Maps**
Notes	✓ Coordinate planes are 2-dimensional planes created via the intersection of a vertical line known as a y-axis along with a horizontal line known as an x-axis. This lesson will teach you more about coordinate planes as maps. ✓ They are perpendicular lines that overlap one another at 0, and that point is known as its origin. ✓ It's utilized to indicate the location of various places on the earth's surface.
Example	*Where is the hospital and Bank?* Find the point of the hospital and bank on the map. Determine, the x and y-coordinates of the hospital and bank point. x-coordinates of H: 1 and B: -2 y-coordinates of H: 4 and B: -4 Then, write the answer as an ordered pair. So, the Hospital is at $(1, 4)$ and the bank is at $(-2, -4)$. **S**: School **F**: Fire Station **B**: Bank **H**: Home
Your Turn!	**Write the coordinates of the specified points.**
	1) Where is the pet store?
	2) Where is the Bank?
	3) Where is the theater?
	4) Where is the science lab?
	5) Where is the locksmith?
	6) Where is the restaurant?
	7) Where is the fire station
	8) Where is the game store?

G: Game store
F: Fire Station
B: Bank
H: Hospital
P: Pet store
S: Science lab
T: Theater
L: Locksmith
R: Restaurant

bit.ly/3XWw4rk

Chapter 17: Answers

Objects on a Coordinate Plane

1) 0
2) −4
3) −2
4) 4
5) 0
6) −4
7) 3
8) 2

Understanding Quadrants

1) ✦
2) ○
3) ◇
4) ⬡

Coordinate Planes as Maps

1) $(4, -4)$
2) $(-3, -3)$
3) $(0, 2)$
4) $(-2, 1)$
5) $(-3, 4)$
6) $(1, 4)$
7) $(1, -4)$
8) $(3, -2)$

Chapter 18: Statistics and Data Analysis

Math topics that you'll learn in this chapter:

- ☑ Pie Graph
- ☑ Graph The Line Plot
- ☑ Distributions in Line Plot
- ☑ Relative Frequency Tables
- ☑ Frequency Charts
- ☑ Mean, Median, Mode, and Range of the Given Data
- ☑ Interpreting Charts to find mean, median, mode, and range
- ☑ Finding an Outlier
- ☑ Finding Range, Quartiles, and Interquartile Range
- ☑ Interpreting Categorical Data
- ☑ Identifying Statistical Questions
- ☑ Completing a Table and Making a Graph: Word Problems

Topic	**Pie Graph**
Notes	✓ A Pie Graph (Pie Chart) is a circle chart divided into sectors, each sector represents the relative size of each value. ✓ Pie charts represent a snapshot of how a group is broken down into smaller pieces.
Example	*A library has 850 books that include Mathematics, Physics, Chemistry, English and History. Use the following graph to answer the questions.* **What is the number of Mathematics books?** Number of total books $= 850$ Percent of Mathematics books $= 38\%$ Then, the number of Mathematics books: $28\% \times 750 = 0.28 \times 750 = 323$ History 17%, English 13%, Mathematics 38%, Chemistry 12%, Physics 20%
Your Turn!	**The circle graph below shows all Bob's expenses for last month. Bob spent $970 on his Rent last month.** 1) How much did Bob's total expenses last month? 2) How much did Bob spend for foods last month? 3) How much did Bob spend for his bills last month? 4) How much did Bob spend on his car last month? 5) How much did Bob spend on his other expenses last month? 6) How much did Bob spend for books car last month? Bob's last month expenses: Rent 25%, Others 9%, Bills 27%, Books 10%, foods 11%, Car 18%

bit.ly/44suVde

Find more at

Topic	Graph The Line Plot
Notes	✓ Draw a number line that encloses all the values included in the data set. ✓ Put an × (or dot) over each data value on this number line. ✓ If a value happens over one time in a data set, put an × over this number for each of the times it happens.
Example	*A researcher working for a research company surveyed people about sleeping habits. Use the data to graph the line plot.* *Sleeping time: 23, 22, 22, 22, 22, 24, 1, 24, 24, 22, 23, 23, 1, 2, 24, 23, 22, 23, 23, 2, 24, 23, 22* First, count how many times each set number appears in the list. 22 appear 7 times in the list, 23 appear 7 times, 24 appear 5 times, 1 appears 2 times, 2 appears 2 time. Then graph it on the line plot.
Your Turn!	Use the data to graph the line plot. 1) The following data is about the number of coffee bags used each day in a café over three weeks. 20, 20, 19, 21, 22, 21, 20, 19, 16, 21, 19, 22, 20, 19, 21, 19, 22, 20, 21, 19, 21 2) The following data is about the daily high temperatures during two weeks. 23°C, 21°C, 21°C, 20°C, 20°C, 21°C, 23°C, 21°C, 23°C, 27°C, 20°C, 21°C, 20°C, 24°C 3) The following data is about the number of sales of a new bag model each day for three weeks. 2, 5, 3, 5, 5, 3, 3, 1, 7, 2, 3, 5, 5, 2, 3, 5, 1, 2, 3, 5, 3 4) Sarah is knitting hats, and every week, she takes a number of knitted hats to the shop for sale. The following data is about the weekly hat sales for three weeks. 15, 15, 14, 13, 13, 9, 14, 12, 12, 15, 14, 15, 16, 14, 13, 15, 13, 15, 12, 9, 13

Statistics and Data Analysis

Topic	**Distributions in Line Plot**
Notes	✓ Step one: Compute the data set's range. ✓ To compute the data set's range, firstly you must determine the greatest data value as well as the least of the data values. Therefore, you subtract the smallest data value from the biggest data value. $$Range = greatest\ value - smallest\ value$$ ✓ Step two: Utilize the range for describing the distribution.
Example	**What does the line plot show?** Look at the line plot. The smallest number is 15 and the greatest is 40. The column for 30 has the most ×s. So, there is a peak at 30, that is the mode of this data. There are no ×s in the columns for 20 to 25. So, there is a gap from 20 to 25. The data has a cluster from 30 to 40. There is a group of ×s in the columns for 30 and 40. Every column has at least one ×, and the columns are next to one another. There is an × in the column for 15, and it is far away from the rest of the ×s. So, there is an outlier at 15 pieces. The data is skewed right. The left and right sides of the distribution are not mirrored images. So, the distribution is roughly asymmetric. The leftmost column with an × is 15. The rightmost column with an × is 40. So, the data is spread out from 15 to 40.

Your Turn! Select all the statements that describe the distribution of the data.

a	The data has a peak at 4.
b	The data has a cluster from 1 to 3.
c	There is a gap from 2 to 3.
d	The data is spread out from 1 to 6.
e	The data has a cluster from 1 to 4.
f	The center of the data is at 2.
g	The data has a peak at 2.
h	The data has a cluster from 3 to 4.
i	The distribution is roughly symmetric.
j	The data is skewed right.
k	The data has a cluster from 4 to 6.
l	The data has a peak at 1.
m	The center of the data is at 4.

1) line plot with values at 1, 2, 3, 4, 5, 6

2) line plot with values at 1, 2, 3, 4, 5, 6

3) line plot with values at 1, 2, 3, 4, 5, 6

4) line plot with values at 1, 2, 3, 4, 5, 6

bit.ly/3PYd4GN

Topic	Relative Frequency Tables
Notes	✓ Frequency is signified by the English alphabet 'f'. Relative frequency is: $$Relative\ Frequency = \frac{Subgroup\ frequency}{Total\ frequency} = \frac{f}{n}$$ ✓ Producing a frequency table: • Step one: Draw 3 columns. The 1st column holds the data values in rising order (from lowest to highest). • Step two: The 2nd column holds the number of times the data value happens utilizing tally marks. Count for each row in the table. Utilize tally marks for calculating. • Step three: Calculate the number of tally marks for each of the data values and put it in the 3rd column.
Example	*Deb wants to subscribe to a plan for education. This plan has weekly hours for different courses. Math 12 hours, chemistry 7 hours and physics 6 hours. Complete the relative frequency table for the data.* | Courses	Math	Chemistry	Physics
---	---	---	---
Relative frequency	___%	___%	___%	 First, find the total number of hours plan, $12 + 7 + 6 = 25$. Write the relative frequency of each course as a fraction with a denominator of 20. Then write as a percent. Math course: $\frac{12}{25} = \frac{12 \times 4}{20 \times 4} = \frac{48}{100} = 48\%$ Chemistry course: $\frac{7}{25} = \frac{7 \times 4}{25 \times 4} = \frac{28}{100} = 28\%$ Physics course: $\frac{6}{25} = \frac{6 \times 4}{25 \times 4} = \frac{24}{100} = 24\%$
Your Turn!	**Write the relative frequency table for the data.**
	1) Maria bakes cupcakes with various flavors. 6 lemon, 13 coffee, 21 carrots, and 10 red velvet.
	2) Eva went to the bakery and bought some bread such as 6 challah bread, 11 yeast bread and 8 pieces of focaccia.
	3) During a month, the maximum air temperature was as follows, six days 34°C, three days 30°C, six days 29°C and fifteen days 26°C.
	4) In a cafe, the number of orders for coffee cups is recorded. The number of cups ordered in the last 20 days is as follows, 40 − 49 cups in three days, 50 − 59 cups in five days, 60 − 69 cups in eleven days, and 70 − 79 cups in one day.

Topic	Frequency Charts
Notes	✓ Any chart illustrating the frequencies of the values of one or more of the variables in a data set. ✓ Frequency charts are created whenever the accumulated data values get placed in ascending order of magnitude together with their parallel frequencies. ✓ You must use frequency table to create a frequency distribution chart. ✓ The primary reason to make this kind of chart is to compare data, how many times the value happens.
Example	*A student counted the number of hours that spend on each of her tests. Use the data to complete the frequency chart below.* *Hours per test:* $1:35, 1:40, 3:00, 2:05, 2:39, 3:22,$ $1:48, 1:57, 3:28, 2:49, 4:10, 3:10, 1:05, 2:55,$ $2:51, 3:30, 3:08, 1:46, 3:55, 3:27.$ | Number of hours	Number of tests
$1 - 1:59$	6
$2 - 2:59$	5
$3 - 3:59$	
$4 - 4:59$	1 | The blank row is for $3 - 3:59$. Count the number of $3 - 3:59$. So, there are 8 hours between $3:00$ and $3:59$.
Your Turn!	Use the data and draw the frequency chart. 1) Every day, Maria bakes various cakes for a cafe. The following data is about the various cakes baked daily during a month. 3, 4, 2, 4, 6, 4, 1, 3, 6, 4, 3, 1, 5, 3, 5, 2, 4, 5, 3, 1, 1, 4, 6, 2, 3, 1, 5, 6, 4, 2 2) Eva went to the shop and bought fruits such as 5 apples, 9 peaches, 11 bananas, 4 pineapples, and 7 melons. 3) The following data is about the daily low temperatures for three weeks. 9°C, 6°C, 7°C, 9°C, 9°C, 6°C, 6°C, 8°C, 8°C, 6°C, 8°C, 9°C, 7°C, 9°C, 6°C, 11°C, 6°C, 8°C, 9°C, 6°C, 7°C, 4) The following data is about the number of cups of coffee that are drunk in a cafe per day. 235, 137, 111, 147, 132, 212, 69, 87, 219, 227, 213, 115, 99, 202, 108, 164, 201, 193, 182, 122, 89

Topic	Mean, Median, Mode, and Range of the Given Data
Notes	✓ **Mean:** $\frac{\text{sum of the data}}{\text{total number of data entires}}$ ✓ **Mode:** the value in the list that appears most often ✓ **Median:** is the middle number of a group of numbers arranged in order by size. ✓ **Range:** the difference of the largest value and smallest value in the list.
Example	**What is the median of these numbers?** **8, 11, 14, 13, 19, 20, 7** Write the numbers in order: 7, 8, 11, 13, 14, 19, 20 The median is the number in the middle. Therefore, the median is 13. **What is the mean of these numbers?** **12, 2, 8, 1, 4, 4, 4, 5** Mean: $\frac{\text{sum of the data}}{\text{total number of data entires}} = \frac{12+2+8+1+4+4+4+5}{8} = \frac{40}{8} = 5$ **What is the range in this list?** **3, 4, 2, 5, 18, 29, 3** Range is the difference of the largest value and smallest value in the list. The largest value is 20 and the smallest value is 3. Then: $29 - 2 = 27$ **What is the mode of these numbers?** **5, 3, 8, 7, 8, 7, 3, 1, 3, 10** Mode: the value in the list that appears most often. Therefore, the mode is number 3. There are three number 3 in the data.
Your Turn!	**Find the values of the Given Data.**

1) 22, 10, 25, 23, 25, 16, 19 Mode: _____, Range: _____ Mean: _____, Median: _____	2) 16, 19, 16, 18, 21 Mode: _____, Range: _____ Mean: _____, Median: _____
3) 6, 11, 5, 2, 1, 5 Mode: _____, Range: _____ Mean: _____, Median: _____	4) 10, 8, 1, 8, 9, 6 Mode: _____, Range: _____ Mean: _____, Median: _____
5) 3, 3, 5, 9, 4, 3 Mode: _____, Range: _____ Mean: _____, Median: _____	6) 14, 14, 8, 9, 13, 14, 15, 11 Mode: _____, Range: _____ Mean: _____, Median: _____

bit.ly/44uaHzW

Topic	**Interpreting Charts to find mean, median, mode, and range**
Notes	These 4 measures are the median, mean, range, and mode. ✓ Mean stands for the average. The mean is determined via the addition of the numbers, and after that, divide via the number of numbers in a group. ✓ The median is the middle number of a data set whenever put in order from the lowest to the highest. ✓ Mode is the number that happens the most. ✓ Range is the difference between the greatest and smallest values.
Example	*Jake paid attention to how many pages of books he read in the past 7 days. What is the range and mode of the number of pages?* To find the range, first find the greatest number, 35. Next find the latest number, 9 Subtract the least number from the greatest number, $35 - 9 = 26$. The range is 26. To find mode, count how many times each number appears. And The number that appears most often (4 times) is 11. The mode is 11. 	Day	Number of pages	 	---	---	 	Saturday	11	 	Sunday	11	 	Monday	35	 	Tuesday	9	 	Wednesday	11	 	Thursday	23	 	Friday	11	
Your Turn!	**A boutique kept a record of how many clothes it sold each day.** 1) What is the median of the number of clothes? 2) What is the range of the number of clothes? 3) What is the mode of the number of clothes? 4) What is the mean of the number of clothes? 	Day	Number of clothes | |---|---| 	Monday	35 | 	Tuesday	35 | 	Wednesday	49 | 	Thursday	28 | 	Friday	33 | 	Saturday	35 | 	Sunday	37 | **Leo looked at the download manager history on his computer to find out how many he had download songs in the past 8 days.** 5) What is the mode of the number of songs? 6) What is the mean of the number of songs? 7) What is the median of the number of songs? 8) What is the range of the number of songs? 	Day	Number of songs | |---|---| 	1st	10 | 	2nd	7 | 	3rd	7 | 	4th	12 | 	5th	9 | 	6th	3 | 	7th	7 | 	8th	3	

bit.ly/3NQxz5D

Topic	Finding an Outlier
Notes	✓ To discover an outlier, find a value that is either a lot bigger or a lot littler than the rest. ✓ One may transform extreme data points into *z* scores which illustrate the number of standard deviations away they are from the mean. ✓ Should the value be a high or low enough *z* score, you can call it an outlier. ✓ An outlier is an extreme value in a data set that is either much larger or much smaller than all the other values.

Example	*Select the outlier in the data set.*
	    28, 44, 48, 35, 30, 33, 27, 3, 43, 41, 36, 37, 44, 28, 29
	First, find the much larger or much smaller value in the data set. The value 3 is an outlier because it is much smaller than all other values.
	
	Select the outlier in the data set.
	    1, 4, 8, 2, 10, 3, 7, 9, 8, 5, 3, 4, 8, 71, 7, 9, 10, 4, 2,
	First, find the much larger or much smaller value in the data set. The value 71 is an outlier because it is much larger than all other values.

Your Turn!	**Leo looked at the download manager history on his computer to find out how many he had download songs in the past 8 days.** 1) 201, 204, 203, 202, 205, 209, 50, 210, 204 2) 5, 34, 37, 32, 38, 39, 40, 42, 43, 40, 37 3) 73, 74, 73, 72, 75, 80, 71, 77, 78, 123, 69 4) 450, 463, 434, 484, 451, 428, 443, 175, 470, 499, 484 5) 11, 21, 91, 41, 21, 31, 31, 51, 11, 41, 31 6) 65, 60, 63, 51, 67, 69, 1, 63, 59, 57, 71

Topic	Finding Range, Quartiles, and Interquartile Range
Notes	✓ To determine IQR, you first subtract the 1st quartile from the 3rd quartile. ✓ The interquartile range denotes the middle half, or middle 50 percent, of the data. The lesser the IQR is for a dataset, the nearer the middle half of the data will be to the median. ✓ IQR illustrates the middle 50 percent of values whenever it is ordered from lesser to greater. ✓ To determine the interquartile range (IQR), firstly determine the median (middle value) of the lower and upper half of your data. ✓ These values will be quartile 1 (Q_1) and quartile 3 (Q_3). IQR is the difference between Q_3 and Q_1.
Example	*Find the quartiles, then find the interquartile range.* 38, 48, 45, 40, 39, 43, 44, 35, 39, 42 First order the data from least to greatest. To find the quartiles, divide a data set into quarters, or four parts. Split the data into a lower half and an upper half. Next, find Q_1, the median of the lower half. And find Q_3, the median of the upper half. Lower half: 35, 38, 39, 39, 40 → Q_1 Upper half: 42, 43, 44, 45, 48 → Q_3 $Q_2 = \frac{40 + 42}{2} = 41$ $Q_1 = 39$, $Q_2 = 41$, $Q_3 = 44$ Now, to find IQR subtract Q_1 from Q_3, $44 - 39 = 5$. So, interquartile range is 5.

Your Turn!

What is the range?

1) 5, 7, 13, 12, 17, 10, 16, 9	2) 10, 20, 16, 27, 10, 7, 23, 25
3) 5, 3, 4, 2, 5, 4, 2, 6	4) 7, 4, 8, 15, 1

In the data set below:
15, 25, 35, 45, 55, 25, 15, 25, 85

5) What is the lower quartile, Q_1?	6) What is the range?
7) What is the upper quartile, Q_3?	8) What is the interquartile range?

Topic	Interpreting Categorical Data
Notes	✓ Categorical data gets analyzed utilizing mode and median distributions, whereas nominal data gets analyzed with mode and ordinal data utilizes both. ✓ Ordinal data can additionally get analyzed utilizing linear trends, univariate statistics, classification methods, bivariate statistics, and regression applications. ✓ To interpret categorical data: • First, we need to organize the data in order from least to greatest. We are given the following data set. • Second, we need to create a frequency table using the given information. The constructed frequency table should look like the following figure. • Last, we will use this information to create a histogram of frequencies.
Example	*Emma went to the shop and bought* 13 *cucumbers,* 3 *oranges,* 4 *bananas and* 6 *melons. What is the mean and mode of her purchase?* *Solution:* To find the mean, count how many numbers are in the group, 5. Then add all the fruits together. Then divide the result by the number of numbers. The mean is 6.5. $$mean = \frac{3+4+6+13}{4} = \frac{26}{4} = 6.5$$ To find mode, find which fruits Emma bought the most, 3, 4, **6**, 13. Emma bought 13 cucumbers, which is more than any other. So, cucumber is the mode.
Your Turn!	1) In a javelin throw competition, five athletes score 55, 49, 58, 55, and 68 meters. What are their mean and mode?
	2) Bob has 8 black pens, 12 red pens, 25 green pens, 14 blue pens, and 3 boxes of yellow pens. If the mean and median are 16 and 14 respectively, what is the number of yellow pens in each box?
	3) At a petting zoo, there were 7 goats, 9 sheep, 2 llamas, 10 ponies, and 12 pigs. Pick the mode of this data set. There may be more than one.
	4) Julia planted some seeds in her garden. The flowers that grew included 15 roses, 13 azaleas, 7 sunflowers, 15 orchids, 9 lilies, and 8 violets. Pick the mode of this data set. There may be more than one. And what is the median?

Topic	Identifying Statistical Questions
Notes	✓ Statistical questions are those you can answer via accumulating data and where there is variability in the data. ✓ This is not the same as a question that foresees a deterministic answer. For instance, "What number of minutes do 6th-grade pupils typically spend on doing homework every week?" is a statistical question. ✓ Therefore, statistical questions are those you can answer via gathering data that varies.
Example	*Is the following a statistical question?* *How much money does Karen spend on groceries in a typical month?* This question can be answered by recording how much money Karen spends on groceries every month. The amount of money she spends probably varies from month to month. So, this is a statistical question. *What is your cousin's favorite Movie?* This question can be answered by a single piece of data. In fact, there is no varied data. So, this is not a statistical question.
Your Turn!	**Determine whether the following questions are statistical or not.**
	1) How many legs does an ant have??
	2) How many hours of sleep do babies get per night?
	3) What day is your sister wedding anniversary?
	4) How much does Jason spend on his house each month?
	5) Which The country's national football team become the first World Cup champion?
	6) How much snowfall does New York typically receive in February?
	7) How many pounds are in one kilogram?
	8) How long is the giraffe's neck?

bit.ly/44stlbx

Topic	Completing a Table and Making a Graph: Word Problems
Notes	✓ You can solve word problems by becoming a detective and searching for clues in the form of keywords and phrases. ✓ Carefully read the text to understand what you are asked to solve. ✓ Write a number sentence then solve it in a single step.
Example	*Complete the table. And graph the data from the table.* *Sue adores her brand-new scented-oil diffuser. She places Three drops of lavender oil in the diffuser every night and it helps her go to sleep.* Figure out the total drops of lavender oil utilized after one night: $1 = 3$, two nights: $2 = 6$, three nights: $3 = 9$, and four nights: $4 = 12$. Utilize the table to write down ordered pairs of numbers. For each pair, write down the number of nights first and then the total number of drops second, $(1,3), (2,6), (3,9), (4,12)$. Then, graph the ordered pairs. Begin with the first pair, $(1,5)$.

Example table:

Nights	Total drops
1	
2	
3	
4	

Your Turn!

Complete the table and graph the equation.

1) Timothy was late to collect apples from the garden. By the time he arrived, his friend Zack had already collected 2 packages. Timothy collected the rest of the apples with Zack.

Timothy	Zack
1	
2	
3	
4	

2) Anne knits 4 gloves in a month. She plans to knit more gloves this month.

Number of months	Total gloves
1	
2	
3	
4	

3) Olivia runs for 20 minutes each day over the summer.

Number of days	Total minutes
1	
2	
3	
4	

4) At the market, melon cost $3 per 5 pounds.

Weight of melon	price
5	
10	
15	
20	

bit.ly/473jMBF

Chapter 18: Answers

Pie Graph

1) $3,880
2) $426.8
3) $1,047.6
4) $698.4
5) $349.2
6) $388

Graph The Line Plot

1)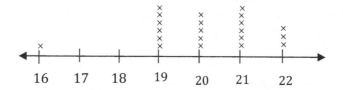

2)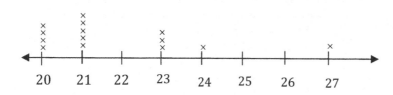

3)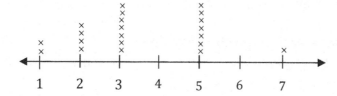

4)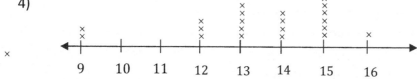

Distributions in Line Plot

1) C, d, k, l, m
2) A, e, j
3) B, g, l, f
4) A, d, h, i

Relative Frequency Tables

1)

Maria's cupcakes				
Various flavors	lemon	coffee	carrot	red velvet
Relative frequency	15%	32.5%	52.5%	25%

2)

Eva's breads			
Breads	Challah	Yeast	Focaccia
Relative frequency	24%	44%	32%

3)

Maximum air temperature during a month				
Temperature	34°C	30°C	29°C	26°C
Relative frequency	20%	10%	20%	50%

4)

Number of cups ordered				
Cup of coffee range	70 − 79	60 − 69	50 − 59	40 − 49
Relative frequency	5%	55%	25%	15%

Frequency Charts

1)

Various cakes	Number of days
1	5
2	4
3	6
4	7
5	4
6	4

3)

Temperatures	Number of days
6°C	7
7°C	3
8°C	4
9°C	6
11°C	1

2)

Fruits	Number of weights
Apple	5
Peaches	9
Banana	11
Pineapple	4
Melon	7

4)

bottles	Number of days
50 − 99	4
100 − 149	7
150 − 199	3
200 − 249	7

Mean, Median, Mode, and Range of the Given Data

1) Mode: 25, Range: 15, Mean: 20, Median: 22

2) Mode: 16, Range: 5, Mean: 18, Median: 18

3) Mode: 5, Range: 9, Mean: 5, Median: 5

4) Mode: 8, Range: 9, Mean: 7, Median: 8

5) Mode: 3, Range: 6, Mean: 4.5, Median: 3.5

6) Mode: 14, Range: 7, Mean: 12.5, Median: 13.5

Interpreting Charts to find mean, median, mode, and range

1) 35
2) 21
3) 35
4) 36
5) 7
6) 7.25
7) 7
8) 9

Finding an Outlier

1) 50
2) 5
3) 123
4) 175
5) 91
6) 1

Finding Range, Quartiles, and Interquartile Range

1) 12
2) 20
3) 4
4) 14
5) 20
6) 85
7) 50
8) 30

Interpreting Categorical Data

1) Mean: 57, Mode: 55
2) 7
3) 10 pigs
4) 15 roses, 15 orchids, Median: 11

Identifying Statistical Questions

1) This is **not** a statistical question.
2) This is a statistical question.
3) This is **not** a statistical question.
4) This is a statistical question.
5) This is **not** a statistical question.
6) This is a statistical question.
7) This is **not** a statistical question.
8) This is a statistical question.

Completing a Table and Making a Graph: Word Problems

1)

Timothy	Zack
1	3
2	4
3	5
4	6

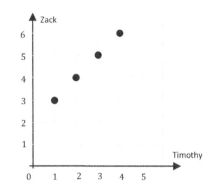

2)

Number of months	Total gloves
1	4
2	8
3	12
4	16

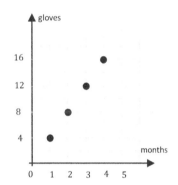

3)

Number of days	Total minutes
1	20
2	40
3	60
4	80

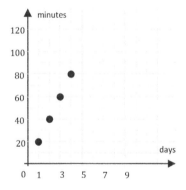

4)

Weight of melon	price
5	3
10	6
15	9
20	12

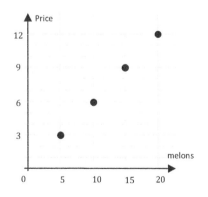

Time to Test

Time to refine your skill with a practice examination

Take a practice MAP Math Test to simulate the test day experience. After you've finished, score your test using the answer key.

Before You Start

- You'll need a pencil and scratch papers to take the test.
- There are two types of questions:

    Multiple choice questions: for each of these questions, there are four or more possible answers. Choose which one is best.

    Grid-ins questions: for these questions, write your answer in the box provided.
- It's okay to guess. You won't lose any points if you're wrong.
- The MAP Mathematics test contains a formula sheet, which displays formulas relating to geometric measurement and certain algebra concepts. Formulas are provided to test- takers so that they may focus on application, rather than the memorization, of formulas.
- After you've finished the test, review the answer key to see where you went wrong and what areas you need to improve.

Good luck!

MAP Grade 6 Math Practice Test 1

2024

Total number of questions: 40

Total time for two parts: 60 minutes

You may use a calculator on this test.

MAP Grade 6 Mathematics Reference Materials

AREA

Triangle $\quad A = \dfrac{1}{2}bh$

Rectangle Parallelogram $\quad A = bh$

Trapezoid $\quad A = \dfrac{1}{2}h(b_1 + b_2)$

VOLUME

Rectangle Prism $\quad V = Bh$

LENGTH

Customary	Metric
1 mile = 1,760 yards (yd)	1 kilometer (km) = 1,000 meter (m)
1 yard = 3 feet (ft)	1 meter (m) = 100 centimeters (cm)
1 foot (ft) = 12 inches (in.)	1 centimeter (cm) = 10 millimeters (mm)

VOLUME AND CAPACITY

Customary	Metric
1 gallon (gal) = 4 quarts (qt)	1 liter (L) = 1,000 millimeters (mL)
1 quart (qt) = 2 pints (pt)	
1 pint (pt) = 2 cups (c)	
1 cup (c) = 8 fluid ounces (fl oz)	

WEIGHT AND MASS

Customary	Metric
1 ton (T) = 2,000 Pounds (lb)	1 kilogram (kg) = 1,000 grams (g)
1 pound (lb) = 16 ounces (oz)	1 gram (g) = 1,000 milligrams (mg)

1) Mira paid $35.28 for 8 gallons of milk. What was the price per gallon of milk?

   [ ]

2) A T-shirt costs $12. Alice has $84. The inequality below can be used to find the number of T-shirts, x, that Alice can buy with $84.

   $$12x \leq 84$$

   Which statement describes all the possible numbers of T-shirts that Alice can buy with $84?

   A. She can buy 5 T-shirts or fewer.

   B. She can buy 7 T-shirts or fewer.

   C. She can buy 12 T-shirts or fewer.

   D. She can buy 96 T-shirts or fewer.

3) The temperature in Anchorage, Alaska on the coldest day in October was -5 degrees Fahrenheit. If the coldest day in Anchorage in November was colder than this, which of the following could be its possible temperature in degrees Fahrenheit?

   A. -3

   B. 5

   C. 0

   D. -6

4) Abby has a rectangular room that is 14 feet wide and 18 feet long. She wants to add a border of carpeting around the room, extending 1 foot out from each side. What will be the area of the room and the carpet border combined?

   A. 320 square feet

   B. 572 square feet

   C. 856 square feet

   D. 1024 square feet

5) A school cafeteria sold 10 pizzas for $12 each and collected $60 for the school fund. The total cost was paid using the school's debit card. The change in the balance of the school's account can be represented by the expression shown: $10(-12) + (-60)$

   Which integer represents the change in the balance of the school's account due to the sale of pizzas?

   A. -120

   B. -48

   C. -180

   D. -240

6) A juice maker mixed 3 cups of orange juice with every 4 cups of apple juice to make a fruit juice blend. Which ratio of cups of orange juice to cups of apple juice will make the same fruit juice blend?

   A. $5:8$

   B. $12:20$

   C. $24:32$

   D. $6:12$

7) What is the perimeter of the following parallelogram?

   A. $30\ m$

   B. $34\ m$

   C. $66\ m$

   D. $88\ m$

   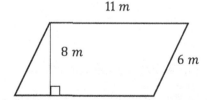

8) In a survey, the number of hours per week that 6 individuals spent exercising were: $2, 3, 5, 6, 8, 10$. Which statement is true about the mean, median, and range of the number of hours spent exercising?

   A. The median is greater than the mean, and the range is 8.

   B. The mean is greater than the median, and the range is 8.

   C. The median is greater than the mean, and the range is 7.

   D. The mean is greater than the median, and the range is 7.

9) What is the value of x that satisfies the equation: $3x - \frac{1}{2} = \frac{7}{2}$?

   A. $x = \frac{4}{3}$

   B. $x = 2$

   C. $x = \frac{3}{4}$

   D. $x = \frac{5}{2}$

10) What is the area of the shaded region?

    A. $98\ ft^2$

    B. $102\ ft^2$

    C. $144\ ft^2$

    D. $168\ ft^2$

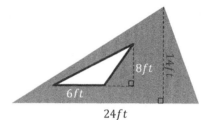

11) The fractions below represent the lengths of 5 different ropes in feet:

    $$\frac{3}{7}, \frac{1}{2}, \frac{2}{3}, \frac{1}{4}, \frac{4}{5}$$

    Which list shows the lengths of the ropes in order from least to greatest?

    A. $\frac{1}{4}, \frac{3}{7}, \frac{1}{2}, \frac{2}{3}, \frac{4}{5}$

    B. $\frac{2}{3}, \frac{1}{2}, \frac{1}{4}, \frac{3}{7}, \frac{4}{5}$

    C. $\frac{1}{2}, \frac{2}{3}, \frac{1}{4}, \frac{4}{5}, \frac{3}{7}$

    D. $\frac{4}{5}, \frac{3}{7}, \frac{1}{4}, \frac{1}{2}, \frac{2}{3}$

12) John made an extra $500 for selling phones. The extra $500 was 10% of the total value of the phones he sold. What was the total value of the phones John sold?

    A. $4,500

    B. $5,000

    C. $4,545

    D. $5,500

13) During a 120-minute orchestra concert, the pianist was on stage 40% of the time. What amount of time in minutes was the pianist on stage?

A. 48 minutes

B. 72 minutes

C. 60 minutes

D. 32 minutes

14) What is the volume of the following rectangle prism?

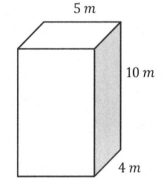

15) John is planning to build a rectangular garden bed in his backyard. He creates a Cartesian coordinate plane to help him decide the dimensions of the bed. He places one corner of the garden bed at (2,3) and the opposite corner at (10,3). If each unit is equal to 2 feet, what is the width of the garden bed in feet?

A. 4 feet

B. 8 feet

C. 6 feet

D. 16 feet

16) What is the prime factorization of 48?

A. $2 \times 2 \times 2 \times 6$

B. $2 \times 2 \times 2 \times 3 \times 2$

C. $2 \times 3 \times 8$

D. 3×16

17) Which set of angle measures CANNOT be the angle measures of a triangle?

   A. $60°, 59°, 61°$

   B. $60°, 60°, 61°$

   C. $150°, 10°, 20°$

   D. $1°, 2°, 177°$

18) According to the line plot, which statement below is correct?

   A. There is an outlier at 10.

   B. The data distribution has no gaps.

   C. The smallest number is -20 and the greatest is 20.

   D. There is a peak at -10

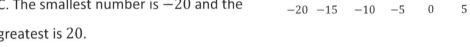

19) Point A is located on the coordinate grid at $(100.5, -\frac{4}{5})$. In which quadrant is point A located?

   A. Quadrant I

   B. Quadrant II

   C. Quadrant III

   D. Quadrant IV

20) What is the value of $7x + 9$, when $x = 8$?

   A. 47

   B. 56

   C. 65

   D. 70

21) The area of a triangle is 48 square inches. The base of the triangle is 8 inches. What is the height of the triangle in inches?

   A. $12\ in$

   B. $14\ in$

   C. $16\ in$

   D. $17\ in$

22) What is the area of the trapezoid given below?

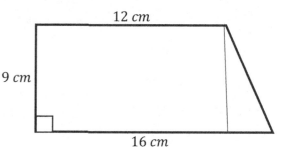

A. $100\ cm^2$

B. $126\ cm^2$

C. $144\ cm^2$

D. $108\ cm^2$

23) 6,000 inches equal to ...?

A. $72,000\ ft$

B. $500\ ft$

C. $50\ ft$

D. $60\ ft$

24) $6(2.123) - 5.387 = \cdots?$

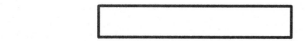

25) A runner records her change of times, in second, for the last four laps around a track as shown below: $-4.2, 3.5, -3.8, 2.7$. Which list correctly compares the times, in seconds, for the four laps?

A. $-4.2 < -3.8 < 2.7 < 3.5$

B. $-3.8 < -4.2 < 2.7 < 3.5$

C. $-4.2 < 2.7 < -3.8 < 3.5$

D. $3.5 < 2.7 < -3.8 < -4.2$

26) Which of the following statements describes this expression?

$$5b - 12$$

A. The expression represents 5 times b minus 12.

B. The expression represents 5 minus b minus 12.

C. The expression represents the product of $5, b,$ and 12.

D. The expression represents the sum of 5 and 12, with b as a variable.

27) Which ordered pair describes point A that is shown below?

A. $(3, -4)$

B. $(-4, 3)$

C. $(-3, 4)$

D. $(4, -3)$

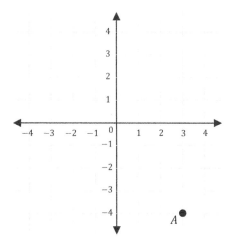

28) Which of the following expressions is equivalent to $7(2w + 4)$?

A. $14w + 11$

B. $9w + 7$

C. $14w + 28$

D. $7w + 11$

29) Which number line represents the solution to $2x - 3 > -1$?

A.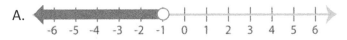

B.

C.

D.

30) Mark and Sarah are both swimming in a pool. Mark can swim 200 meters in 5 minutes, while Sarah can swim 150 meters in 4 minutes. Which of the following statements is NOT true?

A. Mark can swim 400 meters in 10 minutes.

B. Sarah can swim 225 meters in 6 minutes.

C. Mark can swim 500 meters farther than Sarah in 20 minutes.

D. Sarah can swim 300 meters in 8 minutes.

31) 5×10^{-3} is equal to

   A. 0.005

   B. 5,000

   C. 0.05

   D. 50×10

32) The following triangles are similar. What is the value of the unknown side?

   A. 12

   B. 6

   C. 10

   D. 8

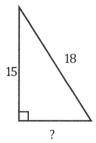
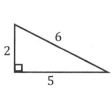

33) If $5x + 2 = 19.5$, what is the value of $3x + 20$?

34) A company produced 450 units in 6 hours. How many units can the company produce in 8 hours if they work at the same rate?

   A. 500 units

   B. 600 units

   C. 650 units

   D. 720 units

35) A bottle contains 20 fluid ounces of shampoo. How many cups of shampoo does the bottle contain?

   A. 2 cups

   B. 2.5 cups

   C. 1.25 cups

   D. 1.5 cups

36) Which point represents the value of $\left|-\frac{14}{4}\right|$?

   A. A

   B. B

   C. C

   D. D

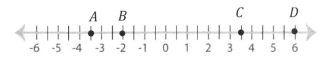

37) Maria has $1000 in her bank account. She wants to spend part of this money on a new laptop. She wants to have at least $400 left in her account after buying the laptop. Which inequality represents all possible values of t, the amount of money in dollars that Maria can spend on the laptop?

   A. $t \leq 400$

   B. $t \geq 400$

   C. $t \leq 600$

   D. $t \geq 600$

38) What is the value of $\frac{3}{7}$ divided by $\frac{2}{5}$?

   A. $\frac{15}{16}$

   B. $\frac{14}{15}$

   C. $\frac{6}{35}$

   D. $\frac{15}{14}$

39) What percentage of the shape is shaded?

   A. 44%

   B. 95%

   C. 88%

   D. 90%

40) Which of the following values of x makes this inequality true? $3x - 5 < 13$

A. 6

B. 8

C. 9

D. 0

This is the end of Practice Test 1

MAP Grade 6 Math Practice Test 2

2024

Total number of questions: 40

Total time for two parts: 60 minutes

You may use a calculator on this test.

MAP Grade 6 Mathematics Reference Materials

AREA

Triangle	$A = \dfrac{1}{2}bh$
Rectangle Parallelogram	$A = bh$
Trapezoid	$A = \dfrac{1}{2}h(b_1 + b_2)$

VOLUME

Rectangle Prism	$V = Bh$

LENGTH

Customary	Metric
1 mile = 1,760 yards (yd)	1 kilometer (km) = 1,000 meter (m)
1 yard = 3 feet (ft)	1 meter (m) = 100 centimeters (cm)
1 foot (ft) = 12 inches (in.)	1 centimeter (cm) = 10 millimeters (mm)

VOLUME AND CAPACITY

Customary	Metric
1 gallon (gal) = 4 quarts (qt)	1 liter (L) = 1,000 millimeters (mL)
1 quart (qt) = 2 pints (pt)	
1 pint (pt) = 2 cups (c)	
1 cup (c) = 8 fluid ounces (fl oz)	

WEIGHT AND MASS

Customary	Metric
1 ton (T) = 2,000 Pounds (lb)	1 kilogram (kg) = 1,000 grams (g)
1 pound (lb) = 16 ounces (oz)	1 gram (g) = 1,000 milligrams (mg)

1) Which expression is equivalent to $5(12x - 16)$?

   A. -20

   B. $-20x$

   C. $60x - 16$

   D. $60x - 80$

2) Which ordered pair describes point A that is shown below?

   A. $(-1, 2)$

   B. $(2, -1)$

   C. $(1, -2)$

   D. $(-2, 1)$

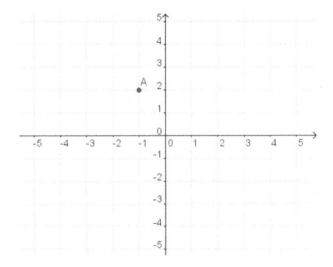

3) To produce a special concrete, for every $13 kg$ of cement, 3 liters of water is required. Which of the following ratios is the same as the ratio of cement to liters of water?

   A. $91 : 21$

   B. $14 : 4$

   C. $39 : 6$

   D. $9 : 39$

4) Find the opposite of the numbers $15, 0$.

5) What is the value of x in the following equation? $-60 = 115 - x$

   A. 175

   B. −175

   C. 55

   D. −55

6) Which of the following graphs represents the following inequality?

   $$-8 \leq 5x - 8 < 2$$

   A.

   B.

   C.

   D.

7) The ratio of boys to girls in a school is 4: 5. If there are 765 students in the school, how many boys are in the school?

   A. 612

   B. 510

   C. 425

   D. 340

8) Martin earns $20 an hour. Which of the following inequalities represents the amount of time Martin needs to work per day to earn at least $100 per day?

   A. $20t \geq 100$

   B. $20t \leq 100$

   C. $20 + t \geq 100$

   D. $20 + t \leq 100$

9) $(55 + 5) \div 12$ is equivalent to ...

   A. $60 \div 3.4$

   B. $\frac{55}{12} + 5$

   C. $(2 \times 2 \times 3 \times 5) \div (3 \times 4)$

   D. $(2 \times 2 \times 3 \times 5) \div 3 + 4$

10) What is the value of the expression $6(2x - 3y) + (3 - 2x)^2$, when $x = 2$ and $y = -1$?

    A. -23

    B. 41

    C. 43

    D. 49

11) Round $\frac{215}{7}$ to the nearest tenth.

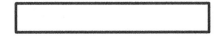

12) A chemical solution contains 6% alcohol. If there is $45 ml$ of alcohol, what is the volume of the solution?

    A. $270\ ml$

    B. $420\ ml$

    C. $750\ ml$

    D. $1,200\ ml$

13) What is the equation of a line that passes through points $(0, 4)$ and $(2, 8)$?

A. $y = x$

B. $y = x + 4$

C. $y = 2x + 4$

D. $y = 2x - 4$

14) What is the volume of a box with the following dimensions?

Height $= 6\ cm$ Width $= 7\ cm$ Length $= 9\ cm$

A. $63\ cm^3$

B. $126\ cm^3$

C. $189\ cm^3$

D. $378\ cm^3$

15) Anita's trick–or–treat bag contains 14 pieces of chocolate, 15 suckers, 16 pieces of gum, and 20 pieces of licorice. If she randomly pulls a piece of candy from her bag, what is the probability of her pulling out a sucker?

A. $\frac{1}{13}$

B. $\frac{3}{13}$

C. $\frac{14}{65}$

D. $\frac{16}{65}$

16) In the following rectangle, which statement is false?

A. AD is parallel to BC

B. The measure of the sum of all the angles equals $360°$.

C. Length of AB equal to length DC.

D. AB is perpendicular to AC.

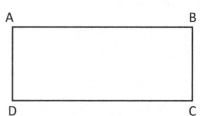

17) The area of a rectangular yard is 90 square meters. What is its width if its length is 15 meters?

   A. 10 meters

   B. 8 meters

   C. 6 meters

   D. 4 meters

18) Which statement about 4 multiplied by $\frac{3}{5}$ must be true?

   A. The product is between 1 and 2

   B. The product is greater than 3

   C. The product is equal to $\frac{75}{31}$

   D. The product is between 2 and 2.5

19) Which of the following lists shows the fractions in order from least to greatest?

$$\frac{3}{4}, \frac{2}{7}, \frac{3}{8}, \frac{5}{11}$$

   A. $\frac{3}{8}, \frac{2}{7}, \frac{3}{4}, \frac{5}{11}$

   B. $\frac{2}{7}, \frac{5}{11}, \frac{3}{8}, \frac{3}{4}$

   C. $\frac{2}{7}, \frac{3}{8}, \frac{5}{11}, \frac{3}{4}$

   D. $\frac{3}{8}, \frac{2}{7}, \frac{5}{11}, \frac{3}{4}$

20) A car costing $300 is discounted 10%. Which of the following expressions can be used to find the selling price of the car?

   A. $(300)(0.4)$

   B. $300 - (300 \times 0.1)$

   C. $(300)(0.1)$

   D. $300 - (300 \times 0.9)$

21) What is the missing price factor of number 420?

$$420 = 2^2 \times 3^1 \times 5^1 \times \ldots$$

Write your answer in the box below.

22) What is the area of the trapezoid below?

A. 84 cm

B. 98 cm

C. 148 cm

D. 172 cm

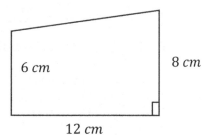

23) By what factor did the number below change from the first to the fourth number?

$$8, 104, 1{,}352, 17{,}576$$

A. 13

B. 96

C. 1,456

D. 17,568

24) 170 is equal to …

A. $-20 - (3 \times 10) + (6 \times 40)$

B. $\left(\frac{15}{8} \times 72\right) + \left(\frac{125}{5}\right)$

C. $\left(\left(\frac{30}{4} + \frac{15}{2}\right) \times 8\right) - \frac{11}{2} + \frac{222}{4}$

D. $\frac{481}{6} + \frac{121}{3} + 50$

25) The distance between the two cities is 3,768 feet. What is the distance between the two cities in yards?

A. 1,256 yd.

B. 11,304 yd.

C. 45,216 yd.

D. 3,768 yd.

26) Mr. Jones saves $3,400 out of his monthly family income of $74,800. What fractional part of his income does Mr. Jones save?

   A. $\frac{1}{22}$

   B. $\frac{1}{11}$

   C. $\frac{3}{25}$

   D. $\frac{2}{15}$

27) What is the lowest common multiple of 12 and 20?

   A. 60

   B. 40

   C. 20

   D. 12

28) Based on the table below, which expression represents any value of f in terms of its corresponding value of x?

   A. $f = 2x - \frac{3}{10}$

   B. $f = x + \frac{3}{10}$

   C. $f = 2x + 2\frac{2}{5}$

   D. $f = 2x + \frac{3}{10}$

x	3.1	4.2	5.9
f	8.6	10.8	14.2

29) $96 kg = ...$?

   A. $96\ mg$

   B. $9,600\ mg$

   C. $960,000\ mg$

   D. $96,000,000\ mg$

30) What percentage of the shape is shaded?

A. 78%

B. 72%

C. 88%

D. 84%

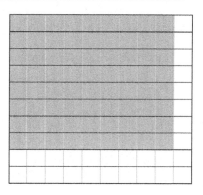

31) The following graph shows the mark of seven students in mathematics. What is the mean (average) of the marks?

A. 13

B. 13.5

C. 14

D. 1.5

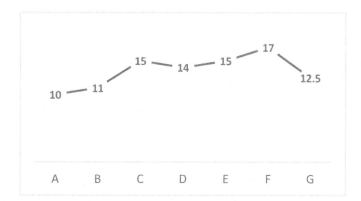

32) Which of the following statements is correct, according to the graph below?

A. The number of books sold in April was twice the number of books sold in July.

B. The number of books sold in July was less than half the number of books sold in May.

C. The number of books sold in June was more than half the number of books sold in April.

D. The number of books sold in July was equal to the number of books sold in April plus the number of books sold in June.

33) What is the ratio between α and β $\left(\frac{\alpha}{\beta}\right)$ in the following shape?

A. $\frac{5}{14}$

B. $\frac{5}{13}$

C. $\frac{13}{5}$

D. $\frac{14}{5}$

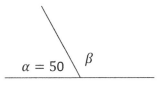

34) When point $A(-5, 4)$ is reflected over the $y-$axis to get point B, what are the coordinates of point B?

A. $(-5, -4)$

B. $(5, -4)$

C. $(5, 4)$

D. $(-5, 4)$

35) In a certain bookshelf of a library, there are 25 biology books, 110 history books, and 65 language books. What is the ratio of the number of biology books to the total number of books on this bookshelf?

A. $\frac{1}{4}$

B. $\frac{1}{8}$

C. $\frac{2}{7}$

D. $\frac{3}{8}$

36) Which of the following is the correct statement?

A. $\frac{3}{4} < 0.7$

B. $25\% = \frac{1}{2}$

C. $6 < \frac{11}{2}$

D. $\frac{4}{5} > 0.7$

37) Daniel is 66 years old, twice as old as Henry. How old is Henry?

[   ]

38) An integer is chosen at random from 1 to 30. Find the probability of not selecting a composite number.

A. $\frac{13}{30}$

B. $\frac{6}{15}$

C. $\frac{11}{30}$

D. $\frac{1}{3}$

39) Which of the following statements can be used for the following inequality?

$$\frac{x}{8} \leq 16$$

A. Sara placed x pens among 16 friends and each friend received fewer than 8 pens.

B. Sara placed 8 pens among x friends and each friend received at most 16 pens.

C. Sara placed x pens among 8 friends and each friend received fewer than 16 pens.

D. Sara placed x pens among 8 friends and each friend received at most 16 pens.

40) If the area of the following rectangular $ABCD$ is 140, and E is the midpoint of AB, what is the area of the shaded part?

A. 100

B. 70

C. 50

D. 60

This is the end of Practice Test 2

MAP Grade 6 Math Practice Tests Answer Keys

Now, it's time to review your results to see where you went wrong and what areas you need to improve!

	MAP Math Practice Test 1				MAP Math Practice Test 2		
1	4.41	**21**	A	**1**	D	**21**	7
2	B	**22**	B	**2**	A	**22**	A
3	D	**23**	B	**3**	A	**23**	A
4	A	**24**	7.351	**4**	−15,0	**24**	C
5	C	**25**	A	**5**	A	**25**	A
6	C	**26**	A	**6**	B	**26**	A
7	B	**27**	A	**7**	D	**27**	A
8	B	**28**	C	**8**	A	**28**	C
9	A	**29**	D	**9**	C	**29**	D
10	C	**30**	C	**10**	C	**30**	B
11	A	**31**	A	**11**	30.7	**31**	B
12	B	**32**	B	**12**	C	**32**	C
13	A	**33**	30.5	**13**	C	**33**	B
14	200	**34**	B	**14**	D	**34**	C
15	D	**35**	B	**15**	B	**35**	B
16	B	**36**	C	**16**	D	**36**	D
17	B	**37**	C	**17**	C	**37**	33
18	D	**38**	D	**18**	D	**38**	C
19	D	**39**	C	**19**	C	**39**	D
20	C	**40**	D	**20**	B	**40**	B

MAP Grade 6 Math Practice Tests Answers and Explanations

MAP Grade 6 Math Practice Test 1
Answers and Explanations

1) The answer is 4.41

To find the price per gallon of milk, we need to divide the total price by the number of gallons:

$price\ per\ gallon = \frac{total\ price}{number\ of\ gallons}$

Substituting the given values, we get:

$price\ per\ gallon = \frac{\$35.28}{8\ gallons} \rightarrow price\ per\ gallon = \$4.41$

Therefore, the price per gallon of milk was $4.41.

So, the answer is $4.41.

2) Choice B is correct

We can solve the inequality by dividing both sides by 12: $x \leq 7$

This means that Alice can buy 7 T-shirts or fewer with $84. Therefore, the answer is B. She can buy 7 T-shirts or fewer. Options A, C, and D are incorrect because they do not represent the correct upper limit of the number of T-shirts that Alice can buy for $84.

3) Choice D is correct

We are told that the coldest day in November was colder than -5 Fahrenheit. The only temperature value that is lower than -5 degrees Fahrenheit is -6 degrees Fahrenheit.

4) Choice A is correct

To find the area of the room and the carpet border combined, we first need to calculate the dimensions of the expanded rectangle. If the border extends 1 foot out from each side, the new width of the rectangle will be $14\ feet + 2(1\ foot) = 16\ feet$, and the new length will be $18\ feet + 2(1\ foot) = 20\ feet$.

The area of the room alone is $14\ feet \times 18\ feet = 252\ square\ feet$. The area of the expanded rectangle (room and border combined) will be:

$(16\ feet) \times (20\ feet) = 320\ square\ feet$

5) Choice C is correct

To solve this problem, we can multiply the cost of each pizza by the number of pizzas sold and then subtract the amount collected for the school fund: $10(-12) + (-60) = -120 - 60 = -180$

Therefore, the change in the balance of the school's account is -180 dollars. The answer is (C).

6) Choice C is correct

We can start by finding the ratio of cups of orange juice to cups of apple juice in the original fruit juice blend. For every 3 cups of orange juice, the juice maker used 4 cups of apple juice. So, the ratio of cups of orange juice to cups of apple juice is $3:4$.

To make the same fruit juice blend, we need to keep the same ratio of cups of orange juice to cups of apple juice. Let's check each answer choice and see if it has the same ratio of cups of orange juice to cups of apple juice:

A. $5:8$ - which is not the same ratio as $3:4$.

B. $12:20$ - This simplifies to $3:5$, which is not the same ratio as $3:4$.

C. $24:32$ - This simplifies to $3:4$, which is the same ratio as the original fruit juice blend.

D. $6:12$ - This simplifies to $1:2$, which is not the same ratio as $3:4$.

Therefore, the answer is (C) $24:32$.

7) Choice B is correct

The perimeter of a parallelogram $= 2(l + w)$

The perimeter of a parallelogram $= 2(11 + 6) = 2(17) = 34\ m$

8) Choice B is correct

The mean of the data is $\frac{2+3+5+6+8+10}{6} = 5.67$, which is greater than the median of the data, which is 5.5. The range of the data is $10 - 2 = 8$.

9) Choice A is correct

The given equation is $3x - \frac{1}{2} = \frac{7}{2}$.

To find the value of x that satisfies this equation, we need to isolate x on one side of the equation by performing operations to cancel out the constants. First, we can add $\frac{1}{2}$ to both sides of the equation to get: $3x - \frac{1}{2} + \frac{1}{2} = \frac{7}{2} + \frac{1}{2}$,

Simplifying this gives: $3x = \frac{8}{2} = 4$

Next, we can isolate x by dividing both sides of the equation by 3: $\frac{3x}{3} = \frac{4}{3}$

Simplifying this gives: $x = \frac{4}{3}$

Therefore, the value of x that satisfies the given equation is $x = \frac{4}{3}$.

10) Choice C is correct

First, find the area of each triangle. Then subtract the area of the inner triangle from the area of the outer triangle. The area of the inner triangle, $\frac{1}{2} \times 8 \times 6 = 24\ ft^2$. The area of the outer triangle, $\frac{1}{2} \times 24 \times 14 = 168\ ft^2$.

To find the shaded area, $168 - 24 = 144\ ft^2$.

So, the area of the shaded region is 144 square feet.

11) Choice A is correct

To put the fractions in order from least to greatest, we need to find a common denominator for the fractions and then compare the numerators. One way to find a common denominator is to multiply the denominators of all the fractions together.

The denominators are 7, 2, 3, 4, and 5, which have a common multiple of 420. We can convert each fraction to have a denominator of 420 by multiplying both the numerator and denominator by a suitable factor:

$$\frac{3}{7} = \frac{180}{420}, \frac{1}{2} = \frac{210}{420}, \frac{2}{3} = \frac{280}{420}, \frac{1}{4} = \frac{105}{420}, \frac{4}{5} = \frac{336}{420}$$

Now we can compare the numerators to put the fractions in order from least to greatest:

$$\frac{105}{420} < \frac{180}{420} < \frac{210}{420} < \frac{280}{420} < \frac{336}{420}$$

Converting these back to fractions, we get: $\frac{1}{4} < \frac{3}{7} < \frac{1}{2} < \frac{2}{3} < \frac{4}{5}$

Therefore, the correct list of the lengths of the ropes in order from least to greatest is A.

12) Choice B is correct

To find the total value of the phones John sold, we can use the information provided in the problem. We know that the extra $500 he made was 10% of the total value of the phones he sold.

www.EffortlessMath.com

Let's start by setting up an equation to represent this information. We can use "x" to represent the total value of the phones he sold: 10% of x = $500

To solve for x, we need to isolate the variable. We can do this by dividing both sides of the equation by 10% (which is the same as dividing by 0.1): x = $500 ÷ 10%

To divide by 10%, we need to convert it to a decimal by moving the decimal point two places to the left: x = $500 ÷ 0.1 → x = $5,000

Therefore, the total value of the phones John sold was $5,000. The answer is B.

13) Choice A is correct

To find the amount of time the pianist was on stage, we need to calculate 40% of 120 minutes:

40% of 120 minutes = $\left(\frac{40}{100}\right)$ × 120 minutes = 48 minutes

14) The answer is 200

Use volume formula: $Volume = l \times w \times h$

Then: $Volume = 10 \times 5 \times 4 = 200 \ m^3$

15) Choice D is correct

To find the width of the garden bed, we need to calculate the distance between the x−coordinates of the two corners. In this case, the x−coordinates are 2 and 10. The distance between them is:

$10 - 2 = 8$

Since each unit on the Cartesian coordinate plane is equal to 2 feet, the width of the garden bed is $8 \times 2 = 16$ feet.

Therefore, the answer is option D, 16 feet.

16) Choice B is correct

The prime factorization of a number is the unique representation of that number as a product of prime numbers. To find the prime factorization of 48, we need to factor it into its prime factors.

We can start by dividing 48 by the smallest prime number, which is 2. We get:

$$48 \div 2 = 24$$

So, 2 is a factor of 48. Now, we divide 24 by 2 again: $24 \div 2 = 12$

So, 2 is a factor of 48 twice. Next, we divide 12 by 2: $12 \div 2 = 6$

So, 2 is a factor of 48 three times.

Continuing with the factorization, we divide 6 by 2:

$$6 \div 2 = 3$$

Now, we have obtained a prime number, so we stop. The prime factorization of 48 is therefore:

$$48 = 2 \times 2 \times 2 \times 2 \times 3$$

We can also write this as: $48 = 2^4 \times 3$

Therefore, the correct answer is B. $2 \times 2 \times 2 \times 3 \times 2$.

17) Choice B is correct

The sum of the interior angles of a triangle is 180 degrees. Among the options, the sum is equal to 180 degrees except for option B:

$60° + 60° + 61° = 181°$

So, option B is the answer to the question.

18) Choice D is correct

There is an × in the column for 15, and it is far away from the rest of the ×s. So, there is an outlier at 15. The smallest number is −20 and the greatest is 15.

The column for −10 has the most ×s. So, there is a peak at −10, which is the mode of this data.

There are no ×s in the columns for 0 to 10. So, there is a gap from 0 to 10.

Therefore, the correct answer is D.

19) Choice D is correct

We know that in Quadrant IV, the x−coordinate is positive and the y−coordinate is negative. Point A has a positive x−coordinate and a negative y−coordinate, which means it is located in Quadrant IV. Therefore, options A, B, and C can be eliminated.

The correct answer is D: Quadrant IV.

20) Choice C is correct

Substituting the value of x in the given expression, we get $7(8) + 9$, which simplifies to $56 + 9 = 65$. Therefore, the value of $7x + 9$, when $x = 8$, is 65.

21) Choice A is correct

Let x be the height of the triangle, then use this formula:

$A = \frac{b \times h}{2} \rightarrow 48 = \frac{8 \times x}{2} \rightarrow 8x = 96 \rightarrow x = 12 \ in$

22) Choice B is correct

Area of a trapezoid: $\frac{a+b}{2} \times h = \frac{12+16}{2} \times 9 = 126 \ cm^2$

23) Choice B is correct

1 feet = 12 inches. Then: $6{,}000 \ in \times \frac{1 \ ft}{12 \ in} = \frac{6{,}000}{12} ft = 500 \ ft$

24) The answer is 7.351

$6(2.123) - 5.387 = 12.73 - 5.387 = 7.351$

25) Choice A is correct

The given list of lap times is: $-4.2, 3.5, -3.8, 2.7$. To compare the lap times, we need to arrange them in ascending or descending order. The correct order is: $-4.2 < -3.8 < 2.7 < 3.5$

Therefore, the answer is A. $-4.2 < -3.8 < 2.7 < 3.5$, which is the only option that has the correct order of lap times.

26) Choice A is correct

In the expression $5b - 12$, the coefficient 5 is multiplying the variable b, and the minus sign indicates that 12 is being subtracted from the product of 5 and b. Therefore, the expression represents 5 times b minus 12.

27) Choice A is correct

The coordinate plane has two axes. The vertical line is called the y −axis and the horizontal line is called the x −axis. The points on the coordinate plane are specified using the form (x, y). Point A is three units to the right of the origin on the of the x −axis, therefore its x −value is 3 and it is four units down, therefore its y −value is -4. The coordinate of the point is: $(3, -4)$

28) Choice C is correct

To simplify the expression $7(2w + 4)$, we can distribute the 7 to both terms inside the parentheses:

$7(2w + 4) = 7(2w) + 7(4) = 14w + 28$

Therefore, the expression that is equivalent to $7(2w + 4)$ is option (C) $14w + 28$.

29) Choice D is correct

Add 1 to both sides of $2x - 3 > -1$: $2x - 3 + 3 > -1 + 3 \rightarrow 2x > 2$

Divide both sides of $2x > 2$ by 2: $x > 1$

30) Choice C is correct

The question provides information about the swimming rates of Mark and Sarah, who are both swimming in a pool. Mark can swim 200 meters in 5 minutes, which means he can swim 400 meters in 10 minutes, 600 meters in 15 minutes, and so on. Sarah, on the other hand, can swim 150 meters in 4 minutes, which means she can swim 225 meters in 6 minutes, 300 meters in 8 minutes, and so on.

Now, we need to identify the statement that is NOT true. Let's consider each option:

A. Mark can swim 400 meters in 10 minutes.

This statement is true. Mark's rate is given as 200 meters in 5 minutes, so he can swim 400 meters in 10 minutes.

B. Sarah can swim 225 meters in 6 minutes. This statement is true.

C. Mark can swim 500 meters farther than Sarah in 20 minutes.

This statement is NOT true. We need to calculate the distance covered by Mark and Sarah in 20 minutes to determine if this statement is true or not.

Mark can swim 200 meters in 5 minutes, so in 20 minutes, he can swim 800 meters. Sarah can swim 150 meters in 4 minutes, so in 20 minutes, she can swim 750 meters. Therefore, Mark can swim $800 - 750 = 50$ meters farther than Sarah in 20 minutes, not 500 meters.

D. Sarah can swim 300 meters in 8 minutes.

This statement is true. Sarah's rate is given as 150 meters in 4 minutes, so she can swim 300 meters in 8 minutes. Therefore, the statement that is NOT true is C.

31) Choice A is correct
$5 \times 10^{-3} = 0.005$

32) Choice B is correct
Find the corresponding sides and write a proportion.

$\frac{6}{18} = \frac{2}{x}$. Now, use the cross-product to solve for x:

$\frac{6}{18} = \frac{2}{x} \rightarrow 6 \times x = 18 \times 2 \rightarrow 6x = 36$.

Divide both sides by 6. Then: $6x = 36 \rightarrow x = \frac{36}{6} \rightarrow x = 6$

The missing side is 6.

33) The answer is 30.5

$5x + 2 = 19.5 \rightarrow 5x = 19.5 - 2 = 17.5 \rightarrow x = \frac{17.5}{5} = 3.5$

Then, $3x + 20 = 3(3.5) + 20 = 10.5 + 20 = 30.5$

34) Choice B is correct

If the company produced 450 units in 6 hours, then they produced 75 units per hour $\left(\frac{450 \text{ units}}{6 \text{ hours}} = 75 \frac{units}{hour}\right)$. To find out how many units they can produce in 8 hours, we multiply the rate by the time: $75 \frac{units}{hour} \times 8 \text{ hours} = 600 \text{ units}$.

35) Choice B is correct

Since there are 8 fluid ounces in a cup, we can convert 20 fluid ounces to cups by dividing by 8:

$20 \div 8 = 2.5$

Therefore, the bottle contains 2.5 cups of shampoo.

36) Choice C is correct

$\left|-\frac{14}{4}\right| = \frac{14}{4} = \frac{7}{2} = 3.5$. Point C represents the value of $\left|-\frac{14}{4}\right|$.

37) Choice C is correct

The given inequality, $t + 400 \leq 1,000$, tells us that the sum of the amount of money that Maria can spend on the laptop and the minimum amount she wants to have left in her account cannot exceed the amount of money she has in her account. To find all possible values of t, we need to isolate t on one side of the inequality by subtracting 400 from both sides:

$t + 400 - 400 \leq 1,000 - 400 \rightarrow t \leq 600$

Therefore, the possible values of t are less than or equal to 600. Therefore, the answer is C.

38) Choice D is correct

To divide fractions, you multiply the first fraction by the reciprocal of the second fraction.

So, $\frac{3}{7}$ divided by $\frac{2}{5}$ is the same as $\frac{3}{7}$ multiplied by $\frac{5}{2}$, which is $\frac{3}{7} \times \frac{5}{2} = \frac{15}{14}$.

Therefore, the value of $\frac{3}{7}$ divided by $\frac{2}{5}$ is $\frac{15}{14}$.

39) Choice C is correct

This shape is 50 parts, and 44 of the parts are shaded. Then to write 44 out of 50 as a percentage:

$\frac{44}{50} = \frac{44 \times 2}{50 \times 2} = \frac{88}{100} = 0.88 = 88\%$

40) Choice D is correct

The given inequality is: $3x - 5 < 13$

To find out which value of x satisfies this inequality, we need to isolate the variable x on one side of the inequality sign.

First, we add 5 to both sides of the inequality to eliminate the constant term on the left side: $3x - 5 + 5 < 13 + 5$

This simplifies to: $3x < 18$

Next, we divide both sides of the inequality by 3 to isolate the variable x: $\frac{3x}{3} < \frac{18}{3}$

This simplifies to: $x < 6$

Therefore, any value of x less than 6 would make the inequality true.

MAP Grade 6 Math Practice Test 2
Answers and Explanations

1) Choice D is correct

$5(12x - 16) = (5 \times 12x) - (5 \times 16) = (5 \times 12)x - (5 \times 16) = 60x - 80$

2) Choice A is correct

The coordinate plane has two axes. The vertical line is called the y-axis and the horizontal line is called the x-axis. The points on the coordinate plane are addressed using the form (x, y). Point A is one unit on the left side of the x-axis, therefore its x-value is -1 and it is two units up, therefore its y-value is 2. The coordinate of the point is: $(-1, 2)$

3) Choice A is correct

$91 :: 21 = 13 :: 3$

$13 \times 7 = 91$ and $3 \times 7 = 21$

4) The answer is −15, 0.

The opposite number of any number x is a number that if added to x, the result is 0. Then:

$15 + (−15) = 0$ and $0 + 0 = 0$

5) Choice A is correct

$−60 = 115 − x$. First, subtract 115 from both sides of the equation. Then: $−60 − 115 = 115 − 115 − x → −175 = −x$. Multiply both sides by $(−1)$: $x = 175$

6) Choice B is correct

$−8 ≤ 5x − 8 < 2 →$ (Add 8 to all sides): $−8 + 8 ≤ 5x − 8 + 8 < 2 + 8 → 0 ≤ 5x < 10 →$ (Divide all sides by 5): $0 ≤ x < 2$

7) Choice D is correct

The ratio of boy to girls is $4:5$. Therefore, there are 4 boys out of 9 students. To find the answer, first divide the total number of students by 9, then multiply the result by 4.

$$765 ÷ 9 = 85 → 85 × 4 = 340$$

8) Choice A is correct

For one hour he earns $20, then for t hours he earns $20t$. If he wants to earn at least $100, therefore, the number of working hours multiplied by 20 must be equal to 100 or greater than 100. $20t ≥ 100$

9) Choice C is correct

$(55 + 5) ÷ (12) = (60) ÷ (12)$. The prime factorization of 60 is: $2 × 2 × 3 × 5$

The prime factorization of 12 is: $3 × 4$. Therefore: $(60) ÷ (12) = (2 × 2 × 3 × 5) ÷ (3 × 4)$

10) Choice C is correct

Plug in the value of x and y and use the order of operations rule. $x = 2$ and $y = −1$

$6(2x − 3y) + (3 − 2x)^2 = 6(2(2) − 3(−1)) + (3 − 2(2))^2 = 6(4 + 3) + (−1)^2 = 42 + 1 = 43$

11) The answer is 30.7

$\frac{215}{7} ≅ 30.71 ≈ 30.7$

12) Choice C is correct

6% of the volume of the solution is alcohol. Let x be the volume of the solution.

Then: 6% of 45 ml: $0.06x = 45 \Rightarrow x = 45 \div 0.06 = 750$

13) Choice C is correct

The slope of the line is: $\frac{y_2-y_1}{x_2-x_1} = \frac{8-4}{2-0} = \frac{4}{2} = 2$. The equation of a line can be written as:

$$y - y_0 = m(x - x_0) \rightarrow y - 4 = 2(x - 0) \rightarrow y - 4 = 2x \rightarrow y = 2x + 4$$

14) Choice D is correct

The volume of a box = $length \times width \times height = 6 \times 7 \times 9 = 378$

15) Choice B is correct

$Probability = \frac{number\ of\ desired\ outcomes}{number\ of\ total\ outcomes} = \frac{15}{14+15+16+20} = \frac{15}{65} = \frac{3}{13}$

16) Choice D is correct

In any rectangle, sides are not perpendicular to diagonals.

17) Choice C is correct

Let y be the width of the rectangle. Then; $15 \times y = 90 \rightarrow y = \frac{90}{15} = 6$

18) Choice D is correct

$4 \times \frac{3}{5} = \frac{12}{5} = 2.4$

A. $2.4 > 2$

B. $2.4 < 3$

C. $\frac{75}{31} = 2.419 \neq 2.4$

D. $2 < 2.4 < 2.5$ This is the answer!

19) Choice C is correct

Let's compare each fraction: $\frac{2}{7} < \frac{3}{8} < \frac{5}{11} < \frac{3}{4}$. Only choice C provides the right order.

20) Choice B is correct

To find the discount, multiply the number (100% − rate of discount)

Therefore; $300(100\% - 10\%) = 300(1 - 0.1) = 300 - (300 \times 0.1)$

21) The answer is 7.

$420 = 2^2 \times 3^1 \times 5^1 \times 7^1$

22) Choice A is correct

Area of a trapezoid: $A = \frac{1}{2} h (b_1 + b_2) = \frac{1}{2} (12)(6+8) = 6(14) = 84$

23) Choice A is correct

$\frac{104}{8} = 13, \frac{1,352}{104} = 13, \frac{17,576}{1,352} = 13$. Therefore, the factor is 13.

24) Choice C is correct

Simplify each option provided.

A. $-20 - (3 \times 10) + (6 \times 40) = -20 - 30 + 240 = 190$

B. $\left(\frac{15}{8} \times 72\right) + \left(\frac{125}{5}\right) = 135 + 25 = 160$

C. $\left(\left(\frac{30}{4} + \frac{15}{2}\right) \times 8\right) - \frac{11}{2} + \frac{222}{4} = \left(\left(\frac{30+30}{4}\right) \times 8\right) - \frac{11}{2} + \frac{111}{2} = \left(\left(\frac{60}{4}\right) \times 8\right) + \frac{111-11}{2} = (15 \times 8) + \frac{100}{2} = 120 + 50 = 170$ (This is the answer)

D. $\frac{481}{6} + \frac{121}{3} + 50 = \frac{481+242}{6} + 50 = 120.5 + 50 = 170.5$

25) Choice A is correct

1 yard = 3 feet. Therefore, $3,768 \, ft \times \frac{1 \, yd}{3 \, ft} = 1,256 \, yd$

26) Choice A is correct

3,400 out of 74,800 equals $\frac{3,400}{74,800} = \frac{17}{374} = \frac{1}{22}$

27) Choice A is correct

Prime factorizing of $20 = 2 \times 2 \times 5$. Prime factorizing of $12 = 2 \times 2 \times 3$

lowest common multiple (LCM) = $2 \times 2 \times 3 \times 5 = 60$

28) Choice C is correct

Plug in the value of x into the function f. First, plug in 3.1 for x.

A. $f = 2x - \frac{3}{10} = 2(3.1) - \frac{3}{10} = 5.9 \neq 8.6$

B. $f = x + \frac{3}{10} = 3.1 + \frac{3}{10} = 3.4 \neq 8.6$

C. $f = 2x + 2\frac{2}{5} = 2(3.1) + 2\frac{2}{5} = 6.2 + 2.4 = 8.6$ This is correct!

Plug in other values of x.

$x = 4.2 \rightarrow f = 2x + 2\frac{2}{5} = 2(4.2) + 2.4 = 10.8$ This one is also correct.

$x = 5.9 \rightarrow f = 2x + 2\frac{2}{5} = 2(5.9) + 2.4 = 14.2$ This one works too!

D. $f = 2x + \frac{3}{10} = 2(3.1) + \frac{3}{10} = 6.5 \neq 8.6$

29) Choice D is correct

$1\ kg = 1,000\ g$ and $1\ g = 1,000\ mg$

$96\ kg = 96 \times 1,000\ g = 96 \times 1,000 \times 1,000 = 96,000,000\ mg$

30) Choice B is correct

This shape is 100 parts, and 72 of the parts are shaded. Then write 72 out of 100 as a percentage: 72%

31) Choice B is correct

$Average\ (mean) = \frac{sum\ of\ terms}{number\ of\ terms} = \frac{10+11+15+14+15+17+12.5}{7} = 13.5$

32) Choice C is correct

A.   The number of books sold in April is: 490

The number of books sold in July is: $780 \rightarrow \frac{490}{780} = \frac{49}{78} \neq 2$

B.   The number of books sold in July is: 780

Half the number of books sold in May is: $\frac{1250}{2} = 625 \rightarrow 625 < 7,800$

C.   The number of books sold in June is: 300

Half the number of books sold in April is: $\frac{490}{2} = 245 \rightarrow 300 > 245$ (it's correct)

D.   The total of books sold in April and June is: $490 + 300 > 780 \rightarrow 790 > 780$

33) Choice B is correct

α and β are supplementary angles. The sum of supplementary angles is 180 degrees.

$\alpha + \beta = 180° \rightarrow \beta = 180° - \alpha = 180° - 50° = 130°$

Then, $\frac{\alpha}{\beta} = \frac{50}{130} = \frac{5}{13}$

34) Choice C is correct

When points are reflected over the y-axis, the value of y in the coordinates doesn't change, and the sign of x changes. Therefore, the coordinate of point B is $(5, 4)$.

35) Choice B is correct

The number of biology books: 25. Total number of books $25 + 110 + 65 = 200$

The ratio of the number of biology books to the total number of books is: $\frac{25}{200} = \frac{1}{8}$

36) Choice D is correct

A. $\frac{3}{4} < 0.7$, $\frac{3}{4} = 0.75$. Therefore, this inequality is not correct.

B. $25\% = \frac{1}{2}$, $25\% = \frac{1}{4}$, not $\frac{1}{2}$.

C. $6 < \frac{11}{2}$, $\frac{11}{2} = 5.5$. Therefore, this inequality is not correct.

D. $\frac{4}{5} > 0.7$, $\frac{4}{5} = 0.8 \to 0.8 > 0.7$, this inequality is correct.

37) The answer is 33

Henry is x years old, then $2x = 66 \to x = \frac{66}{2} = 33$

38) Choice C is correct

There are 30 integers from 1 to 30. The set of numbers that are not composite between 1 and 30 is: $A = \{1, 2, 3, 5, 7, 11, 13, 17, 19, 23, 29\}$

11 integers are not composite. The probability of not selecting a composite number is:

$Probability = \frac{number\ of\ desired\ outcomes}{number\ of\ total\ outcomes} = \frac{11}{30}$

39) Choice D is correct

Let's write the inequality for each statement.

A. $\frac{x}{16} < 8$, It is not true.

B. $\frac{8}{x} \leq 16$, It is not true.

C. $\frac{x}{8} < 16$, It is not true.

D. $\frac{x}{8} \leq 16$, This is the inequality provided in the question.

40) Choice B is correct

Since E is the midpoint of AB, then the area of all triangles DAE, DEF, CFE, and CBE are equal.

Let x be the area of one of the triangles, then: $4x = 140 \rightarrow x = 35$

The area of DEC $= 2x = 2(35) = 70$.

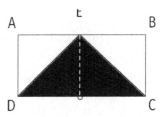

Effortless Math's MAP Grade 6 Online Center

... So Much More Online!

Effortless Math Online MAP Grade 6 Math Center offers a complete study program, including the following:

- ✓ Step-by-step instructions on how to prepare for the MAP Grade 6 Math test

- ✓ Numerous MAP Grade 6 Math worksheets to help you measure your math skills

- ✓ Complete list of MAP Grade 6 Math formulas

- ✓ Video lessons for MAP Grade 6 Math topics

- ✓ Full-length MAP Grade 6 Math practice tests

- ✓ And much more…

No Registration Required.

Visit **EffortlessMath.com/MAP6** to find your online MAP Grade 6 Math resources.

Receive the PDF version of this book or get another FREE book!

Thank you for using our Book!

Do you LOVE this book?

Then, you can get the PDF version of this book or another book absolutely FREE!

Please email us at:

info@EffortlessMath.com

for details.

Author's Final Note

Congratulations on completing this practice book! You've made it to the end – fantastic job!

I would like to extend my heartfelt gratitude for choosing this book to assist you in preparing for your child's MAP Grade 6 Math test. Amidst a wide array of options, I am truly honored that you opted for this practice book.

It took me years to develop this practice book for the MAP Grade 6 Math, as I aimed to create a thorough and all-inclusive resource to help students make the best use of their precious time while preparing for the exam.

Drawing from my extensive experience of over a decade in teaching and tutoring math, I have incorporated my personal insights and notes into the development of this book. It is my earnest hope that the information and practice tests provided within these pages will contribute to your child's success in the MAP Grade 6 Math exam.

If you have any questions, please feel free to contact me at reza@effortlessmath.com, and I will be more than happy to help. Your feedback will enable me to greatly enhance the quality of my future books and make this one even better. Additionally, I acknowledge that there may be a few minor errors in this book. If you come across any, please let me know so that I can rectify them as soon as possible.

If you found value in this book and enjoyed using it, I would love to hear from you. I kindly request that you take a moment to post a review on the book's Amazon page.

I personally read every single review to ensure that my books genuinely benefit students and test takers. By leaving a review, you will help me continue assisting students in their math education.

I wish you and your child all the best in your future endeavors!

Reza Nazari
Math teacher and author

Made in the USA
Monee, IL
09 September 2023